TEELINE SHORTHAND   Made Simple

The Made Simple series
has been created
especially for self-education
but can equally well
be used as
an aid to group study.
However complex the subject,
the reader is taken
step by step,
clearly and methodically,
through the course. Each volume
has been prepared by experts,
taking account of
modern educational requirements,
to ensure the most
effective way of
acquiring knowledge.

In the same series

Accounting
Administration in Business
Advertising
Basic
Biology
Book-keeping
British Constitution
Business Calculations
Business Communication
Business Law
Calculus
Chemistry
Child Development
Commerce
Computer Electronics
Computer Programming
Computer Programming
  Languages in Practice
Computer Typing
Cost and Management Accounting
Data Processing
Economic and Social Geography
Economics
Education
Electricity
Electronics
Elements of Banking
English
Financial Management
First Aid
French
German
Graphic Communication

Italian
Journalism
Latin
Law
Management
Marketing
Marketing Analysis and Forecasting
Mathematics
Modelling and Beauty Care
Modern European History
Money and Banking
MSX
Music
Office Practice
Personnel Management
Philosophy
Photography
Physical Geography
Physics
Politics
Practical Typewriting
Psychology
Russian
Salesmanship
Secretarial Practice
Social Services
Sociology
Spanish
Statistics
Systems Analysis
Teeline Shorthand
Typing

TEELINE SHORTHAND Made Simple

Harry Butler

MADE SIMPLE
BOOKS

Made Simple Books
An imprint of Heinemann Professional Publishing Ltd
Halley Court, Jordan Hill, Oxford OX2 8EJ

OXFORD   LONDON   MELBOURNE   AUCKLAND   SINGAPORE
IBADAN   NAIROBI   GABORONE   KINGSTON

Printed and bound in Great Britain
by Richard Clay Ltd, Bungay, Suffolk

First published 1982
Reprinted 1984
Reprinted 1985
Reprinted 1986
Reprinted 1987
Reprinted 1989

British Library Cataloguing in Publication Data

Butler, Harry, *1913–*
  Teeline shorthand made simple.   (Made
  simple books, ISSN 0265–0541)
  1. Shorthand—Teeline
  I. Title   II. Series
  653′.428   Z56.2.T4

ISBN 0 434 98500 7

Preface

When you start to learn Teeline, you embark on a rewarding adventure, and this course could well be the key to your success. Teeline can earn you money. It can save you time. Whatever your work, Teeline can help you.

The system was first published in 1968 and has become increasingly popular because it is simple, logical and gets results. In evening institutes, teachers find that Teeline classes are always full, and colleges of further education and comprehensive schools report excellent examination results.

Teeline is a new way of using an old skill—that of writing, which has been with us for more than three thousand years. Handwriting is slow and cumbersome, yet it cannot be completely replaced even in these days of electric typewriters, word processors and tape recorders. However much we progress, pen, pencil and paper are still needed.

In Teeline we have a logical and modern system of fast writing with a light memory load, which makes it much easier to learn than traditional systems. The theory can be learned in less than a quarter of the time taken by other methods but it is still capable of high speeds. There have been passes at 140 words a minute in Royal Society of Arts examinations and there are regularly prize winners in the Higher Stage examinations of the London Chamber of Commerce and Industry.

Here within the covers of one book is all you need to know to become a proficient shorthand writer in the realms of commerce, international trade, industry, journalism or medicine.

The book is planned so that the first chapters are common to all learners. Then follow sections on specialized subjects which can be studied or omitted as desired, and subsequent chapters deal with some advanced writing methods and building up speed. Finally there are chapters on how to teach Teeline and on organizing home classes.

Those who need shorthand only for taking lecture notes or making study notes need learn no more than the first eight chapters. By this time, the principles introduced will enable them to write twice as fast as they would in ordinary longhand.

No doubt this will suffice for some, but for most people the object of learning a shorthand system is to put it to commercial use—to apply it to the earning of money. You can do this with Teeline much faster than with older shorthand systems. What is more, if you have a second language you can use Teeline for that, too, without having to re-learn anything.

Teeline follows ordinary spelling. There is no 'writing by sound' with signs to be learned for sounds instead of letters. The inventor of Teeline, the late James Hill, wrote: 'Words written in Teeline do not need to be translated back into longhand as phonographic shorthand does. They simply require to be expanded or reconstituted, as a pure concentrated extract or essence is diluted back to its natural consistency.'

Teeline is a symbol system of shorthand, but the symbols are streamlined versions of the ordinary letters everybody already knows. Most of the vowels and 'silent' letters are discarded because when a word is reduced to its skeleton it can still be recognized in the context of the sentence. It takes only a moment to realize that 'Tk th bk to th clsrm' is the skeleton of the sentence 'Take the book to the classroom' and that the former can be written in much less time than the latter. With Teeline the time is shorter still.

The two basic principles of the system are:

1. The omission of unnecessary letters from words.
2. The elimination of unnecessary movements in forming handwritten characters.

From these two concepts springs the entire simple, logical system of Teeline. For thousands Teeline has been an Open Sesame to fruitful and exciting careers.

It can do the same for you.

HARRY BUTLER
Shorthand Consultant,
National Council for the
Training of Journalists

Acknowledgements

The author places on record his thanks to the following examination bodies for giving permission to reproduce some of their text passages as specimen papers:

The London Chamber of Commerce and Industry, Commercial Education Scheme, Marlowe House, Station Road, Sidcup, Kent, DA15 7BJ.

The Royal Society of Arts Examinations Board, Murray Road, Orpington, Kent, BR5 3RB.

The National Council for the Training of Journalists, Carlton House, Hemnall Street, Epping, Essex, CM16 4NL.

Reference to these bodies is given with each examination passage in the text.

Thanks are also due to Mr Alberto Gallazzi for his careful validation of the first 22 chapters and to Mrs Pauline Hosking, of Seven Kings High School, Ilford, Essex, whose students were the first to use them in class.

How to Study

To become proficient in any system of shorthand requires regular *daily* practice and Teeline is no exception. Delve into the book frequently. Study it on the bus or in the train.

At home, allocate a set amount of time each day to study and working through the exercises. For this you will need a notebook with ruled lines and a ballpoint pen.

Avoid a study plan which provides for one long period twice a week; a regular short working period each day is much better, even if it is only for a quarter of an hour.

With each chapter, copy the outlines given as examples and make a point of saying each word to yourself as you do so. This advice will be repeated from time to time as it is important to your progress. Always copy the examples before working the exercises.

Don't rush. Make sure you thoroughly understand one chapter before going on to the next, and resist the temptation to look too far ahead. Take things as slowly as you wish, and be thorough. In that way the end of the book will be reached much more quickly than if you rush from one chapter to the next and then constantly have to refer back for things which have only been half-learned.

If it is intended to learn the twin skill of typewriting, an excellent textbook is *Practical Typewriting Made Simple*, by Margaret Davis, from the same publisher. By working through the two books in parallel it will soon be possible to get additional practice both in Teeline and typewriting by transcribing the Teeline exercises directly on to the typewriter, thus reaching proficiency in both subjects at the same time.

Contents

PREFACE   v

ACKNOWLEDGEMENTS   vii

HOW TO STUDY   viii

1. THIS IS TEELINE   1
   - Exercise 1   2
   - Exercise 2   4

2. THE TEELINE ALPHABET   5
   - Exercise 3   7
   - Exercise 4   9
   - Exercise 5   10
   - Exercise 6   13
   - Exercise 7   14

3. HOW TO WRITE WORDS   16
   - Special Forms   18
   - Punctuation   19
   - Exercise 8   20
   - Exercise 9   23
   - Exercise 10   26

4. WAYS WITH 'H'   29
   - Exercise 11   32
   - Exercise 12   34

5. DOUBLE VOWELS   36
   - Exercise 13   37
   - Exercise 14   40

6. SIMPLE WORD GROUPS   42
   - Exercise 15   44
   - Exercise 16   46

7. MORE ABOUT VOWEL INDICATORS   48
   - Exercise 17   50
   - Exercise 18   52
   - Exercise 19   55
   - Exercise 20   59

8. A LITTLE LOOK BACK   62

9. WAYS WITH 'C': I. CK, 'SOFT' C, -NCE, -NCH   67
   Exercise 21   68
   Exercise 22   71

10. WAYS WITH 'C': II. HOW TO WRITE THE CN BLEND   73
    Exercise 23   76

11. WAYS WITH 'C': III. HOW TO WRITE THE CM BLEND   79
    Exercise 24   80
    Exercise 25   82

12. TAKING DICTATION   84
    How to Record   86

13. WAYS WITH 'C': IV. THE CNV BLEND   89
    Exercise 26   89
    Exercise 27   91
    Exercise 28   93
    Speed Building   96

14. WAYS WITH 'R': I. BLENDS WITH F, T AND D   97
    Exercise 29   99
    Exercise 30   102
    Exercise 31   106
    Exercise 32   110
    Exercise 33   111
    Speed Building   113

15. WAYS WITH 'R': II. THE 'R' PRINCIPLE   114
    Exercise 34   117
    Exercise 35   119
    Exercise 36   123
    Speed Building   125

16. WAYS WITH 'R': III. BLENDS WITH M, L AND W   127
    Exercise 37   130
    Exercise 38   133

17. LOOKING BACK FOR THE FUTURE   136

18. WAYS WITH 'N': I. ADDING N TO T, D AND P   141
    Exercise 39   143
    Exercise 40   146
    Speed Building   149

19. WAYS WITH 'N': II. BLENDS WITH V, W AND X   150
    Exercise 41   152
    Exercise 42   156
    Exercise 43   158
    Speed Building   160

20. HOW TO WRITE '-TION'   162
    Exercise 44   163
    Exercise 45   166
    Speed Building   169

21. COMMON PREFIXES   170
    Exercise 46   172
    Exercise 47   176
    Speed Building   178

22. COMMON SUFFIXES   179
    Exercise 48   183
    Exercise 49   185
    Exercise 50   189
    Exercise 51   192
    Exercise 52   194
    Speed Building   195

23. A NEW WAY WITH FIGURES   196
    Exercise 53   202

24. THE POLISHING TOUCH   205

25. TEELINE IN THE OFFICE   208
    Specimen Examination Papers   211

26. THE MEDICAL SECRETARY   216
    Prefixes   217
    Suffixes   218
    Specimen Examination Papers   220
    Further Reading   222

27. THE BILINGUAL SECRETARY 223
 Specimen Examination Papers 223
 Further Reading 227

28. TEELINE FOR REPORTERS 228
 Public Administration 230
 Magistrates' and Coroners' Courts 231
 Parliamentary and Political 232
 Specimen Examination Papers 234

29. ADVANCED TEELINE 237
 The 'PL' Principle 237
 Extended Use of 'TR' 239
 Lightly Sounded 'N' 239
 Exercise 54 240
 An '-NTH' Blend 241
 A 'B' Blend 241
 Exercise 55 243
 Additional Suffixes 243
 Additional Prefixes 245
 'Nation' Words 246
 Words Containing 'Arch' 247
 Combining Vowels 247
 Exercise 56 248
 Advanced Word Grouping 248
 'G' and 'J' 255

30. BUILDING TO HIGH SPEED 257
 Dictation Tapes 265
 Examinations 265
 Further Reading 266

31. HOW TO TEACH TEELINE 267

32. HOME CLASSES IN TEELINE 272

APPENDIX 1. Alphabetical list of Special Forms 274

APPENDIX 2. Towns in the United Kingdom and Eire 279

APPENDIX 3. Countries of the World and their Capitals 291

INDEX 303

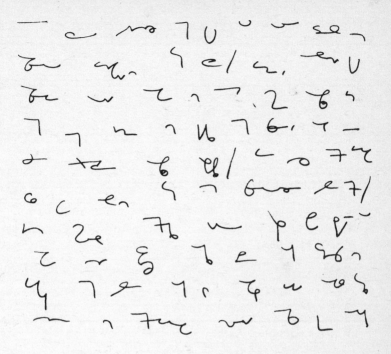

This shorthand was written at 120 words a minute by Stephen Warren, a 20-year-old trainee journalist with the *Paddington Mercury*, and was taken at random from his notebook, the feint-ruled lines of which do not reproduce here. Mr Warren taught himself Teeline but joined a speed class when he could write at 60 words a minute. Here is the key (the hyphens indicate where he has grouped words together):

There now remains the question of what should-be done about-our involvement in-the scheme. I-do-not-think there-is-any question about-it: we-have well and truly got ourselves in at-the deep end and perhaps the best-thing we-can do is-to extricate ourselves as-quickly-as-possible. It may-be that it-will cause a-lot-of discussion in-the town, but-we-must risk that. I-am glad-to-say that-this view has-the full support of all my colleagues on-this side of-the chamber and I-hope the rest of-the council will-see eye-to-eye with-us in-this matter, and that-it-will not-have to-be put to-the . . .

THE TEELINE ALPHABET

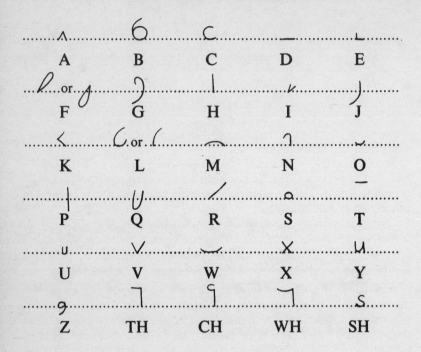

A	B	C	D	E
F or	G	H	I	J
K	L or	M	N	O
P	Q	R	S	T
U	V	W	X	Y
Z	TH	CH	WH	SH

1

THIS IS TEELINE

Teeline shorthand was invented by the late James Hill of Nottingham. He applied the principles of work study to ordinary longhand and after many years of trial and error he produced a system which is at once simple, logical, fast and accurate.

One of his early slogans was: 'If you can write, you can write Teeline'— and that is perfectly true. It has been known for people to make out shopping lists in Teeline after only three lessons, and it can be used in offices just as quickly.

Teeline is different from all other modern systems. All the symbols used are based on the longhand letters you already know. And it follows ordinary spelling. All unnecessary consonants and vowels are removed, and only the skeleton of a word is written. Here are some examples:

Accommodate contains two C's, but only one is needed, so 'acommodate' can be instantly recognized for the word. It also has two M's, but only one is wanted, so that reduces the word to 'acomodate'. But that is not all. The final E is unnecessary and the word can still be read correctly when it is omitted, so the Teeliner writes 'acomodat' and has no trouble in recognizing it.

So: ignore all double letters and 'silent' letters. That is the first thing to be done. Look at these examples:

Normal spelling	Teeline spelling
spell	spel
will	wil
hatch	hach
watch	wach
please	ples
recommend	recomend
light	lit
height	hit
wake	wak
debt	det
more	mor
sign	sin

Next, all unwanted vowels are omitted. Consonants are the skeleton of any word, but vowels are really useful only if they start a word or if they

1

are sounded finally. Only occasionally is it necessary to insert a vowel in the middle of a word, and then only for the sake of distinction or easy reading. Before you read the next paragraph, cover it with your hand or a piece of paper and move your cover downwards line by line as you read.

This example demonstrates that vowels are relatively unimportant in words. On the next line, each dot represents a consonant and only the vowels are shown. Try to read this:

ou. .a. .e. . .o a. . i. . .ea.e.

Next, here is the same phrase with all the consonants but only a dot for the vowels, and see how easy it is to read:

. .r F.th.r wh. .rt .n h. .v.n

Here are some examples of words condensed even further, but still capable of recognition:

have	hv
your	yr
before	bfr
vowel	vwl
contains	cntns
meet	mt
week	wk
book	bk

and so on. At first glance it might be thought that 'bk' (book) would be confused with 'bk' for 'bake', but this is not so. You always follow the sense of the sentence. Thus 'The bk is on the tbl' could only be read as 'The book is on the table'. To read it as 'The *bake* is on the table' would be nonsense. Similarly, 'Go and mt him at the station' could only be 'Go and *meet* him at the station'. No one would ever say 'Go and *might* him at the station'.

Exercise 1

Write the following in normal spelling. The key is on the opposite page, but cover it up and refer to it only as a last resort, if at all.

1. Tk the bk to the grl in the clsrm.
2. I shl go hm at fv.
3. Pt the bx on the tp shlf in the rm.
4. I wnt into the rm to se the grl.
5. I tk the bs to the vlg to mt my fthr.
6. Ths bx cntnd chclts.
7. Hv we any bks abt Tln?
8. Cn we tl hm if we ar lkly to hv any rm in the cr?
9. To mny cks spl the brth.
10. Ths is qt smpl to rd and rt.

Key

1. Take the book to the girl in the classroom.
2. I shall go home at five.
3. Put the box on the top shelf in the room.
4. I went into the room to see the girl.
5. I took the bus to the village to meet my father.
6. This box contained chocolates.
7. Have we any books about Teeline?
8. Can we tell him if we are likely to have any room in the car?
9. Too many cooks spoil the broth.
10. This is quite simple to read and write.

Points to remember:

1. Omit all double and 'silent' letters and any final vowels that are not sounded.

2. Omit all vowels in the middle of words unless they are wanted for distinction (i.e. to distinguish 'man' from 'men', etc.).

3. All initial vowels must be written. In this way we can distinguish 'every' from 'very', 'other' from 'throw', etc.

4. All final vowels, *if sounded*, must be written so that it is possible to tell 'marry' from 'mar', 'carry' from 'car', etc.

Another way we condense words is to make one letter do the work of two. In many words containing PH, we substitute the letter F:

phrase	*becomes*	fras
photograph		fotograf
telephone		telefon
triumph		triumf

Similarly, where GH occurs in a word and it is sounded like F, then we write F:

cough	cof
tough	tof
enough	enof

Where the GH is silent (as in 'dough', 'though', 'thought') then it is ignored, following the rule that all silent letters are omitted.

These are two examples of what James Hill meant when he said that he applied the principles of work study to ordinary longhand.

Another instance of making one letter do the work of two is DG.

Whenever these letters occur together in a word, omit the D and write only the G: eg (edge), heg (hedge), bag (badge). There will be no confusion, because in Teeline you always *follow the sense of the sentence.*

A final example is Y. This sign is used for OY when those letters come in the middle or at the end of a word: by (boy), ryl (royal), lyl (loyal), enjy (enjoy) and so on. When Y comes at the end of a word in longhand spelling, we use I, as in esi (easy), mni (money or many—the context will tell you which), hni (honey), cri (cry).

Exercise 2

Write the following in normal spelling. The key is below, but cover it up and refer to it only as a last resort, if at all.

1. The by tk a gd fotograf of the anml.
2. I am sr he wl enjy the bk abt the rlwa trns.
3. He ws on the eg of the clf.
4. The by hs a bad cof.
5. The pla ws a grt triumf.
6. Thr is a lt of mni in the sf in the rm.
7. Se if he cn cm to the fon to spk to me.
8. I hp to se the by tmrw.
9. Wl she be abl to cm to the cls tmrw?
10. It is esi to se the wa we rt in Tln.

Key

1. The boy took a good photograph of the animal.
2. I am sure he will enjoy the book about the railway trains.
3. He was on the edge of the cliff.
4. The boy has a bad cough.
5. The play was a great triumph.
6. There is a lot of money in the safe in the room.
7. See if he can come to the phone to speak to me.
8. I hope to see the boy tomorrow.
9. Will she be able to come to the class tomorrow?
10. It is easy to see the way we write in Teeline.

Points to remember:
 Whenever possible, make one letter do the work of two.
 When PH and GH have the sound of F, then write F. When DG occur together in a word, ignore the D and write only the G.
 When OY occurs medially or finally, use only Y. When a final Y occurs in a word and it is sounded, write I.

THE TEELINE ALPHABET
Th   Tln   Alfbt

The Teeline alphabet is given opposite page 1. It contains no thick strokes but it is important that the size and shape of the symbols are preserved. Here it is again, but this time notice the size of the strokes:

A	B	C	D	E	F	G	H	I

J	K	L	M	N	O	P	Q	R

S	T	U	V	W	X	Y	Z

By studying them it will be seen that the signs for the vowels A E I O U are all smaller than the other strokes. The 'tail' at the beginning of B is the same length as L. The second F and the letters G, J, P and Q all go through the line of writing, as does the 'tail' on Z. T is a short stroke above the line. All other strokes rest on the line of writing. Now let us look at each letter in detail in order to appreciate the cleverness of the alphabet:

......Λ...... This is derived from the Roman A. It is written about the size shown here. People who use a large writing hand may well write it bigger, but it must retain the same size in proportion to other letters. Later, you will see how ......Λ...... can be reduced to ......⟍....... or ...../......... These signs are called **vowel indicators** and will be explained in due course.

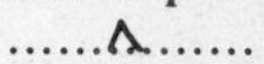

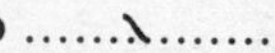

......6...... This stroke is written from the top downwards in one continuous stroke. It is derived from ......𝑏....... and has a well-defined curve, finishing with a large circle.

5

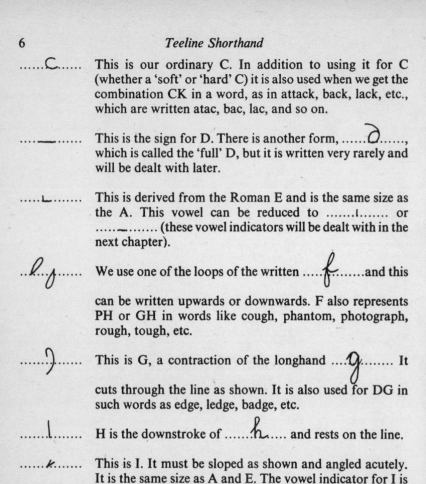

...... C ...... This is our ordinary C. In addition to using it for C (whether a 'soft' or 'hard' C) it is also used when we get the combination CK in a word, as in attack, back, lack, etc., which are written atac, bac, lac, and so on.

..... ___ ...... This is the sign for D. There is another form, ... *∂* ......, which is called the 'full' D, but it is written very rarely and will be dealt with later.

..... ⌐ ...... This is derived from the Roman E and is the same size as the A. This vowel can be reduced to .... ι .... or ..... ___ .... (these vowel indicators will be dealt with in the next chapter).

.. *ℓ* .. *ɟ* ...... We use one of the loops of the written ..... *ƒ* .... and this can be written upwards or downwards. F also represents PH or GH in words like cough, phantom, photograph, rough, tough, etc.

.......) ...... This is G, a contraction of the longhand ... *g* .... It cuts through the line as shown. It is also used for DG in such words as edge, ledge, badge, etc.

.... l .... H is the downstroke of .... *h* ..... and rests on the line.

...... ∠ .... This is I. It must be sloped as shown and angled acutely. It is the same size as A and E. The vowel indicator for I is ...... ∕ ....which can be written upwards or downwards. It is derived from the written ... *ι* ....

.......) .... J is a single downstroke, slightly curved at the bottom. It goes through the line, without loop or dot.

When joining two or more strokes together, the second generally begins where the first leaves off. They are written in one movement, without pause and without lifting the pen from the paper. Once a stroke has been written do *not* try to 'improve' it by going over it.

Always leave a margin on the left-hand side of your page. This is useful for writing any notes or instructions.

Exercise 3

Copy the following letters and write the longhand equivalents on the line below in your notebook. Cover the key below and refer to it only as a last resort:

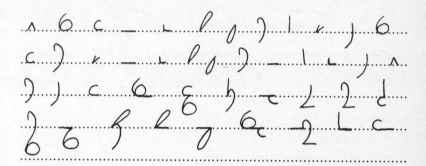

Key

A B C D E F F G H I J B C G I D E F F G D H E J
A G J C BD CB HG DC JD GD HC GB DB FG FD
DF BDC DGD HD CD

Take care in writing your strokes at first. Do not try to write them too quickly—speed will come automatically, as you become more familiar with the signs.

Use a pen, pencil or ballpoint for writing, and use a notebook with ruled lines (but not too closely ruled, or your writing will be impaired).

Remember: a second stroke generally begins where the first one leaves off, as in ordinary writing. Do not pause between each stroke and do not lift the pen from the paper.

Here is another set of letters:

...... Only the angle is needed for K. It is the same size as C. Make sure you have noticed the difference between ...... I and ...... K.

...... L is a single stroke, boldly curved and generally written downwards. For ease in joining, the bottom of the curve is left off when joining to some of the letters and it is written like this: .... Although L is usually written

downwards, it is written *upwards* after G (......), H

(......), J (......) and P (......) so that

the strokes do not go too far below the line of writing.

...... M is a single arch written from left to right ...... with the initial hook and the middle stem omitted.

...... The ordinary form of ...... is contracted to ...... When following other strokes, ... sometimes becomes ...... but it must always be kept narrow.

...... This sign is a short, shallow curve, the bottom part of the letter O. In a few special cases, a full O is used.

...... P is the same size as H, but it is written through the line as is the downstroke in a written longhand ......

...... Q is the joining loop between Q and U ...... It is

written through the line, and as Q is generally followed by U, it is used for the combination of QU (another example of one stroke doing the work of two!). Examples:

...... quite ...... quake ...... require.

...... R is *always* written upwards at the angle shown here. It is

joined to strokes in this fashion: ...... HR,

...... JR, ... PR, ...MR,

...... NR, ... LR and so on. It must never

be written downwards. After B, R can be joined ......

or ...... The latter may appear to be faster but in

fact is not so.

......O...... The ordinary handwritten S is modified to become a small

circle. Compare.......6..... B and......O......S. This circle can be written in any direction when attached to straight strokes: ...`......`...... or ......`......`....., but the anticlockwise motion is recommended. When joined to G or N, it goes

inside the hook: ......Ͽ....... SG or ....ϼ...... SN. It is

always written inside curves: ...σ̄........ SM....ͽ...... WS.

‾‾‾ T is the short horizontal cross-stroke of the written T and as far as possible it is placed in the same position. It is the same length as ......‾‾‾‾ D. It is this T which gives Teeline its name.

Exercise 4

Copy the following letters and write the longhand equivalents on the line below in your notebook. Cover the key below and refer to it only as a last resort.

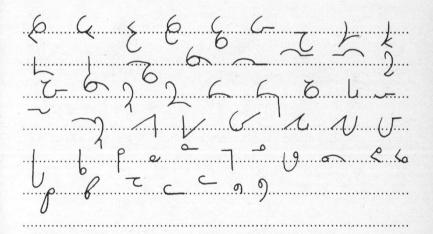

Key

BK LK KL BL LB LD DL JL JK PM PBM MB BM
MD MT TM GO OLD GN GM LM LMP OB HO OD
TO MGN RP PR LR RL RQ QT PQ PS SP SO ST TP
TS QS SM SK KS SF FS TC CD CT SN SG

Try to make each stroke a perfect copy of those shown here, but do so the first time. *Do not* write over the top of a stroke in an effort to 'improve' it; otherwise you will get a stroke which could be quite unreadable.

Teeline is read like ordinary writing—from left to right and from top to bottom. From left to right: .... MNT, ...

TMR, ... RP, ... PR. From top to bottom: .... HB, ... HBK, ... LP, etc.

So far, you have been reading and copying the Teeline letters. The time has now come for you to strike out on your own. Remember that when writing words you join the letters in one motion, without any pauses between strokes or taking the pen off the paper.

Think before you write. In the following exercise, look at the combinations of letters; think what they are, and then write them without pausing while doing so.

Exercise 5

Cover the key on the opposite page. Do not look at it except for checking your work at the end of the exercise. Look first at the combinations; think of the symbols; then write the outline without any pause and without lifting the pen from the paper. This may not be easy at first, but it will soon come. Put the strokes on one line of your notebook, and the long-hand equivalent underneath.

SD	DM	RQ	RQR	RQRS	SG	HS	GS	MMS
MSM	LSR	RG	RLS	PMS	SPN	NG	ND	NT
LOC	CLOC	JST	SGST	MD	MT	DCS	SCL	

Left-handed writers can write Teeline just as easily as right-handed people.

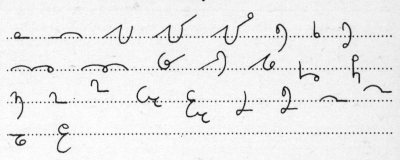

S is normally written with an anti-clockwise motion ......😊........

to all straight strokes: ....🙂...... SD, ...🙂....... SP, ...🙂......

HS, ...🙂........ SR, ...🙂....... RS. It is always written inside

curves: ......🙂.....SB, ...🙂.....SL, ...🙂......LS, ...🙂......

SM, ...🙂..... MS. It is always written inside the G and N hooks,
since they count as curves, but remember to keep them narrow:

........🙂..... SG, ...🙂...... SN.

If S comes between two straight strokes making an angle, it is

written *outside* the angle: ....🙂........ RST, ...🙂...... PSR

.....🙂..... RSP, ...🙂....... PSD.

If S comes between a straight stroke and a curve (or vice versa),

then write it inside the curve: .....🙂....... PSM, ...🙂....... HSL,

....🙂....... RSM, ...🙂.... RSN.
S is written inside the B circle: ......🙂.... BS, ...🙂....... BST.

Remember to make the circle of B larger than S: ......🙂..... B, but

.......🙂.... LS.

One of the most frequent letters in written English is T. That is why it is represented by the simple stroke ....; D is closely related and is

often pronounced like T; for instance, we write *stopped* but pronounce

it *stopt*. Although T is written .... T and D is ....._.........., it is perfectly safe to join these to other strokes and leave the sense of the

passage to tell us whether it is T or D: ......|........ post or posed—the

context will tell us which; .....⌒⎺..... late or laid; .....⌐⎯...... not or nod.

Sometimes it is possible to distinguish by putting an outline in the T position, and we always do this when we can, since it is an aid in reading back:

mt	md	st	sd	bt	bd

ft	fd	tf	df

Always disjoin T or D after R. Put the T 'high' and the D 'low', as in ...../........ rt but ..../⎯........ rd.

The combinations -ted, -det, -ded, etc., are shown by putting one stroke above or below the other: .... td ...⎯⎯....... dt

......_.......... dd .... tt, etc., as in .... mt, ... mtd, ... sttd, ...⎯⎯⎯.... dtd, ...⚬.......... sdd and so on.

Always think of an outline before you write it. Don't put half of it on paper and then pause to ponder on what comes next. Work it out in your mind before putting pen to paper. In a short time you will start to think of the outlines more quickly and most words will come to mind automatically.

Exercise 6

Cover the key below. Do not look at it until you check your work at the end of the exercise. Read again the foregoing paragraphs and then start.

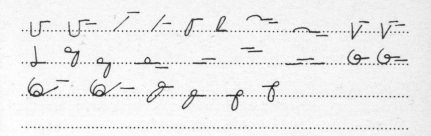

Key
QT QTD RT RD FT FD MTD MDD PRT PRTD HST or HSD
STF SDF DSTD or DSDD DT TD DTD LST or LSD LSTD
or LSDD BSRT BSRD FST FSD DSF TSF

The two signs for F (...... *l* ...... and ..... *ᶴ* ....) can be written either way for convenience. The ...... *l* ...... can be written ..... *ʖ* ...... or ...... *ʌ* ......; and the second sign ..... *ᶴ* .... can be written ..... *ᶮ* ...... or .... *ᶮ* ..... It is a matter of personal choice, but remember to use the first form before D ... *l* .... and the second form before T ... *ᶴ* ...., so that the T and the D keep to their respective positions as far as possible.

Now we come to the last section of the basic alphabet:

...... *u* .... U is the same size as the other vowels. It is important to keep it very narrow so that it does not become confused with ...... *u* ...... O. This is easily done by taking a little extra care in writing at the start. U has an indicator, which is ...... *ı* .... (the same as E but there is no confusion when taken in context).

......∨....... V must be kept upright so that it is never confused with ....ʋ...... I and, of course, being a consonant it is also larger.

......⌣....... The middle stem of the W is omitted, making W the reverse of M.

......✗........ This is the ordinary written X and it is the only letter in the Teeline alphabet in which the hand has to be lifted from the paper, but you will find that often it blends with another letter and can be written very quickly indeed. Whenever a word begins with 'ex' that syllable is shown by blending

the ......✗......., as in ......⫯⸝....... express, ...⫯⌐...... explain, ...⫯⁄........ expert, ...⋏........ excellent, etc.

......Ц....... This is the written Y with the longhand tail and loop omitted.

......9....... This form is used when Z begins a word. When Z occurs medially or finally, an S is generally used.

Exercise 7

Write in Teeline:

LY	LU	LX	XL	TX	XT	BX	XB	ZN	WT
WD	GY	JY	SLW	WSL	ZM	VW	WTD	SRVV	HW
JW	WG	WP	XP	XH	WI	UT	UD	OB	UB
VB	BV	DW	SXTT	YW	YM	YN			

Practise writing W, O, U for pen control like this:

..⌣....⌣....Ц....⌣....⌣....Ц....⌣....⌣....Ц....⌣....⌣....Ц........

It is essential that you show the difference between these letters: any variation will lead to confusion.

When reading Teeline, try to do it as quickly as possible. A useful additional exercise is to read a page several times until you can go through it without hesitation. This is a great aid to speed.

Key

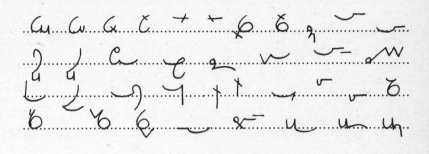

Although one stroke follows another without lifting the pen, it will be noticed that there are two letters where a penlift is required. The first is when K is joined to H, J and P, when the outlines

......k..... HK .....ʃ....... JK, ...k...... PK are quicker and

more distinctive than if the K is put on the end of the stroke.

The other letter is X, which is more often than not blended with

the following letter: ......Č...... XL, ...Ç..... LX, ...↓......

HX, ...ｲ........ XP, ...⤳...... MX, ...⤳....... XM, etc.

Remember, also, that T and D are always disjoined after R, and

they are disjoined, too, when following each other: ....

TD, ...⹀...... DT, etc.

Many of the letter combinations in the exercises make words. FT, for instance, makes 'foot', 'feet', 'feat' and 'fate', MN is 'man', 'men', 'mine', 'main', etc. Do not be worried about these variants, because the context of the passage, plus your own common sense, will tell you which is the correct word. If any distinction is needed (as in the case of 'man' and 'men'— 'the man/men went for a walk', for instance) then a vowel is inserted. How to do this is described in Chapter 3.

3

HOW TO WRITE WORDS
Hw t rt wrds

There are two ways of writing vowels. First, we have the signs:

............⋀............∟............𝑘............⋁............u............

A   E   I   O   U

Second, there are brief signs which are known as **indicators,** which were shown in the last chapter.

In general, consonants are more important than vowels. In Chapter 1, consonants were described as the skeleton of a word. The vowels might be said to be the flesh that surrounds the skeleton and are only needed for the better recognition of an outline.

Most vowels can be omitted in fast writing, but they are *always* shown if they start a word or are sounded at the end of a word. Usually, they are joined to the consonants in the order in which they come.

Here are the indicators again:

Letter	*Indicator(s)*
⋀	⋋⋅⊣ or ⋰⋅⋅⅂
∟	⋅⋁ or ⋅⋅⋅⋗
𝑘	⋰ (it can be written upwards or downwards)
u	⋅⋁

Vowels signs are written *smaller* than consonants; therefore the indicators are also written small. If written correctly, there is no con-

fusion between ....— E and ....— D, because the former is

shorter than the latter. The same can be said for ....⋰...... I and

.........⋰...... R.

........◌̇........   ⌣........   ⌡........   ⌐⌐........

ab (Abe),   ad (add or aid)   al (all)   ag (age)

16

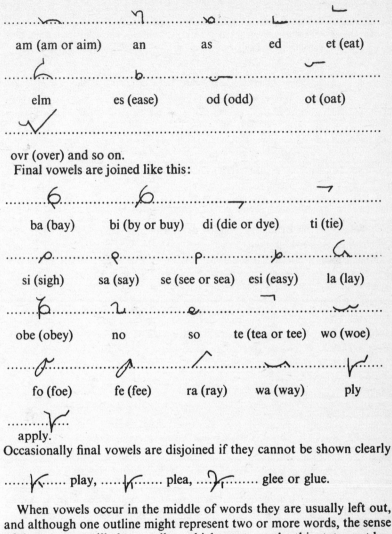

am (am or aim)   an   as   ed   et (eat)

elm   es (ease)   od (odd)   ot (oat)

ovr (over) and so on.
Final vowels are joined like this:

ba (bay)   bi (by or buy)   di (die or dye)   ti (tie)

si (sigh)   sa (say)   se (see or sea)   esi (easy)   la (lay)

obe (obey)   no   so   te (tea or tee)   wo (woe)

fo (foe)   fe (fee)   ra (ray)   wa (way)   ply

apply.

Occasionally final vowels are disjoined if they cannot be shown clearly

.... play, ... plea, ... glee or glue.

When vowels occur in the middle of words they are usually left out, and although one outline might represent two or more words, the sense of the sentence will always tell us which one to read—this statement has been repeated several times because it can easily be forgotten, and in the early stages it is necessary to give a constant reminder of this.

If a vowel is needed in the middle of a word, then it is generally disjoined like this:

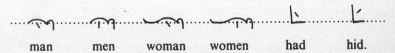

man   men   woman   women   had   hid.

It is quite usual for beginners to write in a lot of vowels which, as they become more expert, they generally leave out. There is no harm in this and it is certainly not 'wrong' to do so. Here are some examples of words with the medial vowels indicated, and which later on will be left out:

hub   ham   home   had   heed   honey

lamb or lame   limb or lime   marry   merry

alone   align   pin   pan   page   peg

rug   rag or rage.

Adelaide   Lagos   Calgary   Ottawa   Bombay   Salisbury

Glasgow   York   Nairobi.

Special Forms

For very frequent words, simple forms are used to save time in writing, and it is necessary to memorize these. There are very few in Teeline, and they will be given as they occur. The best way to memorize them is by writing them out a number of times. Teeline is a skill—a writing skill—and like any other skill it is only learned by *doing*. No one ever learns shorthand merely by looking at it on a printed page. The more often it is written, the greater will be the proficiency. So memorize these special forms by writing them out over and over again until they come automatically—in fact, until you think of the outline immediately you hear the word. Here is the first series:

a   at ('A' in the 'T' position)   the

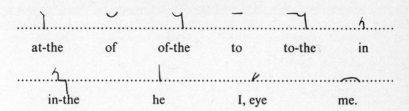

at-the	of	of-the	to	to-the	in

in-the	he	I, eye	me.

(Strictly speaking, 'in' is an ordinary form, but it is of such frequent occurrence that it is included here for your convenience.)

Punctuation

A fullstop or period is an upward stroke written through the line and about twice the length of an R: ..../......... All other marks are the same as in longhand except that a dash, if it is necessary, is shown as

.... We allow ourselves the luxury of two short dashes under an outline to indicate a proper name, like this: .... Ray, ... May, ... Mary, but when writing at speed these can be omitted. Other punctuation marks are the same as in longhand: question mark ......?......, exclamation mark ......!......, quotation marks .... and ...., colon ......:......, semi-colon ......;......, comma ......,.........

Writing tips:

Use a full U before and after S: .... us, use, ... used, ... usual, ... sue, ... suds.

Use a full A before R: .... air, ... airy.

Exercise 8

Read the sentences first, then copy them and transcribe into longhand. Cover the key below and refer to it only as a last resort.

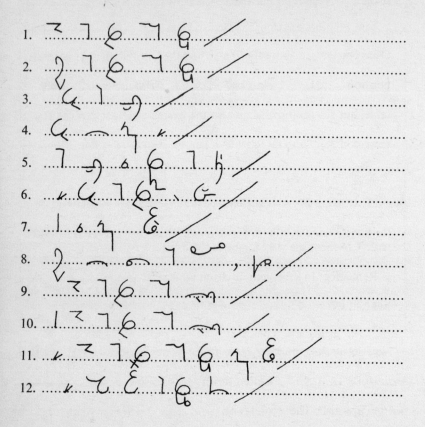

1.

2.

3.

4.

5.

6.

7.

8.

9.

10.

11.

12.

Key

1. Take the book to the boy.
2. Give the book to the boy.
3. Look at the dog.
4. Look me in the eye.
5. The dog is behind the hedge.
6. I like the book a lot.
7. He is in the class.
8. Give me some of the sweets, please.
9. Take the book to the man.
10. He took the book to the man.

11. I took the box to the boy in the class.
12. I will call at the boy's home.

You will notice that in ...... *Ɛ*...... *class* and ...... *Ɛ*...... *call*, the

C has been raised above the line, so that the L is written in its normal

position. ...... *Ɛ*...... *class* and ...... *Ɛ*...... *call* are equally accep-

table, but the positions shown in the exercise are preferable. The

same comment applies to *will*—it can be written ....*ᒪ*..... or

.....*ᒪ*......

.... *sweets* is written above the line in the T position; on

the line it would be ...*ᒪ*...... *swedes*. Wherever possible, outlines

with T in them are written above the line for distinction.

Remember to keep your circle on B larger than S: ......*б*...... B

but ......*б*...... LS.

Now let us take another look at the vowel indicators. 'A' has two

indicators: ......*ᴨ*...... written downwards as shown, and ...*ꓥ*..........

written upwards. The second form (...*ꓥ*.......) is *always* written before

V, W and X like this: .....*ꓥ*...... Avory, ...*ꓥ*...... aver, ...*ꓥ*.....

average, ...*ᴧ*...... awe, ...*ᴧ*.... away, ...*ᴧ*...... awake/awoke,

......*X*...... axe.

'E' also has two indicators: ......*ᴵꓘ*...... and .....*:..?*.... Remember

to keep them short. The second form (...*:..?*.....) is used after the

downstrokes ......*ᑫ*....... N and ......*|*........ P, as in .....*ᑫ*...... knee,

.......*ᒪ*...... pea. It is not often needed.

'O' has no indicator: ....✗...... open, ...┆....... Po, ...⌒.......

no, ...⌒....... so, etc., but when it is joined to N, we omit the hook on

the N and write ....⌐..... for ON. Take care to keep the curve shallow

so that it cannot be mistaken for a Y: ....⌐..... on or one, ...6.......

bone, ...6....... boy (notice the difference?). When O is attached to

M, it is turned on its side:

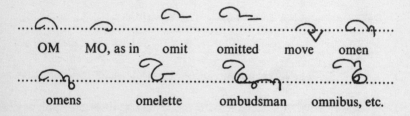

OM	MO, as in	omit	omitted	move	omen

omens	omelette	ombudsman	omnibus, etc.

'U' is the same as E: ....⌐.... but there is never any confusion.

Before P, the full .....⌒........ is used: ....4...... up ......4/..... upper

........4/.... supper (or super) ....4....... upon.

Special forms to be memorized:

on	on-the	my	it	do/day

today	to-do	we	you	with	with-me

with-the	go.

('It' is really a full outline, but it is included here for your convenience.)

Exercise 9

Read the sentences with the key covered in the usual way, then copy and transcribe.

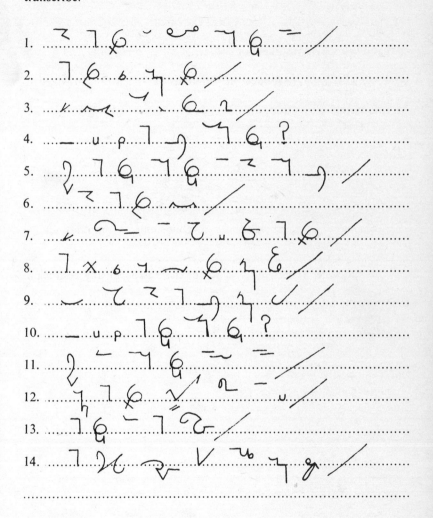

1.
2.
3.
4.
5.
6.
7.
8.
9.
10.
11.
12.
13.
14.

Key

1. Take the box of sweets to the boy today.
2. The book is on the box.
3. I awoke with a bad knee.
4. Do you see the dog with the bone?
5. Give the bone to the boy to take to the dog.

6. Take the book away.
7. I omitted to tell you about the box.
8. The axe is on my box in the class.
9. We will take the dog in the car.
10. Do you see the boy with the bone?
11. Give it to the boy to do today.
12. Open the box Avory sent to you.
13. The boy ate the omelette.
14. The girl moved her toys on the sofa.

Remember that T and D are always disjoined when they

immediately follow R: .... RT, ... RD;

.... aver, ... avert, ... averred,

.... right (or write), ... road (or read, red, rude).

The A indicator is written upwards before V, W and X.
The E indicator is written .... after N and P.
All indicators represent 'long' or 'short' vowels, since we follow
ordinary spelling, and not how the words are sounded.

There are a few occasions when we use the full vowel sign instead of
an indicator for ease in joining, and they are these:

Always use a full ..... ∧ .... after H, M, N and P, so that its presence

can be clearly shown and to make an easier joining: .... hay,

.... may, ... nay, ... pay, ... repay,

.... dismay. This affects only a few words.

Always use a full I before L or V: .... ill or isle, ...

illness, ... ill-will, ... island, ... Ivor,

.... ivory, ... Ivy. At all other times use the indicator:

.... item, ... idle or idol, ... if, ...

fie.

A full ......*u*....... is used before P: ......*Ч*...... up, ...*Ч*...... sup,
......*Ч*...... upon, and before and after S, as in ......*Q*...... us or use,
......*Q*...... useless, ...*Q*...... sue.

When writing words, bear these points in mind:

To make an easier joining between B and C or G or N, use an indicator:

back   bag   beg (or bug)   big

bog   ban   band (or banned)

Ben   bend (or bent)   bind   bone

bond.

Always insert a joined vowel between J and B or C: .... jab,
.... job, ... Jubb, ... Jack.

Finally, *always* show an R in a word (......... girl, ...
part, ... hard, ... cart, ... card, ...
her, ... burly) and write a W *whenever it follows* a vowel:

tomorrow   owe   owed   know   new   news

saw   views   review   bow   how   cow

allow   Harlow.

Exercise 10

Cover the key opposite, read the sentences, then copy and transcribe them:

1. ....
2. ....
3. ....
4. ....
5. ....
6. ....
7. ....
8. ....
9. ....
10. ....
11. ....
12. ....
13. ....
....
14. ....
15. ....
....
16. ....

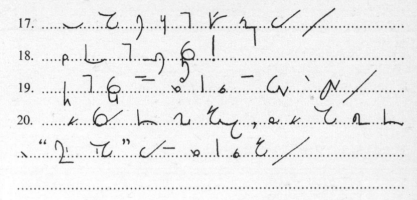

Key

1. Tell Ivy to take the class today.
2. If I see Ivy, I will tell her.
3. My view is the same as hers.
4. I saw him on the way to the school.
5. Do you know if he is at home?
6. How do you manage to do it?
7. To my dismay, he took all the sweets.
8. May I see the book, please?
9. He is ill today but will go to school tomorrow.
10. The band will play all day today.
11. We will go to the island with Ben tomorrow.
12. We may allow the girl to hear part of the play.
13. The girl looks pale, but the boy is at play in the yard.
14. He is hardly an idle boy, as he reads many books.
15. He will review the play in the paper if we allow him to see it.
16. He is in a good job.
17. We will go up the hill in the car.
18. See how the dog begs!
19. Pay the boy today as he is to leave at five.
20. I bear him no ill-will, so I will send him a 'get well' card as he is ill.

You have now mastered the most difficult part of Teeline. Please re-read Chapters 1 and 2 and re-work the exercises, this time writing from the key and checking your outlines with the exercises. Do not be discouraged if you seem to make a few mistakes, because it is almost impossible to write a 'wrong' outline. Many words are capable of being written more than one way, just as some people have different ways of writing letters and words in

longhand. Some people write ...... △ ..... for S, and others write

.... S .... or ... ◠ ......; some write . *and* ... for 'and'

and others write ..... ⊹ ...., but they mean the same.

Remember: if you can write, you can write Teeline, and from now on everything you learn will be a logical progression from these chapters.

4

WAYS WITH 'H'
Was wi 'H'

The letter H occurs quite frequently in English spelling. It often comes after T or C or W or S: TH (think, breathe, thick, that); CH (church, charm, lunch); WH (where, who, wholesale, which); SH (shall, push, sharp). It is convenient to have signs for these combinations and you will recognize three of them instantly:

.........┐...... TH, a combination of .... ‾ and ....|......., which you have already seen in the special form ....┐...... *the*.

.........┐...... CH, which is a small C on top of the H stroke.

.........┐.... WH, a combination of ......⌣..... and ......|......., written so that the H rests on the line.

.......S...... SH, a sign like the longhand S, but written the same size as here.

These signs help a lot in the formation of hundreds of words. In the examples which follow, disjoined vowel indicators are included to help you work out the isolated words, but in a sentence they would rarely be written:

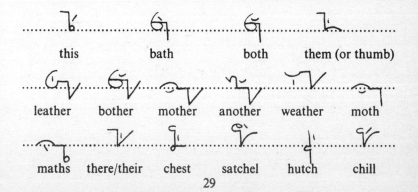

| this | bath | both | them (or thumb) |

| leather | bother | mother | another | weather | moth |

| maths | there/their | chest | satchel | hutch | chill |

29

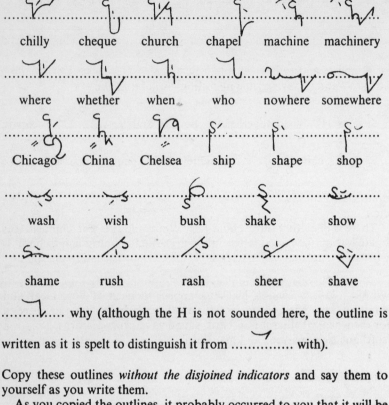

chilly	cheque	church	chapel	machine	machinery

where	whether	when	who	nowhere	somewhere

Chicago	China	Chelsea	ship	shape	shop

wash	wish	bush	shake	show

shame	rush	rash	sheer	shave

.... why (although the H is not sounded here, the outline is

written as it is spelt to distinguish it from .... with).

Copy these outlines *without the disjoined indicators* and say them to
yourself as you write them.

As you copied the outlines, it probably occurred to you that it will be
necessary to distinguish between *ship*, *shape* and *shop*. You are quite

right, and these three words are always vocalized: .... ship,

.... shape, ... shop—for without the indicators one

would never know which word was intended: 'She went to the shp'
could be either *ship* or *shop*. So always insert the vowels.

Another example is .... (ths), which could be *this*, *these*, *those*

or *thus*. These outlines make it quite clear which is which: ....

this, ... these, ... those, ... thus. Always put
the vowels or indicators in the last three.

There is one more thing about H. Although it is an upright stroke, it leans over to the left when followed by V, so that it blends with the V:

.... have, ... heavy, ... behave. This is a blend

of H and V and in later chapters many other clever ways of blending strokes—and so saving time in writing—will be shown.

Just as HV blend together, so do CH and V: .... chives,

.... chivvy, ... achieved. (Incidentally, the same can be

done with P: .... pave, ... pivot, ... paved, etc.)

There is one other thing about CH. Where the H is not sounded, it is treated as an unwanted letter and is discarded; so although 'school' is written in longhand with a CH, the H is an unwanted consonant, and we

write .... school. The same applies to 'chemist', 'chemical' and similar words. The CH sign is written wherever both letters are needed for the word, whether it is a 'hard' sound as in *church*, *charge*, etc., or a 'soft' one as in ma*ch*ine and ma*ch*inist.

Special forms to be memorized:

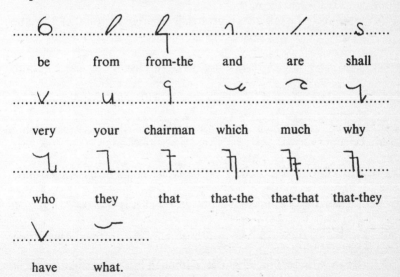

be	from	from-the	and	are	shall
very	your	chairman	which	much	why
who	they	that	that-the	that-that	that-they
have	what.

Teeline Shorthand
Exercise 11
Cover the key, read the sentences, then copy and transcribe them.

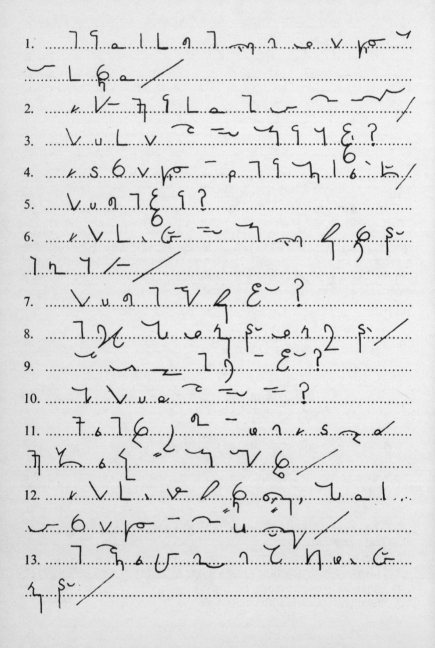

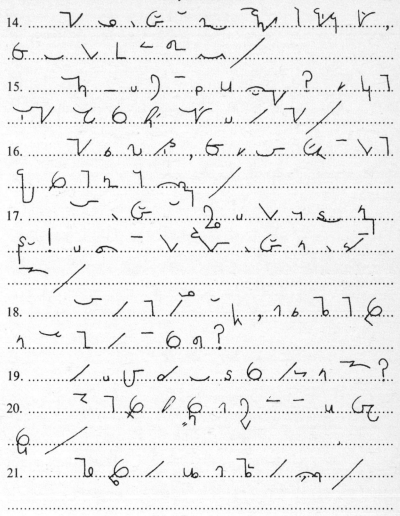

14. ....

15. ....

16. ....

17. ....

18. ....

19. ....

20. ....

21. ....

Key

1. The chairman said he had seen the man and was very pleased with what had been said.

2. I heard that the chairman had said they would meet tomorrow.

3. Have you had very much to do with the chairman of the club?

4. I shall be very pleased to see the chairman when he is at home.

5. Have you seen the club chairman?

6. I have had a lot to do with the man from the big shop at the end of the road.

7. Have you seen the teacher from the school?

8. The girl who was in the shop was in good shape.

9. Which way did they go to school?

10. Why have you so much to do today?

11. That is the book Joe sent to us and I shall make sure that the volume is kept with the other books.

12. I have had a visit from Ben Smith, who said he would be very pleased to meet your mother.

13. The machine is quite new and will help us a lot in the shop.

14. There was a lot of new machinery at the church hall, but we have had it sent away.

15. When do you go to see your mother? I hope the weather will be fine while you are there.

16. There is no rush, but I would like to have the cheque by the end of the month.

17. What a lot of goods you have on show in the shop! You seem to have achieved a lot in a short time.

18. What are the rates of pay, and is this the book in which they are to be seen?

19. Are you quite sure we shall be ready in time?

20. Take the box from Ben and give it to your little boy.

21. Those books are yours, and these are mine.

Exercise 12

Cover the key on the opposite page. Then write the following sentences in Teeline:

1. I do not know whether we shall be at the party tomorrow, as the weather is so bad.

2. What do you wish to do with the boxes of chocolates? Shall we give them to the church bazaar?

3. These are the boxes Joe had in the shop. These are the old boxes and those are the new.

4. Are we allowed to see the goods they sent? Shall we ask if we may open the boxes and see what is inside?

5. I shall be with May and Ivy on the island very shortly.

6. Let me know if Charles will be there tomorrow.

7. Have you seen the new machinery which the man sent to the school?

8. The chairman sent another man to do the job.

9. I shall see John and Al at the church hall today.

10. They are very good at school.

Key

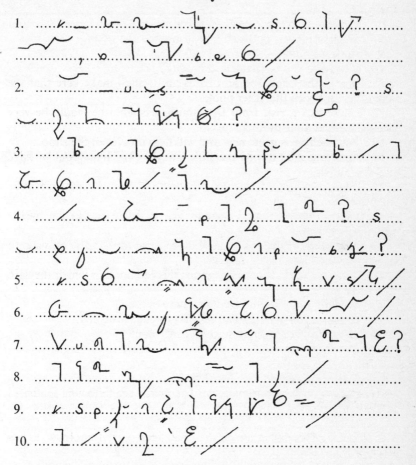

You will have noticed that in 'bazaar' (....⟨shorthand⟩.......) the S inside the B is slightly distorted. This occasionally happens—as in 'best' (....⟨shorthand⟩.......), for instance—but it cannot be read as anything else but S. The outline for 'John' is ....⟨shorthand⟩..... and for distinction we generally use ......⟨shorthand⟩..... for 'Joan', with two indicators joined together. You will learn more about these later.

5

DOUBLE VOWELS
Dbl   vwls

Sometimes consecutive vowels occur at the beginning of a word, and one feels that both should be shown. Examples are the AU in August, author, authority, austere and so on. Then there are EI words like either and eider, or IO words such as ionize, iodine and iota, etc.

There is an easy way of dealing with these. With the AU words, we write the A and ignore the U: .... author, ... August, ... autumn, ... authentic, ... or .... audit, ... aubergine. The use of the A without the U is sufficiently suggestive of the word.

For EI and IO words, it is usual to write the I only: .... 'ither' for 'either' (but if you habitually give 'either' an E sound ('eether') you can easily write an E instead of an I and the word will still be recognized).

With IO, use the I and ignore the O, as in .... 'inic' for 'ionic'.

When two vowels come together and both have equal value, write the first of the two; when one of them is dominant, like the I in 'ionic', then write the dominant one.

We follow the same rule when two vowels come together in the middle or at the end of a word, and write that which is the stronger of the two: .... 'vilin' for 'violin', ... 'vilet' for 'violet', ... 'vilent' for 'violent', ... 'pano' for 'piano', ... 'pom' for 'poem', ... 'didem' for 'diadem', and so on.

The above words may seem odd when looked at in ordinary print, but when written in Teeline and seen in context, they presented no difficulty at all.

There remain two more double vowels in frequent use: OO and OU. These are so closely related that we are able to use the same sign for them, and we use one of the consonants which is also a near relative: the

36

........✓...... sign for W, which fits in without any trouble. It works like

this: .....L.ɘ..... house, ... stout, ... out (the same

outline as 'what' but there is no confusion in context), ...⁊.....

outlines, ...⊊..... lounge, ...ᴏ̄..... bout, ... tout,

.....ᴇ̄...... cloud or clout, ...⌣....... doubt, ... snout,

....⊩̄....... pool, ...ᴇ̄...... cool, ...⌒⌐..... noon.

The sign for OO or OU can be joined or disjoined at the whim of the writer and it does not alter the word. Here is another example: 'about'

can be written ....ᴏ̄....... or ...ᴖ̄..... or ......ᴏ̄...... With such a common word the last form is recommended, but it is not 'wrong' to

write ......ᴏ̄...... or ...ᴖ̄..... That is one of the advantages of Teeline—you can write a word several ways, but there is only one way to read it. Those who have seen or tried to learn other systems sometimes find this statement difficult to grasp at first, so it will be repeated from time to time as a reminder.

Special forms to be memorized: ......⌀...... or, ...⌐↑...... one (the

same as 'on'), ...ᴄ....... letter, ... too or two, ...⟨...... kind.

Exercise 13
Cover the key then read these sentences. Afterwards, copy them and transcribe.

1. ....

....

2. ....

3. ....

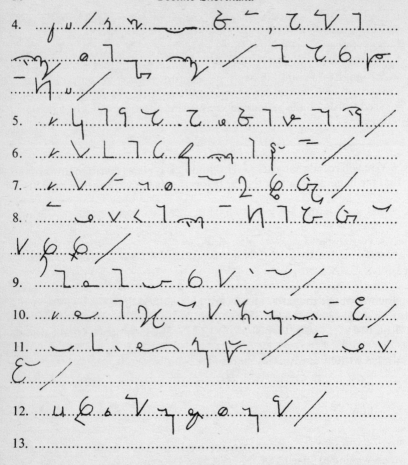

4. ....

....

....

5. ....

6. ....

7. ....

8. ....

....

9. ....

10. ....

11. ....

....

12. ....

13. ....

Key

1. Take the book to the shop and give it to either the boy or the girl.
2. I shall go either to the park or to the show in the church hall.
3. The house is at the end of the road.
4. If you are in any doubt about it, tell either the manager or the deputy manager. They will be pleased to help you.
5. I hope the chairman will tell us about the visit to the match.
6. I have had the letter from the man at the shop today.
7. I have read one or two good books lately.
8. It was very kind of the man to help the old lady with her big box.
9. They said they would be here at two.
10. I saw the girl with her violin on the way to school.
11. We had a swim in the pool. It was very cool.
12. Your book is either on the sofa or on the chair.

Always learn the special forms before beginning any exercise. The best way is to write them over and over, saying them to yourself as you do so. Special forms are never learned properly merely by looking at them on the page; they must be *written* if they are to be learned well. The special forms are easy outlines for frequently-used words, so the better you know them, the more quickly will you write.

You will recall that after G, H, J and P, L is always written upwards so that the hand does not go too far below the line of writing (see page 8):

...... hall, ... hill, ... pool, ... pill, ... hello, ... hollow, ... play, ... apply, ... plea, ... jolly, ... while, etc.

You will notice that after an upward L a finally sounded A or E is always disjoined: ...... play, ... plea. A final I indicator is always written upwards so that it makes a distinctive joining:

....

hilly   Polly   pally   jelly   holly.

Writing a final I indicator at a sharp angle enables it to be shown clearly when writing at speed.

Whenever an upward L is followed by T or D, the letters are disjoined, as they would be after an R:

....

household   play   played   plate   plated   halt

....

halted   guilty   guild   guilt   jilt   jilted

....

child or chilled, etc.

Exercise 14

Cover the key on the opposite page. Read the sentences, then copy them and transcribe.

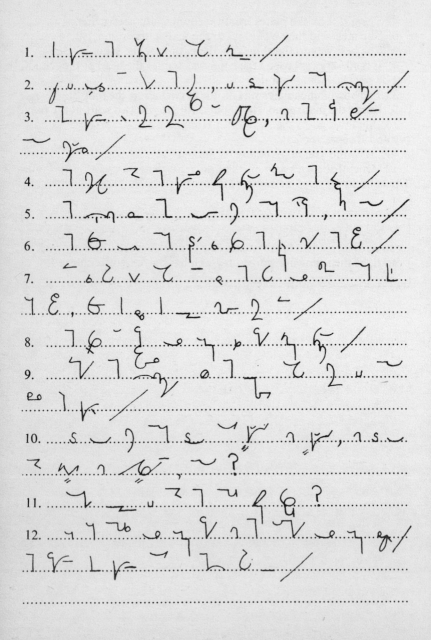

Key

1. He played the violin very well indeed.
2. If you wish to have the job, you should apply to the manager.
3. They played a good game of football and they each scored two goals.
4. The girl took the plates from the lounge into the kitchen.
5. The men said they would go to the match, too.
6. The best way to the ship is by the path near the school.
7. It is all very well to say the letter was sent to the head of the school, but he says he did not get it.
8. The box of chocolates was on the easy chair in the lounge.
9. Either the manager or the deputy will get you two seats at the play.
10. Shall we go to the show with Holly and Polly, and shall we take Ivy and Robert, too?
11. Why did you take the toy from the boy?
12. One of the toys was on the chair and the other was on the sofa. The child had played with them all day.

Never refer to a key except as a last resort. If you are puzzled by an outline, read on for the next two or three words and then go back to it, as the following words may well have given you a clue.

6

SIMPLE WORD GROUPS
Smpl   wrd   grps

Most people learn shorthand in order to write notes quickly. The secretary uses it for taking letters; the newspaper reporter for taking notes of speeches; the student uses it to save time in making notes of lectures, or copying passages from books. It can be used for taking telephone messages, or writing out a reminder to do something, or making out a shopping list. There are scores of ways shorthand can be used. Samuel Pepys wrote his diary in an early system of shorthand (Thomas Shelton's 'Short Writing' of 1626); Bernard Shaw used it for writing his plays; and at least two judges have used it for making notes of trials held in their courts.

Teeline is ideal for all these things. One way in which it is possible to increase one's speed of writing is to use the principle of word grouping—that is, by joining two or more words together in one outline. This saves time and makes it possible to read a group of words at a glance. You are already familiar with a few word groups, for they were given with the series of special forms for memorizing. As a memory refresher, here they are again:

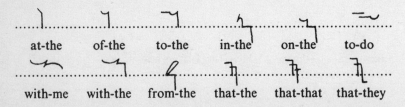

| at-the | of-the | to-the | in-the | on-the | to-do |
| with-me | with-the | from-the | that-the | that-that | that-they |

Sometimes a word can be abbreviated in word groups in much the same way as we group words in speech: .... 'we've' for .... we have, ... 'I'm' for .... I am, ... 'we're' for .... we are, ... 'it's' for .... it is. In addition, an outline can be altered slightly to make a word group, but it can still be recognized. There is an example in the foregoing paragraph, where an E indicator is inserted after the W in 'we are'. This is because

42

.... makes an easier joining than would ...., which

would become distorted at speed.

There are other examples in the earlier outlines. In .... at-the,

.... of-the, for instance, the 'the' is abbreviated to the H, and in

.... 'that-that' the H is attached to the little cross stroke on 'that'.

Words come in patterns. We can often tell which word comes next from the first words in the group. If you heard someone say 'It is a fact—' you would know that the next word would be 'that', even if you did not hear it properly. We do not learn these patterns, because they come automatically. It is the same with word groups. Once you have seen a few examples and practised them, they flow straight from the pen without a second's thought. On the other hand, we do not join words together willy-nilly; we apply grouping only to those words which occur frequently and which together make a distinctive outline.

Here are some examples of word patterns which can be grouped. Write them out several times, and it will help if you say them to yourself as you do so:

| we-have | I-will | we-will | we-w(ill)-be | I-am |

| have-the | I-have | I-have-the | I-have-had | it-is | it-will |

| it-w(ill)-be | who-(ha)s or who-is | it-is-not |

| and-the | to-be | by-the | I-hope | if-the | if-you |

| if-we | if-we-are | if-you-are | if-you-will |

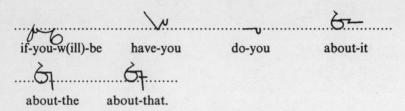

if-you-w(ill)-be   have-you   do-you   about-it

about-the   about-that.

It is best to spend some time copying out these forms. *Say them to yourself as you do so.* This is important, although to the beginner it may not seem necessary. Saying the outlines to yourself as you write them will help to fix the principle in your memory. Writing a different outline each time is also a help. Filling two or three pages of a notebook like this:

etc.

is much more beneficial than doing a whole line of the same group because it is also a good exercise in pen control.

Make sure you are familiar with word grouping before going further. For the time being, do not join more than three words together. As you begin to recognize more word patterns, then more groups can be introduced—but that will be left until later. For the time being, concentrate on using groups of small words, such as those shown here and the few additional simple word groups to be encountered in future exercises.

Special forms to be memorized: .... general-ly, ... nine, ... noon, ... able or able-to, ... accident, ... member (......... members).

Exercise 15

Cover the key on the opposite page. Read the sentences and then copy and transcribe them.

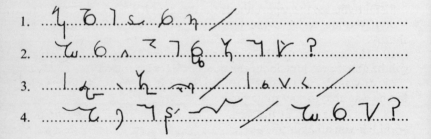

1.

2.

3.

4.

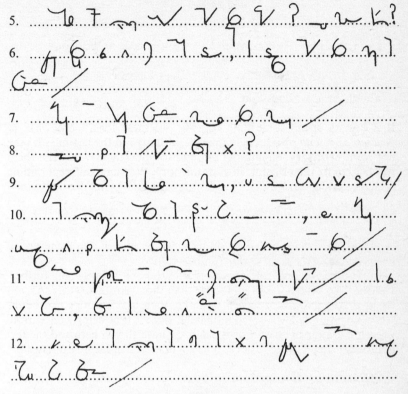

Key

1. I-hope to-be at-the show by nine.
2. Will-you be able-to take the boy's violin to-the hall?
3. He is-not a violent man. He is very kind.
4. We-will go to-the ship tomorrow. Will-you be there?
5. Who-is that man over there by-the chair? Do-you know him?
6. If-the boy is able-to go to-the show, he should-be there by nine at-the latest.
7. I-hope to have-the latest news by noon.
8. Did-you see the report about-the accident?
9. If-you-are to-be at-the house at noon, you should leave very shortly.
10. The manager will-be at-the shop all day today, so I-hope you-will-be able-to see him about-the new book I-wish to buy.
11. It-was pleasant to meet General Smith at-the party. He is very old, but he was able-to stay some time.
12. I saw the man at-the scene of-the accident and if-you-have time I-will tell-you all about-it.

Exercise 16

Cover the key on the opposite page. Then write the following sentences in Teeline.

1. It-is quite easy to write Teeline, but like all skills, you-have to-do a lot of study and write outlines many times over. Do not-be upset if-you find you-have made a mistake. That is-the way to get on.

2. The chairman said if-we-are to-be ready to catch the boat, we should-be at-the garage by noon at-the latest. I-have-had to tell this to all-the members of-the party.

3. If-you-will-be at-the garage early, we-will-be able-to leave in good time. I-hope you-will not-be late.

4. Who-has had the book about-the old church in-the village? I see it-is on-the chair by-the alcove.

5. There-are two baskets on-the chairman's desk. One is-the 'in' basket and-the other is-the 'out' one. There-are always many letters in them, as he is-a very busy man.

6. Will you please let me have-the letters they sent to-the chairman? They should-be on-the top of-the pile in-the 'out' basket.

7. The bad weather seems to-be general.

In the above exercise the new word groups include .....ᴔ........ is-a. This is a typical example of the way you can make up your own word groups:

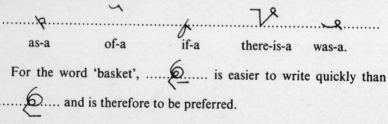

as-a	of-a	if-a	there-is-a	was-a

For the word 'basket', ...ᴓ...... is easier to write quickly than

......ᴓ..... and is therefore to be preferred.

In all future exercises, words that are hyphened should be joined together in a word group. From time to time new word groups will be introduced, so that it can be seen how easy it is to make them up.

The word 'time' may be written .... or .... but at speed the former is more facile and is therefore used in all exercises.

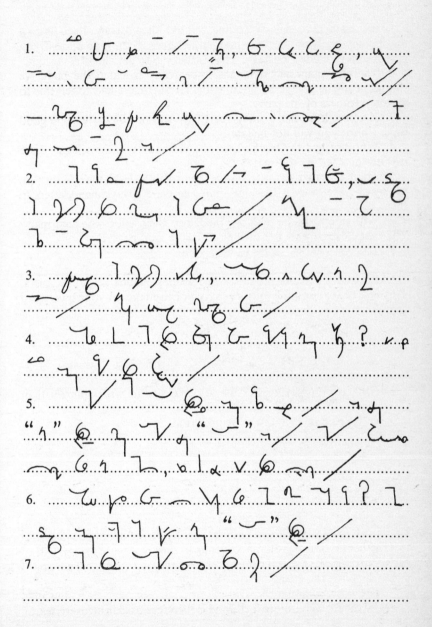

MORE ABOUT VOWEL INDICATORS
Mr   abt   vwl   indctrs

With this lesson you are going to learn how to write hundreds more words with a simple stroke of the pen.

1. A disjoined 'A' indicator *at the end of a stroke* adds '-ang':

hang   bang   rang   sang   Lang   harangue

tang   pang.

Remember that the 'A' is disjoined and comes at the *end* of a stroke; that

is why, in .... rang, the 'A' comes above the line, because R, being an upward stroke, finishes in that position.

Plurals are shown by adding S:

hangs   bangs   harangues   pangs   fangs.

The past tense is shown by adding D:

hanged   banged   harangued, etc.

2. A disjoined 'E' indicator *at the end of a stroke* adds '-eng':

.... Leng (other examples will be given later).

3. A disjoined 'I' indicator *at the end of a stroke* adds '-ing', and this is the most widely-used disjoined indicator of them all:

sing   ring   Ming   ping   wing   owing

48

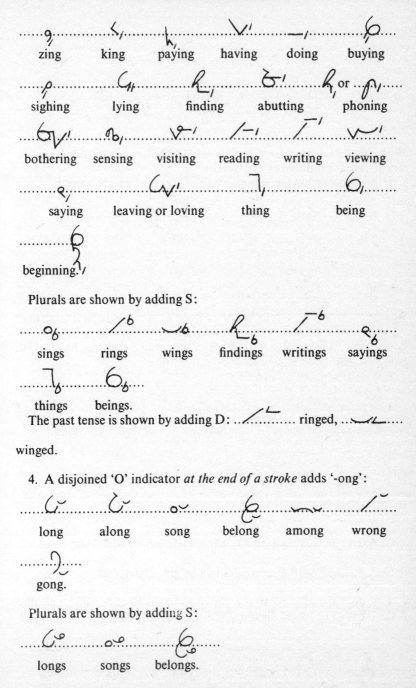

zing　king　paying　having　doing　buying

sighing　lying　finding　abutting　phoning

bothering　sensing　visiting　reading　writing　viewing

saying　leaving or loving　thing　being

beginning.

Plurals are shown by adding S:

sings　rings　wings　findings　writings　sayings

things　beings.

The past tense is shown by adding D: .... ringed, ... winged.

4. A disjoined 'O' indicator *at the end of a stroke* adds '-ong':

long　along　song　belong　among　wrong

gong.

Plurals are shown by adding S:

longs　songs　belongs.

The past tense is shown by adding D:

...../‾.............6.............(‾.....

wronged   belonged   longed.

5. A disjoined 'U' indicator *at the end of a stroke* adds '-ung':

.......ol..............U.1.............../'.............(1.............61......

sung   young   rung   lung   bung.

Plurals are shown by adding S:

....../ᵇ..............(.ᵇ..............6.ᵇ....

rungs   lungs   bungs.

The past tense is shown by adding D: ...6⌐...... bunged, etc.

Copy all the above outlines, saying them to yourself as you do so, and you will quickly get into the habit of writing a disjoined indicator at the end of a stroke for -ang, -eng, -ing, -ong, -ung.

Special forms to be memorized: ....ᗐ..... department (......ⓐ...... departments), ...ᑌᒍ...... equal, -ed (.....ᑌᒍ....... equals), ...⋀........ represent or representative (......⋀ᵦ..... represents or representatives), ...ᒎ..... no, number.

Exercise 17

Read these sentences and afterwards copy and transcribe them. The key appears on page 52.

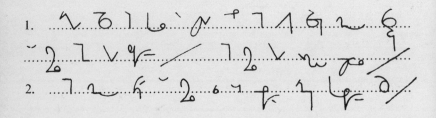

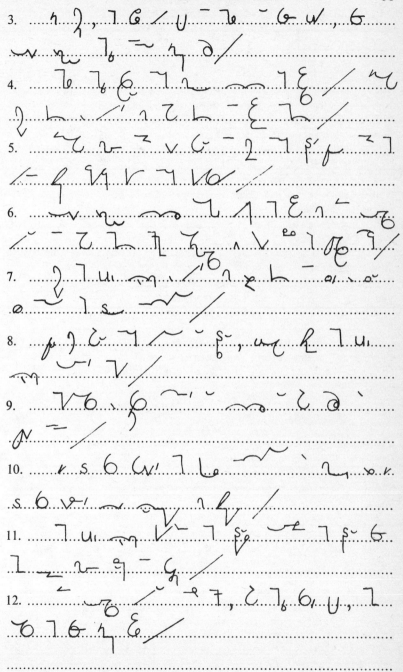

Key

1. I-have to-be at-the house at five to-see the representative about-the new batch of goods they have supplied. The goods have a-number-of defects.

2. The new line of goods is on display in-the household department.

3. In general, the sales are equal to those of last year, but we-have a-number-of things to-do in-the department.

4. Those things belong to-the new member of-the club. I-will give him a ring and tell him to collect them.

5. It-will not take very long to get to-the ship if-we take the road from-the church hall to-the harbour.

6. We-have a-number-of members who represent the school and it would-be wrong to tell them that-they will-not-be able-to have seats at-the football match.

7. Give the young man a ring and ask him to sing a song or two at-the show tomorrow.

8. If-you go along to-the row of shops, you-will find the young man waiting there.

9. There-will-be a big meeting of members of all departments at five today.

10. I shall be leaving the house tomorrow at noon as I shall be visiting my mother and father.

11. The young man harangued the shoppers outside the shop, but they did not stop to listen.

12. It would-be wrong to-say that, all things being equal, they will-be the best in-the class.

Exercise 18

Cover the key, then write the following sentences in Teeline:

1. If-you-are ready, we-will go along to-the church hall right away, as I-wish to make sure that-the girl is there at-the beginning of-the show.

2. There-is-a long queue at-the hall, waiting to-be let in. The meeting is-not due to begin until two.

3. I-hope you-will-be able-to see the men who-are going fishing.

4. The representatives said the ship should-be loaded by tomorrow. If-you-are going to-the ship, you-will no doubt find one of-them there, waiting to-see if-the loading is finished in time.

5. We-have-had news that-the large household department at-the shop is holding a sale of chairs and stools. We-shall be going there to-see if-there-are any easy chairs in-the sale.

6. He is quite equal to-the task and we-are hoping he will-be finishing it shortly.

Key

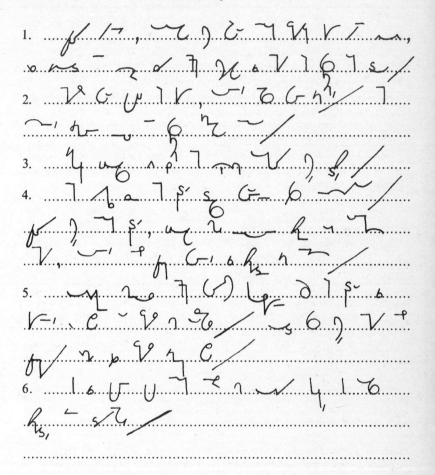

1. ...

2. ...

3. ...

4. ...

5. ...

6. ...

Did you remember that ...⤳....... can stand for OO and OU as well as W? And did you notice the difference in the length of the upstroke in ......⟋...... there/their and .....⟋........ there-are?

We have not quite finished with the very useful principle of using a disjoined indicator for -ang, -ing, etc. In order to speed up writing with no effort at all, there are several other things we can do with this principle.

So far, the indicators have been disjoined for word endings, but it is also possible to use them in the middle of words:

hang	hanging	bang	banging	long	longing

belong	belonging	sing	singing	throng	thronging

wing	winging	ring	ringing	length	lengthening

wrong	wronging	amongst	longer	singer	finger

bangle,	tangle	tangling	dangle	dangling	hunger

hungry

How to Write '-ingly'

Many words end in '-ingly' and in these cases we omit the '-ing' and write only a *disjoined* '-ly'. The fact that it is disjoined tells us that we have to read an 'ing' before it although it is not written (what a time-saver this is!). These examples will show how straightforward it can be:

loving	lov(ing)ly	knowing	know(ing)ly	seeming	seem(ing)ly

according	accord(ing)ly	sing	s(ing)ly.

The word-ending '-ingle' can be written the same way, but without

the final 'I' indicator ......⌒(..... mingle (but note ......⌒⟩...... mangle),
......o(...... single, ...⌐(....tingle (but note .....⌐⟨...... tangle).

You will have noticed that the disjoined indicators represent -ang, -eng, -ing, -ong, -ung. They are *not* used for -ange, -enge, -inge, -onge, -unge, where the 'G' has a soft sound. Thus, we write

change   sponge   lunge   lounge   manger   hinge

Special forms to be memorized: .....⌐⌐...... thought, ...⚬....... accept
(......⚬..... accepted), ...⚬.... business (.......⚬.... businesses).

Exercise 19

Read these sentences and afterwards copy and transcribe them. The key appears on page 57.

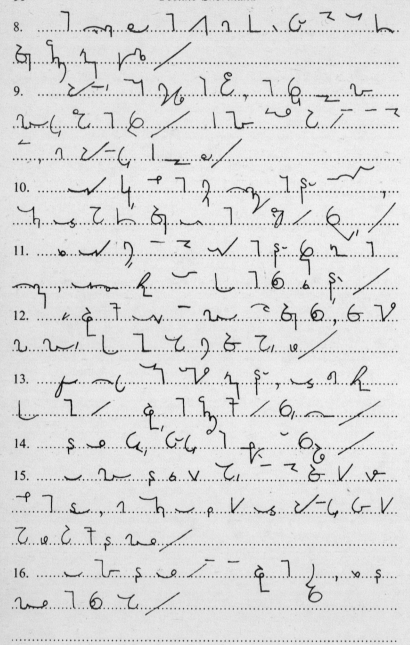

Key

1. The boy was wrongly admonished by-the teacher.
2. The singer cut her finger just as she was about to go on-the stage.
3. He is hoping to equal the record achieved by-the other men.
4. The building of-the house will take longer than we thought.
5. If-we-are to change the plans of-the building, it-will-be best if-we tell them right away.
6. She chose a ring with a single ruby in it.
7. The boy said he was very hungry and was looking longingly at the food.
8. The man saw the representative and had a long talk with him about-the change in-the plans.
9. According to-the girls at-the school, the boy did not knowingly steal the book. He thought it-was all right to take it, and accordingly he did so.
10. We-are hoping to-see the general manager of-the shop tomorrow, when we-shall tell him about-the way the staff are behaving.
11. As we-are going to take over the shop by-the end of-the month, we-must find out how the business is shaping.
12. I accept that we-have to know much about-the business, but there-is no knowing how they will go about telling us.
13. If-we mingle with-the others in-the shop, we-shall soon find how they are accepting the changes that are being made.
14. She was looking longingly at-the display of bangles.
15. We know she is very willing to talk about her visit to-see the show, and when we see her we-shall accordingly let her tell us all that she knows.
16. We thought she was right to accept the job, as she knows the business well.

Remember that for '-ingle' we use a disjoined L: .....⌢⌣(......

mingle, ...o.(...... single; and for '-ingly' we write a disjoined '-ly'. In these cases there is no need to write a disjoined '-ing' as its

presence is implied: ...o.(........ singly, ...⌣⌢(.... lovingly.

The disjoined indicators, with a small C added to them, give us the combinations -ank, -enk, -ink, -onk, -unk, as in:

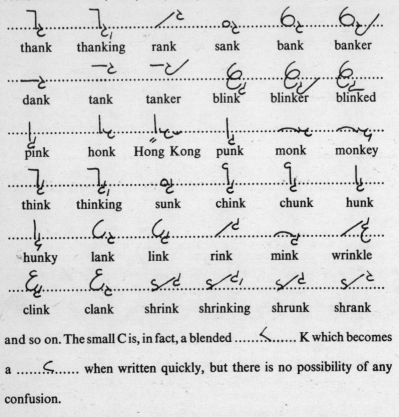

thank	thanking	rank	sank	bank	banker
dank	tank	tanker	blink	blinker	blinked
pink	honk	Hong Kong	punk	monk	monkey
think	thinking	sunk	chink	chunk	hunk
hunky	lank	link	rink	mink	wrinkle
clink	clank	shrink	shrinking	shrunk	shrank

and so on. The small C is, in fact, a blended .... K which becomes

a .... when written quickly, but there is no possibility of any

confusion.

Special forms to be memorized: .... has (H sloped to blend with

the A indicator), ... his (H sloped to blend with the I indicator),

.... however, ... necessary, ... only.

Word groups: .... has-been, ... have-been, ...

had-been, ... we-have-been. (The outline .... 'been', in

these groups, is abbreviated to ....)

Exercise 20

Read these sentences and afterwards, copy them and transcribe. The key appears on page 61.

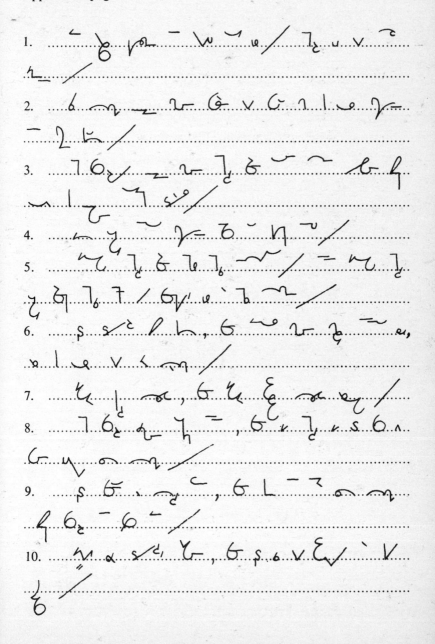

11.

12.

13.

14.

15.

16.

17.

18.

19.

20.

Key

1. It has-been pleasant to have-you with us. Thank you very much indeed.

2. His money did not last very long and he was glad to get home.

3. The banker did not think about what might result from-the way he dealt with-the shares.

4. I-am only too glad to-be of help to-you.

5. I-will think about those things tomorrow. Today I-will think only about-the things that are bothering us at this minute.

6. She shrank from him, but it-was not necessary to-do so, as he was-a very kind man.

7. I-like punk music, but I-like classical music as-well.

8. The bank is-not open today, but I think I shall be able-to let you-have some money.

9. She bought a mink coat, but had to take some money from-the bank to buy it.

10. Ivy is a shrinking violet, but she is very clever at her job.

11. The monkey at the zoo was watched by many people, who thought his antics very funny.

12. I think the chairman is very busy. However, I think he may be able-to see you today or tomorrow.

13. Which way did the tanker go? It slipped out of-the harbour quite early.

14. The ship sank at-the spot where many other ships have sunk.

15. The pink cloth had shrunk a lot by-the time I had finished washing it.

16. We-have-been very busy at the bank.

17. He had-been at school all day, but did not shrink from going to-see the man about-the part time job at-the shop.

18. Has his game finished yet? However it ends, he will still have to go to his part time job at-the shop.

19. I-have yet to-see him be late. He always leaves his house about nine, as he does not have to-be at his shop until then, and he lives only a little way away. However, one day he may be a little late. Who knows?

20. It-is not necessary to thank me, as-the job did not take very long. It-was only necessary to get the engine going.

Do not forget that the disjoined indicators stand for -ang, -eng, -ing, -ong and -ung. They do *not* represent -ange, -enge, etc., as in ch*ange*, ch*ange*r, d*ange*r, r*ange*r, d*ung*eon, l*ing*erie, etc. The disjoined indicators with a small C added represent -ank, -enk, -ink, -onk, and -unk.

8

A LITTLE LOOK BACK
A   ltl   lk   bac

Now you have made so much progress with Teeline, this is a convenient point at which to see how much ground has already been covered. With any system of shorthand, frequent revision is most necessary at the learning stage. The reason for this is easily appreciated: shorthand is a skill, and any skill is mastered only by doing it until it becomes second nature.

When anyone first takes driving lessons, there is a routine to be learned when moving off, another drill for changing gear, a third for driving along a road, and so on. At first, everything is a conscious effort and it is only by constant repetition that one is able to accomplish everything without having to think about it.

It is the same with shorthand—even Teeline, which is relatively easy, since it has a light memory load and has no exceptions to its very few rules.

Let us pause for a moment and consider the basic principle of Teeline. It is this: we follow ordinary longhand spelling, but we discard all unwanted letters. That is all there is to it.

When the late James Hill started to apply work study principles to longhand writing, he realized that symbols would be needed rather than letters, and he cleverly devised his alphabet so that every sign bore some relation to its longhand equivalent. You have already been discovering how ingeniously this works.

One of the beauties of Teeline is that it is almost impossible to write a 'wrong' outline. We know that all initial vowels must be written and that any finally sounded vowels must also be shown; but vowels coming in the middle of words are rarely needed.

However, with an open-ended system like Teeline, you can insert vowels if you wish, and the finished outline will not be incorrect because you have done so. If you wish to write 'take' as TAK instead of TK, it will not be wrong, because the resulting outline can still only be read as 'take'. It is, of course, advisable to omit the A because it is unnecessary and also saves valuable time, but it is not 'wrong' to include it.

When working the exercises it is more than likely that some of your outlines have been different from those shown in the keys, but it does not follow that the shorthand form you have written should be counted as an error. Experience has shown that when writing quickly—at 80, 100 or 120 or more words a minute—some forms are better than others because they keep their shape better and are therefore more acceptable. Those are the outlines used in this book.

Quite a number of words can be written more than one way and it is up to you to decide which you prefer and which comes easiest to

the hand. The word 'coffee', for example, can be written ....,

.........., ..., ... or .... It does not matter

which way it is written, for it can still only be read as 'coffee' in the context.

Even the sentence 'We went into the .... for a ....' can

only be read as 'We went into the cafe for a coffee'. It would be nonsense if the words were reversed.

Here are some other things you have learned:

When consecutive vowels start a word and neither has a dominant sound (AU in August, Australia, is an example), use the first vowel and ignore the second. *But* if one of the vowels is dominant, like the I in eider or either, or the E in aegis, then write the dominant one.

When two vowels come together in the middle of a word, use the dominant one, like the I in violin or violence, or the A in piano or radiant. (The combinations EA as in idea or the OI in boil and toil will be dealt with later and will not worry you.)

When OO or OU occur in a word, we use the same sign as W and this presents no difficulty.

One other thing must be remembered, and that is that R is always shown in a word, even if it is not pronounced, and we always write a W when it follows a vowel.

There are some other consonants which, you have no doubt noticed, act in a certain set way.

T and D are two of them. These letters are represented by an identical stroke, but T is placed above the line and D on it. Yet in practice they tend to move around. How is one to be distinguished from the other?

Let's put it this way: T is always 'written high' whenever possible

and D is 'written low'. T or D after R is an example of this; .... is RT (always disjoined unless another consonant comes between, and the

T is 'written high'), while.........is RD (disjoined, with the D 'written low'). As far as possible we always try to preserve this distinction.

Another example is T or D after an upward L. As you know, L is normally a *down* stroke, but it is always written upwards after G, J, P—and H ('H' includes ....ᒉ...... CH, ...ᒎ...... WH and ....ᒎ......

TH, since these are compound signs). Study these outlines: .....ᒮ.........

child (D written low), ...ᒮ........ hold (D written low), ...ᒮ......... halt

(T written high), ...ᒮ....... plate (T high), ...ᒮ...... played (D low).

The same applies to 'children' (D low) and Chiltern (T high), which you will learn to write later.

When T or D come in the middle or at the end of a word, they may safely be written out of the normal positions, because the sense of the

sentence tells us how to read them: ....ᒫ......... can be post or posed;

......ᑕ...... can be best or based; ....ᒍ...... can be get, got or good.

Bear in mind the sense of the sentence, and that will always help you. Some people like to write ......ᒪ........ for paid and ......ᒋ........ for put;

but that is something entirely up to the individual. In more than twelve years of writing Teeline I have only once encountered a slight confusion

and that was ...ᒪᒪ..., which could have been read as 'had had' or 'had hit'. It so happens that the latter was correct, so ever since I have

been careful to vocalize ......ᒦ...... hit. It is as simple as that: I merely slip in an indicator and that is enough to tell me that the outline is to be read as 'hit' and not 'had' or 'hid'. That snag has only arisen once in thousands of words, and it may never happen again.

Here is something which has not been mentioned before, because it is not a rule of the system but a personal idiosyncrasy: L can also be written upwards or downwards after M and N if you wish. The L can quite easily be written downwards (as it should be) after M:

......ᒩ..... ML, but if you prefer, you may write it upwards: .....ᒧ...... ML, and it does not alter the value of the outline. Personally I prefer the downward form, as I like to be consistent as far as possible. Re-

search into the timing of outlines shows that ......ᒩ...... takes slightly less time to write at speed than does ....⌢⌣...... After N, L may also be written upwards: ......⌒...... NL, or downwards: ......⌒...... NL. Both outlines mean the same. My own preference is for the downward form in ....⌒...... only, since the L seems to balance the ....⌐......; but at

all other times I find it easier to write the upward form: ......⌒........ nail, ...⌒........ knell, ...⌒........ knelt, ...⌒...... Nile, and so on. This is purely a personal matter which is left entirely to the individual; either way is correct.

This is the great thing about Teeline: you might write words differently from other Teeliners, but in the context of the sentence they all mean the same thing. That is why it is almost impossible to write a 'wrong' outline in Teeline.

Another interesting feature of this very logical system is the way one letter can blend with another. Later on you will learn more about blending, but you have already seen what happens with H, which is

an upright stroke: ....|....... When joined to V, it would make an awkward joining: ......↓..... so we slope it to the left in order to blend with the first stroke of the V: ......⋁...... have, ...⋁...... heave, ...⌣........

hover (notice how the R also blends with the V!), ...Ç....... behave, and so on.

The same thing happens with P; it can blend very nicely with V, so avoiding the awkward joining ......|........ So 'PV' words are written like this: .....⋁......... pave, ...⋁........ paving, ...⋁........ pavilion.

Disjoined vowel indicators, written at the end of a stroke, give the syllables -ang, -eng, -ing, -ong and -ung, but they are not used where the G has a soft sound, as in change, danger, singe, hinge, and so on. With a small C added, the disjoined indicators are used for -ank, -enk, -ink, -onk and -unk.

To conclude this brief revision, here is some guidance about the writing of F. This letter is represented by two forms which are the upper and lower loops of the written .... 𝑓 ...... Generally, you write whichever form suits you: ..... ↄ .... and ..... ↄ ..... both represent find or fond or fund (but not found—that will come later). ...... ↄ ...... or .... ↄ ..... both represent cough (we make one stroke do the work of two, remember?); ..... ↄ ...... or ...... ↄ .... can both be fake or folk. You write whichever form suits you, but before T and D you must write the loop which puts the T or D in the normal position: ..... ↄ .... FT, ... ↄ ...... FD.

You may prefer ..... ↄ .... (fine or phone or fun) to ...... ↄ ......, or ..... ↄ .... for father rather than .... ↄ ......; it is entirely a matter for the individual.

If you have any uncertainty, then the best way to decide is to experiment. Try ...... ↄ ...... and ..... ↄ ......; .... ↄ .... fnd and ...... ↄ ..... fnd; ...... ↄ ...... or ...... ↄ ..... or ...... ↄ ...... (they all stand for 'off') and use the form that you find best.

The same applies to the letter S on the straight strokes. Some people say it is easier for them to write .ↄ .ↄ .ↄ .ↄ .ↄ; others prefer ↄ .ↄ .ↄ .ↄ .ↄ In this textbook the latter are given as the more acceptable when written at speed.

Already you have learned to write hundreds of words in Teeline and unbeknown to yourself you are beginning to write quickly and accurately. You will no doubt find the next step even more interesting and, it is to be hoped, fascinating. Remember: in the words of James Hill, if you can write, you can write Teeline.

WAYS WITH 'C': I
CK; 'soft' C; -NCE; -NCH

In the Concise edition of the Oxford Dictionary there are more than 3,400 root words that begin with the letter C. These are the root words only, and do not include the hundreds of derivatives or abbreviations. Neither does it include words which have a C somewhere in the middle or at the end, of which there are thousands.

As a matter of fact, C, T, R and N are among the most important consonants in the English language and, as you will see, Teeline has its own clever way of dealing with them.

Let us deal with C first, since it appears in an enormous number of words. The Teeline sign is written like an ordinary longhand C, but it is also used when we get the combination CK in a word (see p. 6) as in lick (lic), sack (sac), etc. This in itself is ingenious, because it helps us to distinguish between lic(k) and like, sac(k) and sake, bac(k) and bake, and so on. Examples of this are: .... lack, ... lake, ... tack, ...take, ... quick, ...

quake, and in other words where the outline is similar.

It is sometimes helpful, especially at the end of words, to know whether C has a hard or soft sound. In order to provide a useful clue, we put a small circle inside the C in such cases: .... nice or niece, ... or .... race, ... races, ... or .... rice .... face, ... lace, ... piece, ... dice, ... decide, ... office, ... parcel, ... receive. This 'soft C' sign is used *only* in the middle or at the end of words. At the beginning of an outline .... represents SC as in .... school, ... scholastic, ... scherzo.

There is an easy way of writing -NCE in a word: we write nothing at all for the N and disjoin the C. In this way we can tell at a glance that we read '-nce' for the disjoined C:

hence	since	science	chance	balance	once

announce	stance	fence	appearance	elegance

The disjoined C for -NCE can also be used in the middle of words:

balances	balanced	chances	chanced	chancing	enhanced

enhances	fancy	fencing	announcing	announced

Word groups for practice: .... as-soon-as, ... to-see .... o'clock.

Exercise 21

Cover the key and read the sentences. Then copy the outlines and transcribe.

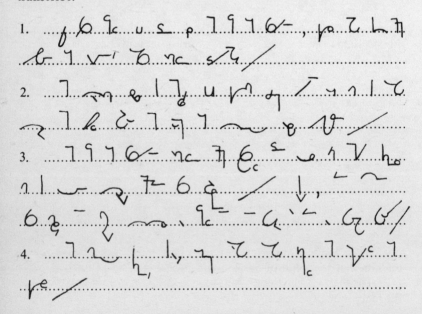

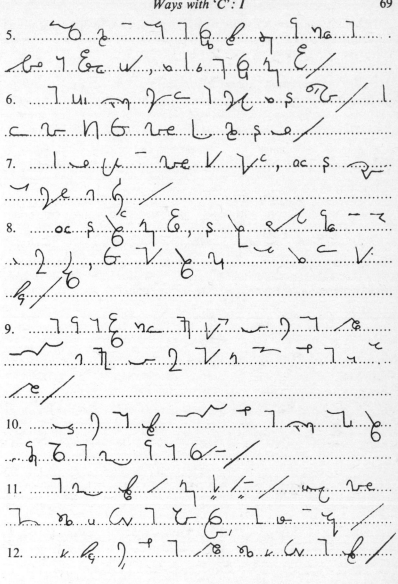

5.

6.

7.

8.

9.

10.

11.

12.

Key

1. If by chance you should see the chairman of-the board, please tell him that-the result of-the voting will-be announced shortly.

2. The man says he thinks your plan is-the right one and he will make the fence along the top of-the meadow as-you request.

3. The chairman of-the board announced that-the balance sheet was in their hands and he would move that-it be accepted. However, it might be necessary to give members a chance to look at it a little longer.

4. The new painting hanging on the wall will enhance the appearance of-the place.

5. It-will-be nice to watch the boy's face as-the chairman announces the results of-the scholastic year, as he is top boy in the school.

6. The young man glanced at-the girl as she smiled. He could not help but notice how nice she was.

7. He was quick to notice her appearance, since she moved with grace and elegance.

8. Since she has-been in-the class, she has-had several chances to take a good job, but there has-been none which has caught her fancy.

9. The chairman of-the club announced that-the party would go to-the races tomorrow and that-they would get there in time to-see the one o'clock race.

10. We-shall go to-the office tomorrow to-see the man who has-been chosen to-be the new chairman of-the board.

11. The new offices are in-the High Road. You-will notice them as-soon-as you leave the old building they used to occupy.

12. I fancy going to-see the races as-soon-as I leave the office.

Points to remember:
A 'soft C' is .... ℰ ......, but *only* in the middle or at the end of words.

The combination NCE is shown by a disjoined ...... ℭ ....

In words containing 'CK', use the C and ignore the K.

'Office' is best written ..... 𝓎 .... Here it is enlarged so you can

see the direction the pen takes: ...𝓎........𝓎......

In many words the letters NCH come together, and since we use a disjoined C for NCE it is logical that for NCH we should use a disjoined CH sign:

bench or bunch lunch   munch   hunch pinch or punch ranch

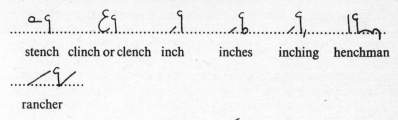

stench   clinch or clench   inch   inches   inching   henchman

rancher

Special forms to be memorized: .... because, ... evidence, evident.

Exercise 22

Cover the key and read the sentences. Then copy the outlines and transcribe.

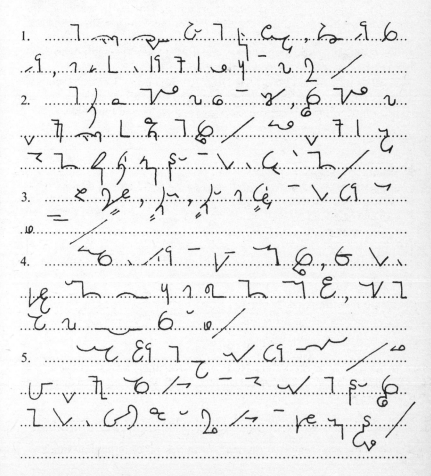

Key

1. The man moved along the path slowly, almost inch by inch, and I had a hunch that he was up to no good.

2. The judge said there-was no case to answer, because there-was no evidence that-the man had stolen the books. It-was evident that he only took them from-the ledge in-the shop to have a look at them.

3. Ask Grace, Joan, John and Lucy to have lunch with us today.

4. It-will-be a wrench to part with-the books, but have a parcel of-them made up and send them to-the school, where they will no doubt be of use.

5. We-will clinch the deal over lunch tomorrow. It-is quite evident that-they will-be ready to take over the shop because they have a large stock of goods ready to place on-the shelves.

> Did you remember that .....⏜..... stands for OO or OU as well as W ?

10

WAYS WITH 'C': II
How to write the CN blend

A great many words contain the syllables CAN, CEN, CIN, CON, COUN or CUN. Whenever the combination of C + *any* vowel + N occurs, we use a sign which at first glance is rather like a squeezed C:

........⌠...... It is in fact a blend of ......⌒...... and ......⌐....... and it is

written the same size as an ......⌐....... but with the hook on the opposite side to show the inclusion of the C.

The important thing to remember is that the CN blend, as it is called, represents C + *any* vowel + N; therefore on first acquaintance it may be necessary to run through the five vowels to try out variants, but always *the sense of the sentence* will provide the vital clue, and in a short time you will cease to ring the changes on the vowels and recognize instantly which vowel is to be read.

Here are some examples of the CN blend with the different vowels:
CAN:

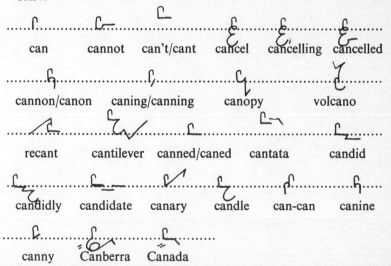

| can | cannot | can't/cant | cancel | cancelling | cancelled |

| cannon/canon | caning/canning | canopy | | volcano |

| recant | cantilever | canned/caned | cantata | candid |

| candidly | candidate | canary | candle | can-can | canine |

| canny | Canberra | Canada |

73

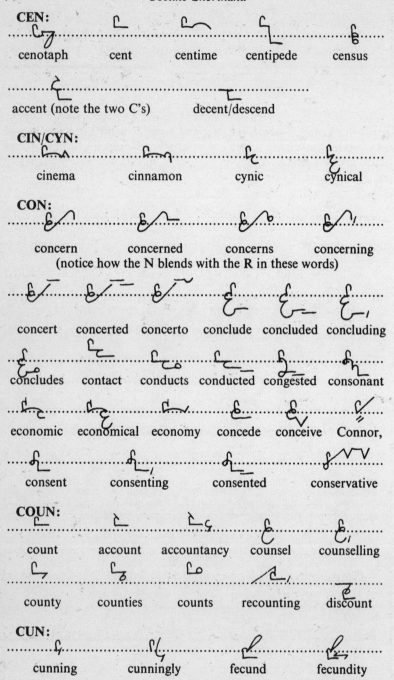

CEN:

cenotaph   cent   centime   centipede   census

accent (note the two C's)   decent/descend

CIN/CYN:

cinema   cinnamon   cynic   cynical

CON:

concern   concerned   concerns   concerning
(notice how the N blends with the R in these words)

concert   concerted   concerto   conclude   concluded   concluding

concludes   contact   conducts   conducted   congested   consonant

economic   economical   economy   concede   conceive   Connor,

consent   consenting   consented   conservative

COUN:

count   account   accountancy   counsel   counselling

county   counties   counts   recounting   discount

CUN:

cunning   cunningly   fecund   fecundity

Remember that the CN blend represents either the 'hard' or 'soft' sound of C. In Teeline you follow the *spelling* of a word.

The ...... ⌠ ...... sign is a most useful one and it will be met with later in words like *centre, control, consider* and so on. In the meantime, it will help you immeasurably if you copy out all the foregoing words several times, *saying them to yourself as you do so*. In this way you will quickly get used to the CN blend.

Special forms to be memorized : .... ⌠ .... can or council, ... ⌠⌠ ......
county council, ... ⟋ℓⱺ ... recognize (...... ⟋ℓⱺ! .. recognizing,
... ⟋ℓⱺ ... recognized), ... ⟋ℓ ... recent, ... ⟋ᵧ ... recently,
.... ℓ .... success, ... ⌒⟍ Mr.

Word groups: .... ⟋ᑫ ..... we-can, ... ᑫⱼ .... if-we-can, ... ⟍ᵧ ......
of-course, ... ↳ᵹ ... not-been.

The CN blend represents C plus *any* vowel plus N, as in
..... ⌠ .... Canberra, ... ⌠⟍ ...... Connemara, ... ⌠ ....
⌒ Cincinatti.

Words containing SF or FS are easy to write: .... ℓ ..... safe,
...... ℓᵧ .... safety, ... ℓ ...... sofa, ... ℓ ...... fuss, ... ℓ ....
fist, ... ℓ .... fast, ... ℓ .... fastest. Use the bottom F loop in the last three words so the T can be shown in position.

Exercise 23

Cover the key and read the sentences. Then copy the outlines and transcribe.

1. _(shorthand outlines)_

2. _(shorthand outlines)_

3. _(shorthand outlines)_

4. _(shorthand outlines)_

5. _(shorthand outlines)_

6. _(shorthand outlines)_

7. _(shorthand outlines)_

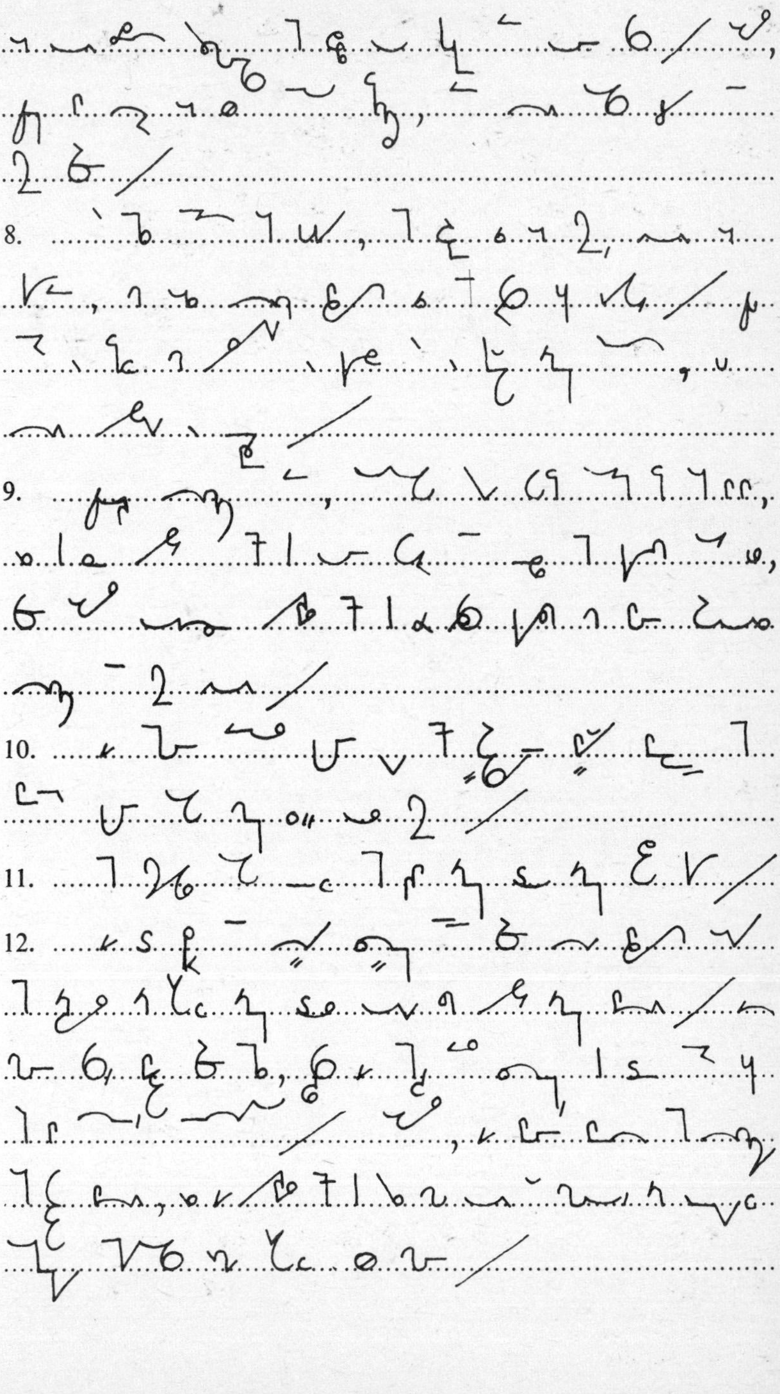

Key

1. We-shall be very happy to-see you at-the council meeting to-morrow if-we-can manage to get there.

2. We-can easily cancel the concert in-the local cinema if-we cannot sell enough tickets to cover the cost.

3. Of-course, we always conduct the business in-the most economical way we-can. In that way we-can be sure of success.

4. I recognize that-the county-council can decide how the money shall be spent, but I think the council should bear in mind the wishes of those who elected them.

5. Your recent letter cancelling the concert at-the cinema gave me a lot to think about, because it shows that-the club members have not-been contacted about-it. I think they will-be very concerned about your attitude in-this.

6. Recently the local youth club saw the play 'The Cat and-the Canary' at-the church hall. They concluded that-it had-been well played, but that it-was not very well staged as-the scenery was very shabby indeed.

7. The High Road is very congested with cars and lorries and-the new one way system has-not-been the success we hoped it would be. Of-course, if-the council make one or two changes, it may well-be easier to get about.

8. At this time of-the year, the accent is on getting away on holiday. and one's main concern is to book up early. If-you take a chance and reserve a place at a hotel in-the autumn, you may receive a discount.

9. If-we-can manage it, we-will have lunch with-the chairman of-the county-council, as he said recently that he would like to discuss the plan with us, but of-course we-must recognize that he is-a busy person and cannot always manage to get away.

10. I thought it-was quite evident that Albert Connor conducted the cantata quite well and-the singing was good.

11. The girls will dance the can-can in-the show in-the school hall.

12. I shall speak to Mr Smith today about my concern over the increase in violence in-the shows we-have seen recently in-the cinema. I-am not being cynical about this, because I think it-is something he should take up at-the council meeting tomorrow. Of-course, I cannot condemn the manager of-the local cinema, as I recognize that he has no way of knowing in advance whether there-will-be any violence or not.

11

WAYS WITH 'C': III
How to write the CM blend

We write the combination C + *any* vowel + M by using an elongated C like this: ......*C*...... It is called the CM blend and is used for the syllables CAM, CEM, CIM/CYM, COM and CUM. Like the CN blend, it can be used anywhere in an outline. It is best written twice as long as a normal ......*C*...... but it should not be written any higher:

.*C*....*C*... NOT .....*C*...... Here are some examples:

CAM:

camel	camber	Cambridge	Camberley	camera

campaign	Camembert	camp	camper	Camberwell.

CEM: ......*C*...... cement, ...*C*...... cembalo (another name for

a harpsichord), ...*C*...... chemist, ...*C*...... chemical, ...*C*...... scheme.

CIM/CYM: ......*C*...... cymbal, ..*C*..... Cimmerian (an ancient nomadic tribe).

COM:

combine	comment	commenting	compact	commence

79

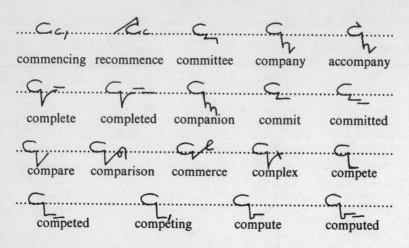

commencing	recommence	committee	company	accompany
complete	completed	companion	commit	committed
compare	comparison	commerce	complex	compete
competed	competing	compute	computed

CUM:

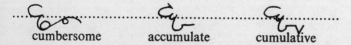

| cumbersome | accumulate | cumulative |

You will notice that the CM blend, like CN, can be used anywhere in an outline and not just at the beginning. Study the examples given and write them out several times, saying them to yourself as you write them.

Special forms to be memorized: ......C...... come, ...⦿..... become (note .....C..... came, ...⦿.... became for distinction), ...⌒...... gentleman, ...⌒...... gentlemen, ...⊥⦿.... experience, ...⊥....... expect, ...⊥....... expected, ...⦡....... recommend, recommended (......⦡....... recommends, ...⦡.⁄.... recommending).

Exercise 24

Cover the key and read the sentences. Then copy the outlines and transcribe.

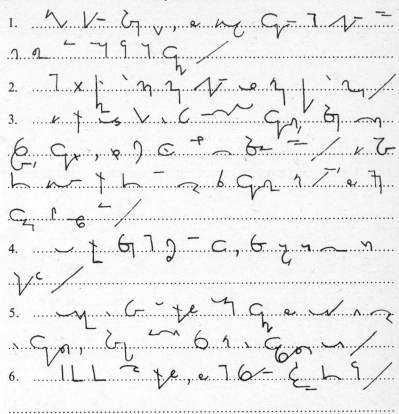

Key

1. I-have heard all-the evidence, so I-will complete the report today and send it to-the chairman of-the company.

2. The accident happened at nine and-the report was in-the paper at noon.

3. I expect we-shall have a letter tomorrow complaining about-the main building complex, as-a gentleman came to-see me about-it today. I told him I-would expect him to make his complaint in writing so that-the committee can discuss it.

4. We expected both the gentlemen to come, but only one made an appearance.

5. We-have-had a lot of experience with-the company so we-are able-to make a comparison, although it-may be in a cumbersome way.

6. He had had much experience, so the board elected him chairman.

Exercise 25

Cover the key, then write the following sentences in Teeline.

1. The camber of-the road near Cambridge was reported on by-the chairman of-the committee.

2. He said the meeting was being held in camera.

3. She did not complain to-the company about-the accident, although we expected her to-do-so in view of all-the evidence.

4. Bert will-be at-the office at nine. He is due to commence at that time.

5. The package was cumbersome because it-was so big, but she did not complain.

6. I-must comply with-the rules of-the game.

7. The chairman will recommend that-the money be paid. He will do-so at-the meeting of-the committee tomorrow.

8. I-will begin my campaign in a month's time.

9. You-will-be happy to know that-the committee has decided to recommend that-the chairman may commence the meeting at any time he likes once there-are five members there.

10. She has composed a song about her visit to-the island and will come to-the concert to sing it.

Key

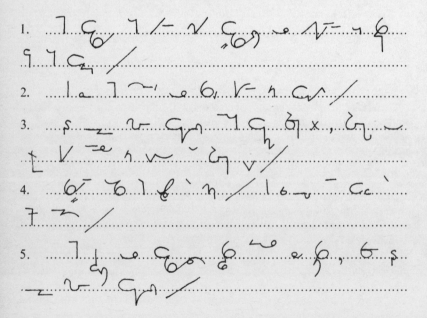

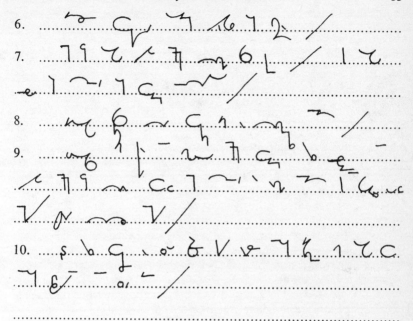

6. ....

7. ....

8. ....

9. ....

10. ....

....

....

Remember: Wherever CK occur in a word, write the C and ignore the K, as in .... or .... package, in sentence 5 above.

12

TAKING DICTATION

Now the time has come for you to try some dictation. There are many people who learn Teeline for the sheer pleasure of doing so, but for the majority the principal object is to be able to make notes faster than is possible in normal longhand. In order to do this it is necessary to practise taking down the spoken word, and that is what we are going to do now.

So far you have been *looking* at words and working them out, either from Teeline into longhand or vice versa. Now you are going to *listen* to words, then work them out and put them into Teeline. This is very new to you and will require an amount of mental effort, but it is possible to attain an astonishing facility at this and—who knows?—you may even achieve the ability to write at a sustained speed of three or four words *a second* for several minutes. Many others have reached this speed with Teeline and with regular practice you can do it, too.

But first it is necessary to go slowly—very slowly. Sometimes, like a baby learning to walk, you will stumble; but with persistence, the skill can be mastered and you will start to build up speed. Like the baby with its first steps, you may find you are unable to keep up; but keep trying, for you are learning a new skill which will be of great use to you.

Some people do not succeed the first time; others do. If you do not make a successful first-time effort, don't get annoyed with yourself. I once had a student who could not get a complete sentence down after three or four attempts so he raised his arms in the air and deliberately snapped his pencil in his frustration. There is no need to go to extremes like that. If you fail in your effort, just remain calm and try again. That is the way to succeed.

For dictation, you will need either someone to read to you at an even speed or a tape recorder. If you are lucky enough to have a reader, then invite him or her first to read the paragraphs below headed 'How to Record', because dictating at a slow speed is not easy and it is possible that your reader will need several attempts to get used to it. In general, it is far more comfortable to read a passage at 200 words a minute than at 20, because 200 is nearer the average speed of normal speech and at 20 words a minute it is more difficult to convey the meaning of what is being said. (As a matter of interest, radio and television news bulletins are timed for reading at three words a second, which is 180 words a minute.)

To begin with, however, we must go slowly so that you can develop the skill of hearing a word, thinking of the outline in a given time and then writing it. At the start you may find your outlines becoming distorted into a mere scribble. That happens to everyone and in due course guidance will be given on how to overcome this. For the time being it is sufficient to write an outline for every word spoken.

An end-opening notebook is most suitable for taking dictation. Some people prefer loose sheets on a clipboard, but the pages of a notebook are easier to turn quickly than are large sheets. It is advisable to use ruled paper and the majority of writers find a wide ruling preferable to a narrow one. Occasionally shorthand is written on plain paper, the writer judging the position of an outline from a previous one. This method is not to be recommended for serious work. Jotting down a note on unruled paper during a telephone call is a different matter, but even this is rarely done by the experienced writer. Some strokes must be written in position and unless there is a line to write on, transcribing from a note on unruled paper is very much a hit-or-miss affair.

Put the date on the page each day, so that time will be saved should it be necessary to refer to previous dictation. This reference back can be done even more rapidly if the date is put at the bottom of the page, so that it can be found merely by flicking over the leaves instead of opening them fully. There is no need to write any longhand in doing this—the date and a figure or a Teeline outline for the month is sufficient.

If a new paragraph is indicated by the person dictating, it can be shown by writing two fullstop signs close together: ..../...... This

automatically includes the fullstop at the end of the preceding sentence as well as showing the new paragraph.

Make a habit of leaving a margin on the left-hand side of the page. This is useful for writing any guidance notes that may be required. If the instruction is given during dictation 'Check the spelling of that name' then a simple cross or some other indication can be put in the margin against that line to act as a reminder. Or again, a comment might be made as an afterthought, such as 'Oh, you'd better let So-and-So have a copy' and 'Copy to——' can be written in the margin.

Insertions given afterwards can be indicated in the same way. It has been noticed that insertions are sometimes troublesome to less experienced secretaries because they are not clearly indicated. A useful way when taking letters is to draw a line across the page after each piece of dictation, but if an insertion is required, then divide the letter from the insertion by drawing a short wavy line.

If more than one insertion is required, mark them 'A', 'B', 'C', etc., in the margin both in the body of the note and against the appropriate insert. This is particularly useful when a memorandum or a long report is being dictated. Never use figures for insertions as this can be confusing, especially where there are figures in the dictation.

A few people like to divide a page into two columns because they prefer to write on short lines. There is no objection to this but it means that time has to be spent on drawing lines down the pages. It will also be found that, generally, fewer outlines will be written on two short lines than on one full one, so there is just as much turning of the page to be done and, in the long run, probably more. The impression that this is also an aid to speed is purely psychological.

When taking dictation, place the notebook on a desk or table. Resting it on the knee can be unsatisfactory and sometimes results in difficulty in turning a page quickly.

Should your practical work at the moment necessitate your taking dictation or telephone messages in scribbled longhand, then start putting Teeline into use without delay. Experience over many years has shown that a badly written shorthand outline can often be read back more easily than longhand scribble.

Use as much Teeline at work as possible. Begin with the special forms. If it is necessary to stop and think of a special form, then it is an indication that it is not known as well as it should be. Set yourself this standard: that until you can write a word without hesitation, you do not 'know' it as well as you should. Special forms cover most of the commonest words in the English language, so it will be realized that being able to write them without a second thought will result in a considerable saving of time when taking dictation.

The ultimate goal, of course, is to take *every* word in Teeline and to achieve this it is necessary in dictation practice to write entirely in shorthand. No longhand should ever be used and it is better to miss a few words than to resort to longhand (incidentally, the use of longhand in a shorthand speed examination could result in disqualification).

Taking dictation at an even speed, whether it be at 30, 50, 100 or more words a minute, is sometimes criticized as being artificial because people seldom speak at a uniform pace. This is quite true but by learning to take shorthand at, say, 120 words a minute for three or four minutes the writer is reaching a standard where it is possible to get words down at an even higher speed for short bursts. Another reason for training at a set pace for several minutes is that it gives added confidence in note-taking and transcribing accurately. Further, it also provides a standard by which progress can be judged.

How to Record

If you are unable to obtain the services of a reader, then put the dictation passages on to tape. This of course has the advantage that you can practise at any time and should you get too far behind, you can switch off, rewind the tape and start again.

In the dictation passages given in this and subsequent chapters you will find the words marked in tens and each diagonal line like this: / will show the end of a section of 10 words.

Take each numbered paragraph separately. Record each one at a speed of 30 words a minute, timing the reading with either a stopwatch or a wristwatch with a large second hand. At 30 words a minute it will mean reading each word in two seconds (this is slower than you think!). In practice you will find that it is possible to read a short word in one second and this will give you an extra second or so which can be spent in speaking the longer word which follows.

For example, if a sentence began 'The management has decided . . .' then the word 'the' can be said in one second, leaving three seconds for the longer word 'management', making a total of four seconds for the two words, but aim at an overall speed of 10 words in 20 seconds.

You can record the entire exercise with longer pauses between each sentence so that they are all put on tape at the same time, but remember to keep the speed down to an even 10 words every 20 seconds.

It is no use speaking the first 10 words at a normal rate, waiting until the hand reaches the 20-second mark and then rapidly saying the rest, for you may well find yourself becoming confused in trying to remember the order of the words.

Do not worry if, when the dictation has finished, you are two or three words behind. It is normal practice to be a few words in arrear; but if you are five or six words behind the speaker then that is too much.

Here is the first dictation practice:

1. I am hoping that you will be able to come / to see us. (13 words) (If you have reached 'come' by the time the voice stops, then your practise has been satisfactory. If you are further behind or have missed anything out, then repeat the sentence until you are able to get it all down.)

2. Will you please tell the manager that I will call / tomorrow. (11)

3. I will collect the parcel when I call at the / shop. (11)

4. The representative said the company will commence their campaign in / a month's time. (13)

5. I expect the committee will discuss your letter at their / meeting tomorrow. (12)

6. It is quite evident that the committee will consent to / the sale of the building. (15)

7. I have nothing to say about the chairman's comments, but / I expect the others will say a lot. (18)

8. Do you think the manager will consent to being sent / to the other shop, or will he leave the company? / (20)

9. The gentleman from the company recommended that we should buy / the goods because they happen to be a good bargain / (20)

10. The recent success of the company is recognized by the / board and it is to be hoped that the increase / will be kept up. (24)

11. We shall be pleased to help you all we can / in your desire to see the scheme go ahead at / once. (21)

12. I cannot see my way to collect all that money / from the company, whether or not it is in aid / of the new ambulance. (24)

Words you may wish to check:

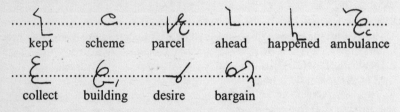

kept　　scheme　　parcel　　ahead　　happened　ambulance

collect　building　desire　bargain

When you have succeeded in getting these 12 sentences down at 30 words a minute, then re-record the exercise at 40 words a minute. That is an average of 10 words every 15 seconds. When you have managed to do that—and do not expect to do it at the first attempt—proceed to the next chapter. But under no circumstances do so until you can take them all at 40 words a minute, remembering, of course, that it is quite usual to finish two or three words behind the speaker.

13

WAYS WITH 'C': IV
The CNV blend

There is one more way of writing 'C' and that is a blend for the combination of C + any vowel + N + V, as we get in words like CoNVey, CoNVerge, CoNValescent and so on. We achieve this blend by the simple expedient of leaning the sign backwards until it becomes part of

the ...... *V* .... sign, like this:

converse	convert	converted	converts	converting	convalescent

converge	converged	convey	conveys	conveyed	convulse

canvas	canvassed	convex	convivial	conveyance	convoy

convoys	convoyed	convoke

Special forms to be memorized: ...... inconvenient, ...
inconvenience, ... for.

Words groups: ...... instead-of, ... best-wishes,
...... to-you, ... that-you-will-be.

Exercise 26

Cover the key below the exercise. Read through the exercise first, then copy the outlines and transcribe into longhand. Try to make your outlines exactly like those given here, paying attention to the narrow hooks on the CN and CNV blends.

1. *[shorthand outline]*

2. *[shorthand outline]*

3. *[shorthand outline]*

4. *[shorthand outline]*

5. *[shorthand outline]*

6. *[shorthand outline]*

7. *[shorthand outline]*

8. *[shorthand outline]*

Key

1. I-hope it-will not-be inconvenient if I ask you to come at one o'clock instead-of two.

2. This letter conveys my best-wishes to-you all, and I-hope that-you-will-be coming to-see us soon.

3. They live on a converted barge on-the river at Cambridge.

4. The show had a lively comic on-the bill and for much of-the time he had us convulsed at his antics.

5. They are buying a new house and have-been to-the lawyer to sign the conveyance.

6. It-will-be no inconvenience to convey your goods in the convoy of vehicles which leaves tomorrow instead-of-the one which leaves today.

7. We hope it-will not-be inconvenient if-the company commence building on-the land in a month's time.

8. The council committee has been to look at-the village square today. Several roads converge at that point and convoys of vehicles pass by there night and day, as it-is-a very busy spot. I think the county council should do something about-it.

Exercise 27

Cover the key below, then write the following exercise in Teeline:

I-am very pleased to-be able-to report that-the company balance sheet shows that-we-have plenty of funds. It-is with pleasure that I-have to tell-you that-the board has requested me to convey their thanks to-you, as-you-have achieved so much this-year. The output of-the company has reached a record total and we-are in no doubt as to-the success of all-the effort you-have made. We hope the coming year will-be just as much a success as this-year.

Key

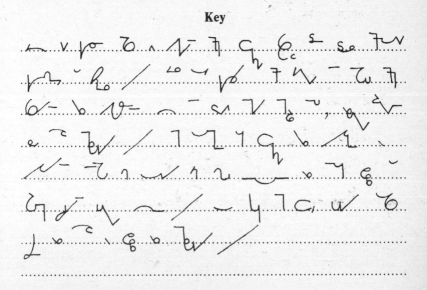

Did you remember that OU, OO and W are all written with
.....ᶸ...... ? (See 'output' above.) The word group 'you-have' may
be written ......ᴫ....... or ......ᴫ...... Use whichever you prefer.

Whenever C or K are followed by T or D, we use the blend ....ᶜ......
This stands for C or K and saves time in writing. Thus ....ᶜ...... ask

but .....ᶜ...... asked, where the use of the blend gets rid of a series of

angles (......ᶜ..... or ....ᶜ...... for 'asked'). It is an extension of the

rule that where C or K come together, we ignore the K and write only the
C. Here are some examples.

......ᶜ..... kick, ...ᶜ....... kicked, ...ᶜ.... lack or lick,

......ᶜ...... lacked or licked, ...ᶜ.... like, ...ᶜ...... liked,

.........ᶜ..... ask, ...ᶜ.... asked, ...ᶜ..... back, ...ᶜ.......

backed (a vowel is always joined between B and C to make an easier

joining—remember?), ...ˡ......... pact, ...ᶜ....... impact, ...ᶜ.......

impacted, ...ᶜᵧᶜ...... neglect, ...ᶜᵧᶜ...... neglected, ...ᵛᶜ........ erect,

....ᵛᶜ........ erected, ...ᶜ...... wrecked, ...ᶠ........ or ....ᶜ........

fact (the former is preferable), ...ᶠ...... respect, ...ᶜ.... exact

(note how the X blends here with the C), ...ᶜᵧ..... exactly, ...ᶜ....

exactitude, ...ᵛᶜ...... convict, ...ᵛᶜ....... convicted, ...ᵛᶜᵖ.....

convicts, ...ᵛᶜ..... convicting, ...ᶜ..... cook, ...ᶜ....... cooked.

Here is an extension of the CN rule which is very useful in a number
of frequently-used words: in order to save time, words ending in KN can
be represented by the CN sign, as in

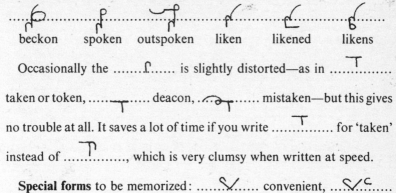

beckon   spoken   outspoken   liken   likened   likens

Occasionally the ....Γ...... is slightly distorted—as in ....

taken or token, ...—...... deacon, ..⌢.... mistaken—but this gives

no trouble at all. It saves a lot of time if you write ....T........ for 'taken'

instead of ......T......., which is very clumsy when written at speed.

Special forms to be memorized: ....Υ...... convenient, ...Υ.ᶜ..... convenience.

Word groups: ...ᴄ~.... a-lot-of, ..⌣ᵍ...... I-am-sure, ..⌣ᵍ..... I-am-sorry.

Exercise 28

Read through the following exercise. Try to do so as quickly as possible, without too many pauses. Then copy the outlines neatly and transcribe.

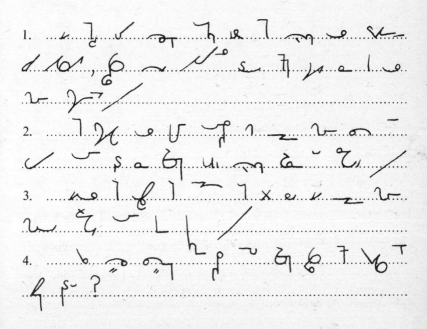

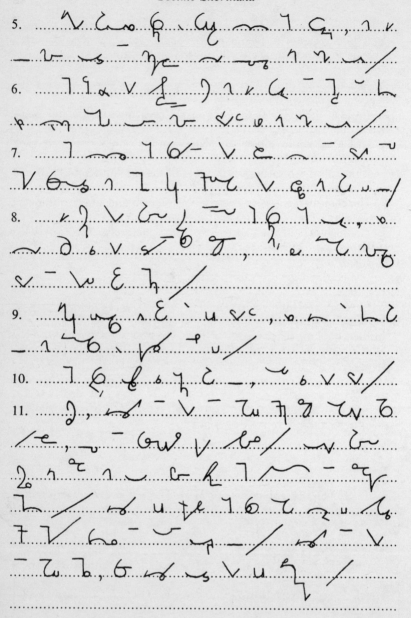

Key

1. I think you-are mistaken when you-say the man was convicted for robbery, because my records show that-the jury said he was not guilty.

2. The girl was quite outspoken and did not seem to care what she said about-the young man accused of stealing.

3. I-was at-the office at-the time of-the accident so I did not know exactly what had happened.

4. Has Miss Smith spoken to-you about-the books that have-been taken from-the shop?

5. I-have always been a loyal member of-the committee, and I do not wish to neglect my duties in any way.

6. The chairman is-a very respected gentleman and I like to think of him as-a man who would not inconvenience us in any way.

7. The members of-the board have asked me to convey to-you their best-wishes and they hope that-you-will have success in all you do.

8. I generally have a-lot-of jobs to-do at-the beginning of-the week, as my department is very short staffed, so it-will not-be convenient to have-you call then.

9. I-hope you-will-be able-to call at your convenience as I-am at home all day and it-will-be a pleasure to-see you.

10. The booking office is open all day, which is very convenient.

11. Gentlemen, I-am-sorry to have to tell-you that-the staff will-have to-be reduced, due to last-year's poor results. We-have a-lot-of goods in stock and we cannot find the room to stockpile them. I-am-sure your experience of-the business will make you realize that there-are limits to what we-can do. I-am-sorry to have to tell-you this, but I-am-sure we-shall have your sympathy.

In the word .... sympathy, notice how it is possible to

raise the SM above the line so that the P goes through it. This also enables us to write the word without going too far below the line. If you wish, you can do the same thing with other words in

which P is the second or third consonant: .... swoop,

.... wipe, ... map, ... cap or cup,

.... copy, etc.

Speed Building

Here is another exercise for you to help build up your speed. Follow the same procedure as that described in Chapter 12 (p. 87). Take the exercise first at 30 words a minute and when you can get it all down, try it again at 40 w.a.m.

Gentlemen, The chairman has been very kind to me and / has consented to allow me a short time in which / to speak to you. I hope that when you have / heard what I have to say, you will not think / that I have taken up too much of your time. / As you know, I am the representative of the toy / department on this committee. (64)

Outlines you may wish to check:

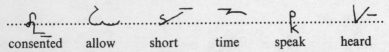

| consented | allow | short | time | speak | heard |

If you wish, you may write 'short time' as a word group like this:

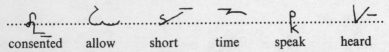, making the final T in 'short' also do duty for the initial T in 'time'.

There were special forms in this passage. If any of them made you hesitate, check them with the alphabetical list in Appendix 1. It is most important that you can write these without hesitation. If any of them made you pause and think, then copy them several times, saying them to yourself as you do so. In this way, they will soon spring readily to mind and will be no problem.

14

WAYS WITH 'R': I
Blends with F, T, and D

We saw briefly in Chapter 10 (p. 74) that R and N can be blended

like this: .... instead of writing

............................., and we use the RN blend in such words as

.... burn or born or borne or barn,

.... churn, ... concern,

.... concerning, ... tavern,

.... Malvern, ... ironic,

.... ironically, ... siren,

.... current, ... earn, and many
others.

We can also blend F and R, and instead of writing

.... or ...., we combine the two

strokes: .... so that one part of the F loop becomes
part of the R:

for or four, far, etc.,   forsaken   frail

frog   forgo   frond   France   French   Francis

Frances	frolic	far-away	effort	farce

farewell	offer	conference

This blend can also be done the other way round and

.... represents RF, as in ....

rough, ... raft (the T is disjoined for convenience),

.... refuse, ... refused,

.... refusal, ... bereft,

.... curfew, ... seraph,

.... graph. You may place the F on whichever side of

the R you prefer. 'For' is still 'for' whether it is written

.... or .... and the same applies

to .... rough, ... graphic,

.... curfew, etc. The choice is up to the individual,

but make sure you keep the R straight.

The combination RFR is shown by *not* blending the F:

refrain	refresh	refract	reefer

Special forms to be memorized: .... firm, form,

.... behalf, ... before,

.... half, ... profit

(............................. profits, ... profited),

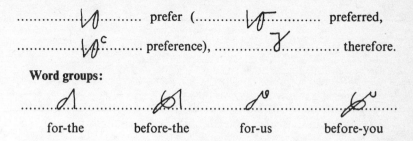

prefer (preferred, preference), therefore.

Word groups:

for-the before-the for-us before-you

Exercise 29

First read the following exercise. Try to do so as quickly as possible, without too many pauses. Then copy the outlines neatly and transcribe.

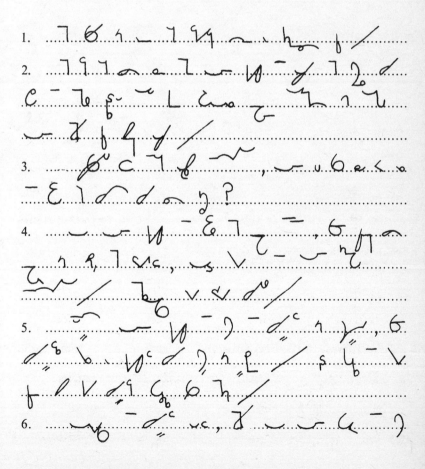

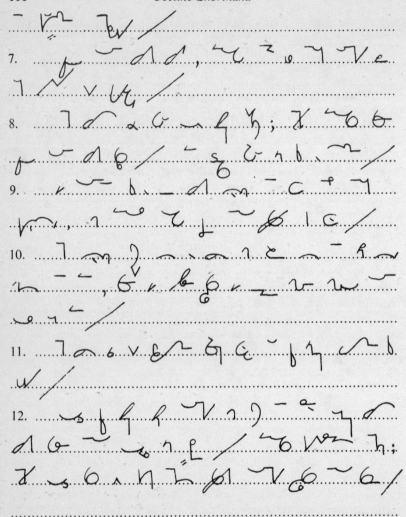

Key

1. The bazaar in aid of-the church made a handsome profit.
2. The chairman of-the firm said they would prefer to offer the goods for sale to those shops which had always dealt with-them and who would therefore profit from-the offer.
3. Before-you come to-the office tomorrow, would you be so kind as to call at-the farm for some eggs?
4. We would prefer to close the deal today, but if-the firm delay in

signing the conveyance, we-shall have to wait until tomorrow. This-will-be very inconvenient for-us.

5. Tom would prefer to go to France in July, but Frances has a preference for going in September. She hopes to have profited from her French lessons by then.

6. We-have-been to France once, therefore we would like to go to Holland this-year.

7. If-we wait for-the ferry, it-will take us to-the other side of-the river very quickly.

8. The farm is-a long way from-the village; therefore it-will-be best if-we wait for-the bus. It should-be along in half a minute.

9. I waited half a day for-the man to come to-see to-the plumbing, and it-was well past two before he came.

10. The man gave me a form and asked me to sign my name to it, but I refused because I did not know what was on it.

11. The firm is very concerned about-the lack of profit in-the current half year.

12. We-shall profit from-the fine weather and go to stay on-the farm for-the last two weeks in September. It-will-be harvest-time then; therefore we-shall be able-to help them before-the weather becomes too bad.

The months of the year are written: ....).................

January, ...6............... February, ...

March (see Chapter 16), ...).............. April (see Chapter

15), ... May, ...)............... June,

...............).../......... July, ...2............... August,

...............[............. September, ...

October, ...V............... November (see Chapter 19),

.... December.

Exercise 30

Transcribe the following into your neatest Teeline:

1. Unless the company decide otherwise, we may have to forgo the basic wage increase for-the time being.
2. The old lady is very frail, but she refuses all offers of help.
3. If-we make a big effort, we may get to-the farm before four.
4. We-are hoping to go to Spain for a month in July or August.
5. Before very long we-shall be writing Teeline quite quickly.
6. Half the goods have already been sold, but if-you go to-the shop early in-the day you-will still be able-to pick up a bargain or two.
7. The conveyance has yet to-be completed; therefore we-have to accept the fact that-the change cannot take place before November. There-is little chance of-the business being taken over before then.

Key

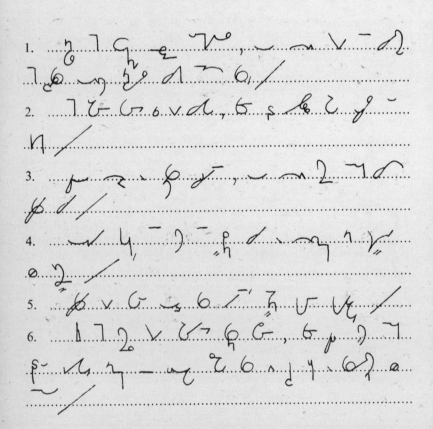

7.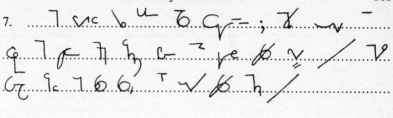

The days of the week are: ....⌒⌐............. Monday

(.............._............. is a special form for '-day'),

.............._............. Tuesday, ...⌣⁻.............
Wed(nesday), ...⩗ᵉ............. Thursday,

..............⧸............. Fri(day), ...⌒_⁼............. Satur-

day (see this chapter), ...⌒⌐............. Sunday. Note also

..............⩗⁻..... holiday (the ...._............. for

'-day' once again), ...⌒⌒_............. May-day,

⩁_⁼

..............⩁_⁼............. yesterday (see this chapter).

The signs ....⟋............. and ....⟋............. are blended into one straight stroke for TR and DR. The strokes are as long as T and R or D and R together, and they can be used initially, medially or finally:

TR:

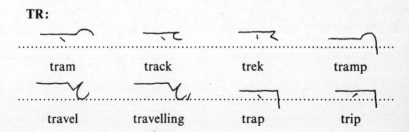

| tram | track | trek | tramp |
| travel | travelling | trap | trip |

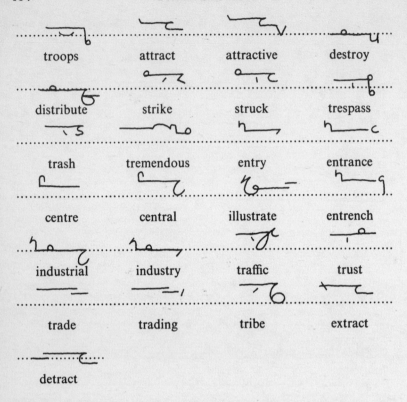

troops	attract	attractive	destroy
distribute	strike	struck	trespass
trash	tremendous	entry	entrance
centre	central	illustrate	entrench
industrial	industry	traffic	trust
trade	trading	tribe	extract

detract

A vowel can be read between the T and the R, as it can with the CM and CN blends. At first it may be necessary to ring the changes on the vowels, as with the CM and CN, but it quickly becomes second nature to realize which vowel is intended from the sense of the sentence. Here are some outlines where vowels are read between the T and the R:

TAR:

tarpaulin	tardy	Tarmac	target
nectar	attar	tariff	tarragon
tart	tartar	tartaric	Tarzan

TER:

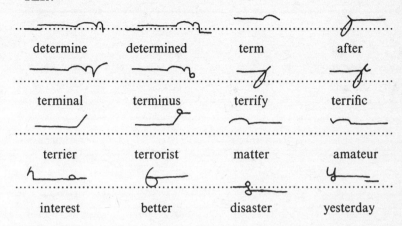

determine	determined	term	after
terminal	terminus	terrify	terrific
terrier	terrorist	matter	amateur
interest	better	disaster	yesterday

TIR:

tire or tyre	tiresome	attire	entire

entirely

TOR:

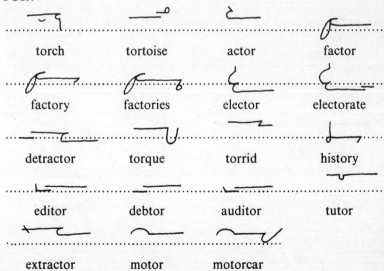

torch	tortoise	actor	factor
factory	factories	elector	electorate
detractor	torque	torrid	history
editor	debtor	auditor	tutor
extractor	motor	motorcar	

TUR (TURE):

picture	future	feature	turmoil

Turk	turf	fixture	turbine

aperture	debenture	suture	lecture

lecturer	lectured	manufacture	manufacturer

You will of course have observed that some outlines can represent

two or more words: .... can be tram, trim or term;

.... can be matter or motor; ....

can be debtor or daughter. It is emphasized again that when seen in context, there will be no confusion. In the unlikely event of someone saying such a phrase as '. . . the matter of the motor . . .' then it is easy to show the difference by simply inserting a disjoined vowel indicator in

the second outline: ....

Like all Teeline, it is easy and logical.

Special forms to be memorized: .... refer, -red,

reference, ... extra, ... extra-ordinary.

Exercise 31

Write in Teeline:

1. I-would like to refer to-the matter of-the new motorcar which was purchased by me last-week. I find there-is-a defect in-the gear lever, which strikes me as being extraordinary.

2. The firm is to launch a big advertising campaign to announce the opening of its new factory.

3. The adaptor would not fit the machine so we-are sending it back to-the manufacturer.

4. The teacher gave an interesting lecture on early English houses which was accompanied by a-number-of very good slides to illustrate that period of history.

5. The cigarette lighter which is manufactured today is much better than those of several years ago.

6. After the lecture, the lecturer made reference to-the picture hanging in-the entrance to-the building. I thought this quite extraordinary, as it had nothing to-do with what he had-been talking about.

7 In future, see that-you alter the aperture of-the camera before-you take a picture!

Key

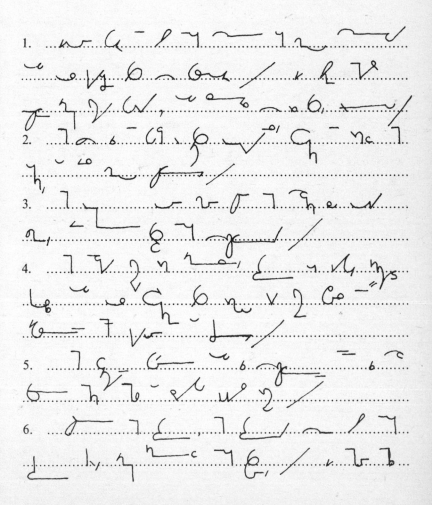

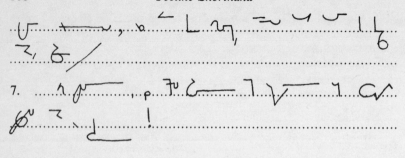

7.

The TR sign .... can represent TR, TAR, TER, TIR, TOR, TUR, TURE or TEUR. You will soon learn which syllable to read between the T and the R.

The rules for ....——————........... DR are the same as for TR, except that when a word begins with DR the outline starts in the D position. Like TR, it can wander around a little when it occurs in the middle or at the end of a word. Here are some DR examples:

DR:

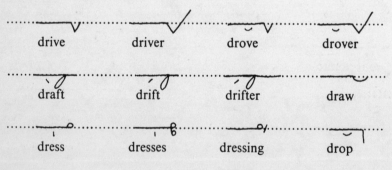

drive	driver	drove	drover
draft	drift	drifter	draw
dress	dresses	dressing	drop

DAR:

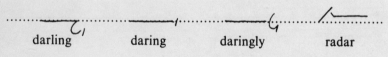

| darling | daring | daringly | radar |
| cedar | | | |

DER:

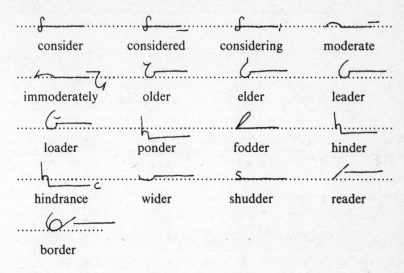

consider	considered	considering	moderate
immoderately	older	elder	leader
loader	ponder	fodder	hinder
hindrance	wider	shudder	reader

border

DIR:

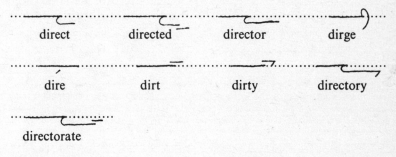

| direct | directed | director | dirge |
| dire | dirt | dirty | directory |

directorate

DOR:

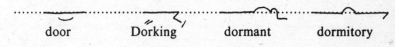

| door | Dorking | dormant | dormitory |

DUR:

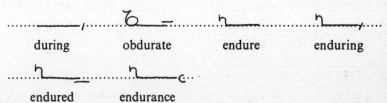

| during | obdurate | endure | enduring |
| endured | endurance | | |

Special forms to be memorized: .... ———— .... dear,

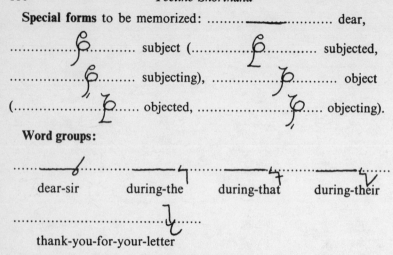

.... subject (................. subjected,

.... subjecting), ... object

(................. objected, ... objecting).

Word groups:

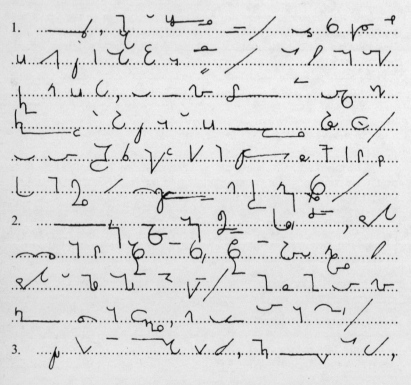

dear-sir   during-the   during-that   during-their

thank-you-for-your-letter

Exercise 32

First read through the exercise, going as quickly as you can. Then copy the Teeline neatly and transcribe.

1.

2.

3.

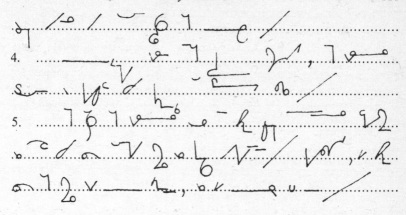

Key

1. Dear-Sir, Thank-you-for-your-letter of yesterday's date. We-shall be pleased to-see your representative if he will call on Tuesday. With reference to-the other point in your letter, we do not consider it would-be any hindrance at all if one of your directors also came. We would welcome his appearance here at-the factory so that he can see how the goods are manufactured and packed in-the boxes.

2. During-the debate on-the suggested housing estate, several members of-the council objected to being subjected to a-lot-of insults from several of those who took part. They said they would not endure some of the comments, and walked out of-the meeting.

3. If-you have to travel very far, then drive with care, as-the roads are wet because of-the drizzle.

4. During-their visit to-the picture gallery, the visitors showed a preference for paintings of country scenes.

5. The object of-the visitors was to find if-the traders charged as much for some of-their goods as had-been reported. Personally, I find some of-the goods very dear indeed, as I daresay you do.

Make sure you learn all special forms before you begin an exercise. This is important for you.

Exercise 33

Transcribe into Teeline, taking care to write it neatly:

I-would like to draw one matter to your notice, and it-is this: that-we-are on-the edge of disaster. I shudder to think what might happen if a disaster did materialize, but we cannot ignore the fact that such a thing might occur. One factor we-must consider is-the need for-a new managing director. I-consider we-should give the job to an outsider and not appoint a man from-the firm's factory, which would-be a blunder. The man we appoint should-be a good leader and a man with a-lot-of drive. He should-be fairly young, because an older man will-be no good at all in-the job. It does not matter if he is lacking in experience; we-must give preference to youth instead-of age.

Key

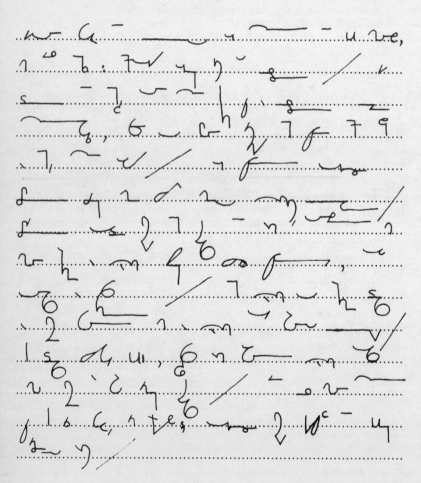

Speed Building

Take the following passage at 30 w.a.m. When you have succeeded in getting it at that speed, try it again at 40 w.a.m.

Dear Sir, First of all I must thank you for / your letter which came today. I am glad to hear / that you are delighted with the examples of the goods / we manufacture. We have already dealt with your request about / future supplies to your factory. I shall be personally interested / in what you may have to say about them when / they are received by you. I hope they will be / satisfactory. (71)

Words you may care to check:

delighted   examples   request   personally

received

Although examples of word groups are given from time to time, do not forget that you can make up your own if you wish.

15

WAYS WITH 'R': II
The 'R' principle

There are four other consonants which are often immediately followed by R. They are B, C, G and P, and give the combinations BR (bridge, bring, broad, brass, bride), CR (creep, crime, cross, crisis, cruel), GR (grab, group, grim, grumble), and PR (price, produce, proper, appropriate).

The presence of the R is shown by writing the following stroke through, or close to, the preceding one. For the word 'bride', for example, we write the B and then intersect the D through the circle on the B like this:

.... Put another way, we show the presence of the R *immediately after* the B by writing nothing for the R, but by inter-

secting the following stroke. Here are some more examples:

.... b(r)im, ... b(r)andy,

.... b(r)eak, ... b(r)ass. The

intersection tells us that we *must* read an R immediately after the B. By

this means we can distinguish at a glance between ....

bran and .... barn, ... brow

and .... borrow. We know straight away that if a

stroke R is written, then we have to read a vowel before it:

.... brass but .... bars,

.... brake or break but .... bark,

and so on. Here are further instances of intersection for R:

....

bridge   brag   brigade   brief

114

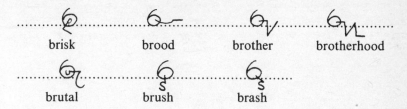

brisk	brood	brother	brotherhood

brutal	brush	brash

If it is not possible to intersect clearly, then the R is shown by placing one stroke close to the other, as in some of these CR examples:

CR:

creep	crawl	cross	across

crave	cramp	cream	crazy

crop	cradle	crack	crook

crash	crease	crew	crib

crooner	croquet	crust	cruiser

cryptic

GR:

grim or grime	growl	great	greater

greatly	grade	greed	greedier

gradual   gradually   grave   gravity

gross   grouse   grotesque   grotty

PR:

prim or prime   protect   product   producer

protector   pressure   predominate

preside   protest   protesting

Where we cannot easily intersect a stroke, then it can be close-placed:

propose   proposed   present   presented

proper   preparatory   problem   pre-pay

preponderance   prejudge   pre-history   prehistoric

apprehensive   apprehend   appreciate   apprentice

To sum up: whenever BR, CR, GR, PR occur in a word, write nothing for the R but intersect or close-place the following stroke

Special forms to be memorized:

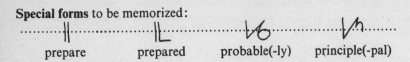

prepare   prepared   probable(-ly)   principle(-pal)

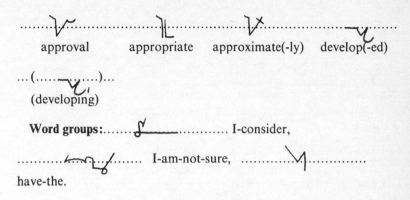

approval   appropriate   approximate(-ly)   develop(-ed)

...(.............)...
(developing)

Word groups:.............. I-consider,

.... I-am-not-sure, ...

have-the.

Exercise 34

Read the following as quickly as you can, then copy and transcribe.

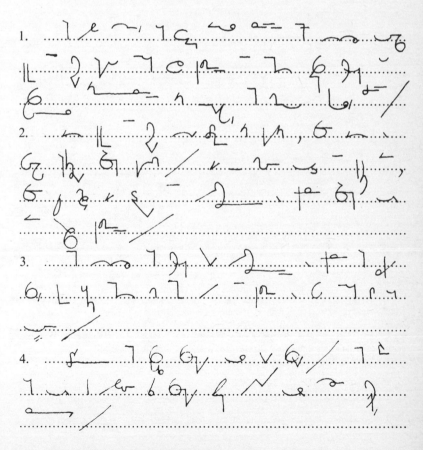

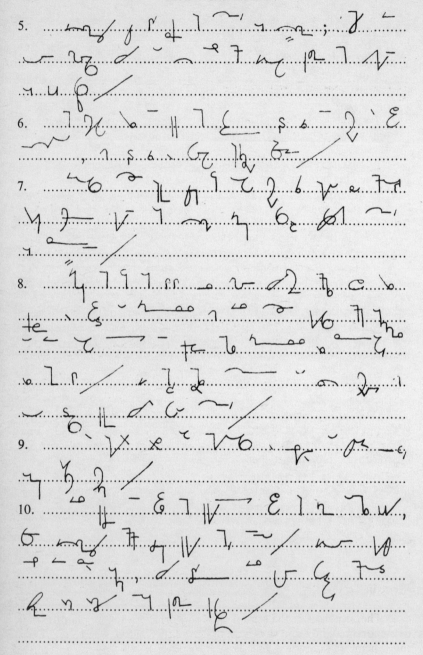

Key

1. At-the recent meeting of the committee it-was stated that members would-be prepared to give approval to-the scheme presented to them by-the group of builders interested in developing the new housing estate.

2. I-am prepared to give my consent in principle, but I-am a little apprehensive about-the plan. I do not wish to prejudge it, but if necessary I shall-have to register a protest about-the way it has-been presented.

3. The members of-the group have registered a protest at-the pressure being put upon them and they are to present a letter to-the council on Wednesday.

4. I-consider the boy's brother was very brave. The account of-the way he rescued his brother from-the river was-a most gripping story.

5. I-am-not-sure if I-can preside at-the meeting on Monday; therefore it would not-be fair of me to-say that I-will present the report on your behalf.

6. The girl has to prepare the lecture she is to give at school tomorrow, and she is-a little apprehensive about-it.

7. It-will-be most appropriate if-the chairman will give his approval so that-we-can have-the greater part of-the money in-the bank before-the meeting on Saturday.

8. I-hope the chairman of-the county council does not forget that-this scheme has produced a clash of interests and it-is most probable that-the opponents of it will try to protect those interests as strongly as they can. I think this-is-a matter of some gravity and we should-be prepared for-a long meeting.

9. At approximately six o'clock there-will-be a display of folk dancing on-the village green.

10. It-is proposed to close the preparatory school at-the end of-this year, but I-am-not-sure that-that is-the proper thing to do. I-would prefer to-see it stay open, for I-consider it-is quite likely that-we-shall find an answer to-the present problem.

Special form to be memorized: .... ʃ .... speech.

Word group: .... ५ .... yours-truly.

Exercise 35

Write in Teeline:

1. The principal of-the school agrees in principle to-the plan for-the new sports pavilion and says he is prepared to-do all he can to-see that-the scheme is submitted in a proper manner to all parents for their approval.

2. Dear-Sir, Thank-you-for-your-letter which I did not receive until today, although it-was dated last Thursday. I think it-will-be most necessary for-you to-be at-the conference to-be held in Camberley at-the end of-the month, if only to protect your interests in-the proposed scheme. It-is quite probable that there-will-be a preponderance of supporters of-the plan at-the conference, so there should-be no problem in presenting your views. However, it-will-be a help if-you-will-be kind enough to keep your speech brief and to-the point when you present them. Yours-truly

3. Dear-Sir, Your kind letter reached me today. It-is most kind of-you to devote so much time to-the problem and I appreciate your gesture very much. Like you, I-consider the matter to-be of great interest and I-am-sorry that-the greater number-of those concerned have not yet got to grips with it. However, I expect interest will build up gradually, as they begin to realize how much pressure is being put upon them to dispose of their property. Once again, thank-you-for-your letter. Yours-truly.

Key

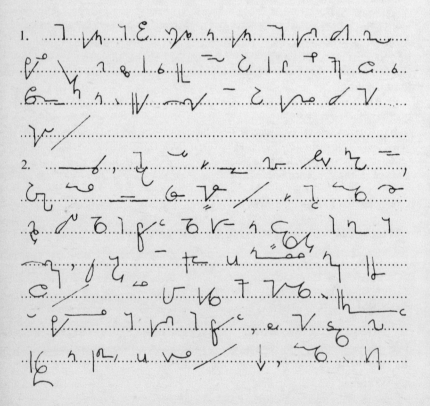

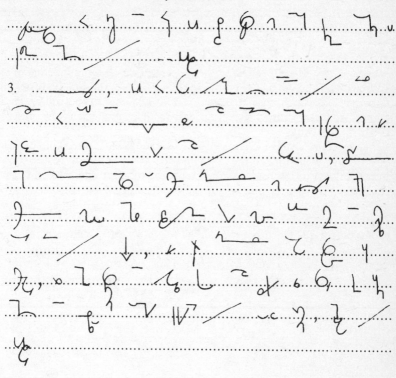

The R principle is used not only with the consonants B, C, G and P
It can also be applied most usefully when R follows the vowels A, O and
U.

In the case of A, the letter after R is intersected through the full A:

arm	army	art	arrange
arranged	article	artisan	argue
arena	arid	arrive	armature

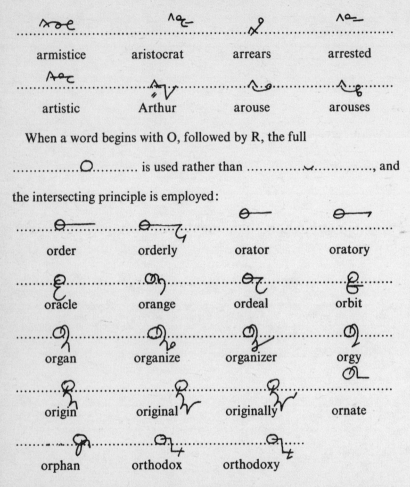

armistice	aristocrat	arrears	arrested

artistic	Arthur	arouse	arouses

When a word begins with O, followed by R, the full

.... O .... is used rather than .... ⌣ ...., and

the intersecting principle is employed:

order	orderly	orator	oratory

oracle	orange	ordeal	orbit

organ	organize	organizer	orgy

origin	original	originally	ornate

orphan	orthodox	orthodoxy	

When writing words beginning with UR, the following letter is either intersected or tucked inside the U, which becomes slightly larger in order to accommodate it (that is why a full O is used in 'OR' words):

uric	urge	urgent	urn

urban	urchin	Uranus	

Special forms to be memorized:

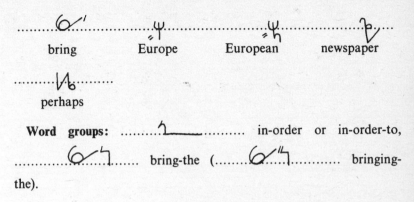

bring   Europe   European   newspaper

perhaps

Word groups: .... in-order or in-order-to, ... bring-the (.......... bringing-the).

Exercise 36

Read through the exercise as quickly as possible. Always try to increase you reading speed. Then copy and transcribe.

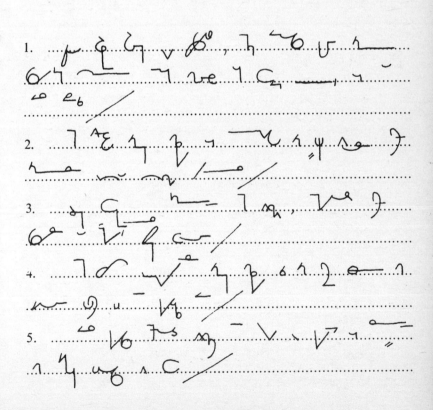

1.

2.

3.

4.

5.

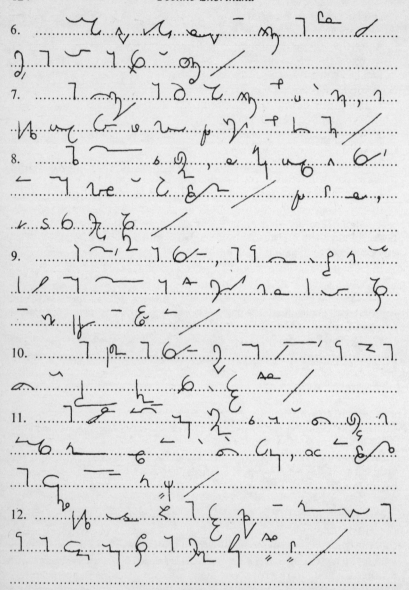

6.

7.

8.

9.

10.

11.

12.

Key

1. If-we accept all-the evidence before-us, then it-will-be quite in-order-to bring-the matter to-the notice of-the committee during one of its sittings.

2. The article in-the newspaper on travel in Europe aroused great interest among many readers.

3. As-the competitors entered the arena, there-was-a great burst of cheering from-the crowd.

4. The farm advertised in-the newspaper is in good order and I-would urge you to purchase it.

5. It-is probable that-we-shall arrange to have a party on Saturday and I-hope you-will-be able-to come.

6. We-will arrive early as-we-have to arrange the contest for guessing the weight of-the box of oranges.

7. The manager of-the department will arrange to-see you at nine, and perhaps you-will let us know if-you agree to-see him then.

8. This matter is urgent, so I-hope you-will-be able-to bring it to-the notice of all concerned. If-you can do-so, I shall be greatly obliged.

9. At-the meeting of-the board, the chairman made a speech in which he referred to-the matter of-the art gallery and said he would object to any proposal to close it.

10. The present the board gave to the retiring chairman took the form of-a picture painted by a local artist.

11. The first item on-the agenda is one of some urgency and it-will-be in-order-to discuss it at some length, since it concerns the company's trade in Europe.

12. Perhaps we-should ask the local newspaper to interview the chairman of-the committee on-the subject of-the grant from-the Arts Council.

Speed Building

Take the following passage at 30 w.a.m. When you have succeeded in doing so, try it at 40 w.a.m. Remember that taking dictation is still very new; therefore it may take several attempts before you get a passage down completely. If you find yourself getting a few words behind, force yourself to catch up. The motto for anyone in the early stages of speed building is 'Keep on keeping on'.

Dear Sir, Your letter of last Wednesday reached me today / so I must present my apologies for a late answer, / but I am sure you will appreciate that the delay / is not due to me. As the manufacturers of the / product to which you refer, I must say I was / surprised at your comments, but I will arrange for you / to receive a new piece for your machine in accordance / with the guarantee we give to all clients. It should / arrive either at the same time as this letter or / just before. I am sorry it has been necessary to / send it back. Yours-truly (105)

Outlines you may care to check:

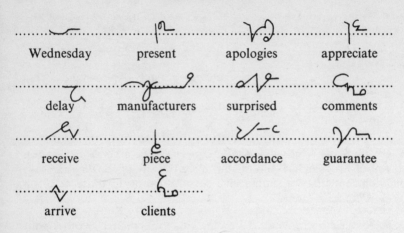

Wednesday	present	apologies	appreciate
delay	manufacturers	surprised	comments
receive	piece	accordance	guarantee
arrive	clients		

Remember to learn the special forms before beginning an exercise. Resist the temptation to skimp this work.

Do not forget that such word groups as 'you-will-be' and 'we-will-be' may be written .... or

..............; .... or

..............., whichever you prefer.

16

WAYS WITH 'R': III
Blends with M, L, and W

There are many words in which R happens to be a neighbouring consonant of M, L and W and there is a simple way of showing the combination, but first we should give some attention to those occasions when R comes *before* M.

The outline .... is one which, at speed, should be written with some care. The reason for this is that it is possible at first glance to mistake it for a distorted upward L and because of this we avoid it as much as possible. There are times when it must be written, as in

.... charm, ... harm; but

generally there is an easy way to avoid this and that is by inserting a joined vowel indicator between the R and the M:

....

     remain   remained or remind   Rome or roam

....

    Roman   remove   removal   remember

....

remembrance   remonstrance   remonstrate   rim

....

    room   ram

When a word contains MR, we show the R by the simple expedient of lengthening the M:

.... (.....................)

more, mere or mar   summer   (simmer for distinction)

....

    merely   merry   America   American

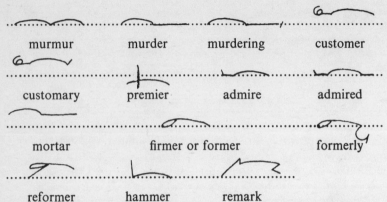

murmur   murder   murdering   customer

customary   premier   admire   admired

mortar   firmer or former   formerly

reformer   hammer   remark

For L + any vowel + R (for example, LAR, LER, LOR, etc.), it is possible to lengthen the L, whether written upwards or downwards:

cutler   paler   parlour   killer

butler   lured   lurid   lurking

antlers   large   roller   curler

slur   slurry   lorry   learn

learner   caller   smaller   similar

lyric   earlier

It will be seen that the LR sign always cuts through the writing line.

For WR, the W is lengthened: .... ~~~~ .... were (or war,

wear, ware, wire—according to context), ... ~~~~ .... weary,

.... ~~~~ .... worried, ... ~~~~ .... work,

.... bower, ... rower,

.... mower, ... aware,

.... awareness, ... warm,

.... warrant, ... ward or word

or weird, ... wardrobe, ...

hardware, ... software, ...

warlike, ... wireless, ... wire-

haired, ... world, ... world-
wide.

Special forms to be memorized:

....

were, our, hour   important   importance   particular

....

particularly   mayor

Word groups:

....

we-were   if-we-were   if-our   have-our

....

half-an-hour

Always write Teeline as neatly as possible. Take pains to do so
now, and it will be more legible when writing at higher speeds.

Exercise 37

Read through the following exercise several times, until you can do so
without pausing. Try to read it as fast as you can read ordinary print.
Then copy it in neat Teeline and transcribe.

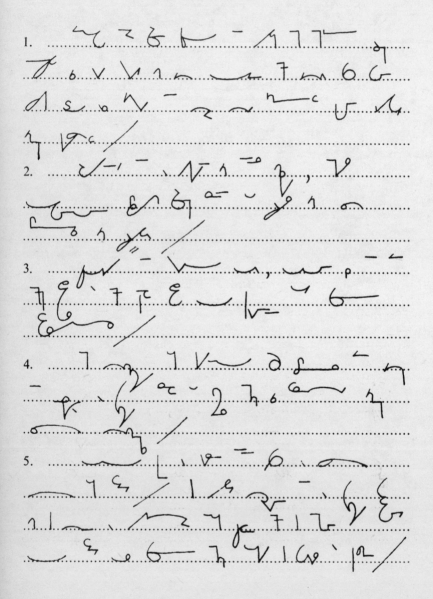

1.

2.

3.

4.

5.

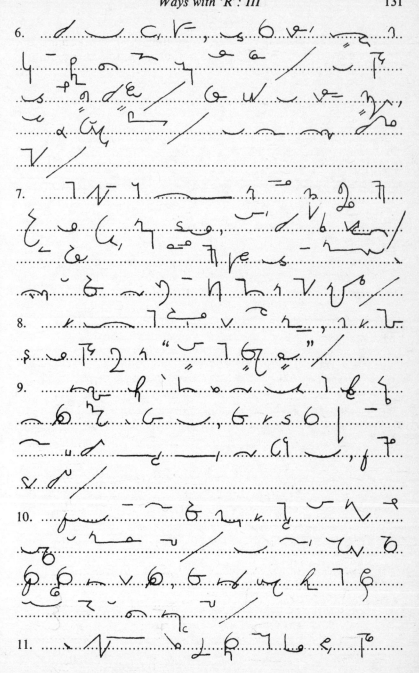

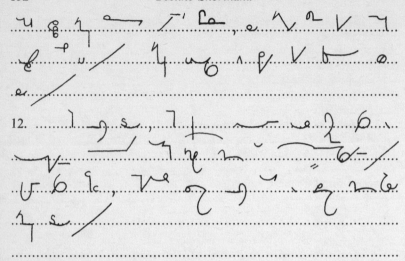

12.

Key

1. It-will take about half-an-hour to reach the theatre as-the traffic is very heavy and I-am worried that I-may be late for-the show as I-have to make my entrance quite early in-the performance.

2. According to a report in today's newspaper, there-is world-wide concern about-the state of affairs in some countries in Africa.

3. If-we-are to have-our way, we-would see to it that-the scholars at that particular school were provided with better classrooms.

4. The manager of-the hardware department considers it important to display a larger stock of goods than is customary in-the summer months.

5. We-were paid a visit today by a former mayor of-the city. He recently moved to a larger locality and he made a remark to-the effect that he thought our city was better than where he lives at present.

6. For our coming holiday, we-shall be visiting America and hope to spend some time on-the west coast. We particularly wish to-see San Francisco. Last year we visited Nigeria, which is-a lovely country. We made many friends there.

7. The report of-the murder in today's newspaper suggests that-the killer was lurking in-the shadows, waiting for his victim. It also states that-the police wish to interview a man of about my age to help them in their inquiries.

8. I admire the actress very much indeed, and I thought she was particularly good in 'What the Butler Saw'.

9. I-am-not often at home as my work at-the office keeps me busy until a late hour, but I shall be happy to meet you for-a drink during my lunch hour, if that-is convenient for-you.

10. If-we-were to meet about noon I think what I-have to-say would-be of interest to-you. Our meeting will-have to-be brief because I-am very busy, but I-am-sure you-will find the subject of-our talk of some importance to-you.

11. A reporter has just been to-the house seeking particulars of-your success in-the story writing contest, so I-have sent her to-the office to-see you. I-hope you-will-be able-to spare her half-an-hour or so.

12. At-the dog show, the premier award was gained by a wire-haired terrier with-the unusual name of Mortar-board. Quite by chance, there-was-a smaller dog with a similar name also in-the show.

Special forms to be memorized: .... immediate,

.... immediately.

Word groups:

....(........)..

first-of-all   (firstly)   so-far

....(........)..

so-far-as   ladies and gentlemen   Mr Chairman

Exercise 38

Read through the following exercise several times, until you can do so without pausing. Try to read it as fast as you can read ordinary print. Then copy it in neat Teeline and transcribe.

1.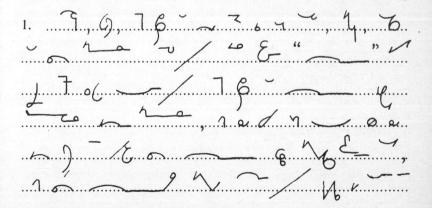

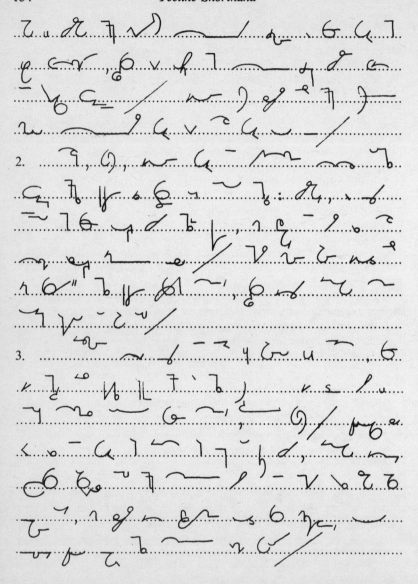

Have you revised your knowledge of the special forms recently? In the learning stage it is essential that they be revised frequently, so that they spring to mind without thinking about them. Always learn new special forms before working the exercises.

Key

1. Mr Chairman, ladies and gentlemen, the subject of my talk is one which, I-hope, will-be of some interest to-you. It-is called 'Murder'— just that single word. The subject of murder usually attracts immediate interest, and so for an hour or so I-am going to recall some murder cases I-have-been connected with, and some murderers I-have met. Perhaps I ought to tell you first-of-all that-the average murderer is-not a bit like the usual criminal, because very often the murder is-the first crime to have-been committed. I-would go so-far-as to-say that-the greater number-of murderers look very much like we do.

2. Mr Chairman, ladies and gentlemen, I-would like to remind members of-this committee that-this proposal is based on two things: firstly, a desire to-do the best we-can for these people, and secondly to raise as much money as-we-can in-order-to do-so. There-is not a-lot I-wish to-say in bringing this proposal before-the meeting, because I-am-sure it-will meet with-the approval of all of-you.

3. It-is-not my desire to take up a-lot-of your time, but I think it-is perhaps appropriate that at this juncture I should refer you to-the minutes of-our last meeting, ladies and gentlemen. If-you-will-be so kind as to look at-the item at-the top of page four, it-will immediately become obvious to-you that-the matter referred to there has still to-be dealt with, and so-far-as I-am concerned we-shall be neglecting our duty if-we delay this matter any longer.

Did you remember that a dash in Teeline is

................................? And did you hesitate over

.... obvious? Words containing '-ious' can

often have two of the vowels omitted:

.... previous, ... serious,

.... various.

17

LOOKING BACK FOR THE FUTURE

This is a somewhat convoluted chapter heading, but when you have finished reading this section its meaning will be perfectly clear. In learning any system of shorthand frequent revision is necessary. With Teeline the revision is not so frequent because the system is simpler, but all the same it is useful to pause and review what has already been learnt.

Of course, 'learning' is one thing, but knowing how to apply your learning is another; and knowing how to apply it *instantly*, in a matter of a second or so, is quite something else.

The successful way to learn a writing skill is to repeat the outlines over and over, knowing instantly what they mean without the effort of having to puzzle them out. On many pages you have worked through so far there has been a statement to the effect that you should write some outlines 'saying them to yourself as you do so'. That is because it has been found that if you say a word mentally as you write it, the principle behind its construction will be retained in the mind more easily.

This, of course, applies only to the learning stage. When you start building up speed, your proficiency will be such that it will no longer be necessary to say everything mentally; but at present, when copying out outlines and when memorizing the special forms, you should certainly do so.

In the previous seven chapters you have come a long way—well over half way through the system, in fact—and you have learned how to write hundreds more words.

First, we went through the clever ways of writing the letter C, and they are worth recalling:

1. When -CK occurs in a word, ignore the K and write only the C. In this way we can distinguish many words at a glance. We can tell whether an outline is 'lack' or 'lake', 'sack' or 'sake', 'knock' or 'nook', 'smock' or 'smoke', and so on.

2. For a 'soft' C you may if you wish (and most people do!) write a C with a small circle tucked inside it, but bear in mind that 'soft' C is written in the middle or at the ends of words *only*. If it were used at the beginning of an outline, it would be read as SC. Although this means that 'certain' and 'curtain' are written with the same Teeline letters, the context will tell you how it is to be read: you would read 'She drew back

the curtain', because 'She drew back the certain' would obviously not make sense.

3. Then there is the ingenious way of writing the letters NCE in a word. You will recall that for this, we simply write a small disjoined C, so that when we see, for instance, D followed by a disjoined C, it is to be read as 'dance' or 'dunce' (context will tell us which—'He was a dunce at school', 'they went to a dance', etc.), or BL followed by a disjoined C is 'balance', and BL followed by a disjoined CD is 'balanced'.

4. The letters NCH can be shown by a disjoined CH (see p. 70 for examples).

5. A sign like a 'squeezed C' gives us the combination of C + *any* vowel + N. This CN sign, as it is called, can be used in hundreds of words and it can be written initially, medially or finally and represent CAN, CEN, CIN, CON, COUN and CUN. It helps us to write several letters at one stroke, as do many other Teeline blends. We sometimes use this blend to represent KN in such common words as

.... spoken, ... taken, and

notice how, in the latter case, we flatten the hook to save time. Other examples of this occasional flattening of the hook are

.... betoken, ... mistaken, and

.... deacon. Do not forget that the CN sign can be

used for a 'soft C' as in .... cinema,

.... centre, ... central,

.... cinder.

6. An elongated C represents CM—as in CAM, CEM, CIM, COM, CUM and CYM—and, like its CN companion, it can be written anywhere in a word—initially, medially or finally.

7. The combination CNV is shown by blending CN with V:

.... and on p. 89 you will find a profusion of examples. Take a look at them now to refresh your memory.

8. Finally, whenever C or K are followed by T or D, we use the

blend ...., as in .... asked,

.... tact or tacked, etc.

Chapters 14, 15 and 16 deal with various ways of representing R. You will remember that R must always be shown wherever it occurs in a word. When it follows T or D, we lengthen the T or D so that the stroke is the same length as T and R or D and R put together. These two blends are used: (*a*) whenever TR or DR come together in a word, or (*b*) when *any* vowel comes between.

We also lengthen L, M and W to show a following R; therefore L lengthened can stand for LAR, LER, LIR, LOR, LOUR, LUR or LYR, and the same rule applies to M and W.

One of the most convenient principles of Teeline is that of indicating R when it immediately follows B, C, G and P. We represent the R in these cases either by intersecting or close-placing (see p. 114) and this can also be done with the vowels A, O and U. Remember that when applying the R principle to O, we use a full O and not the usual symbol (see p. 121).

You will also notice how F blends with R, and F can blend with other consonants as well, as you have already seen in the special forms

.... half, ... form or firm, and

.... profit. This is how F blends with other conson-

ants: .... FL, ... FM,

.... MF, ... FW,

.... WF, ... FB. We get these

blends in such words as .... full, feel, fell, fail, fall,

.... fame, ... famous,

.... muff, ... few,

.... wife, waif, etc.

On several occasions you have been given a blend of X and another stroke, as in the special forms .... expect

.... expected, and in .... explain.

The letter X, in fact, can be easily blended, as in

.... excel .... excellent .... exist .... exclaim

| pixie | x-ray | Rex | wax |

| mix | exam | vex |

It is worth remembering that this blending can be done in other words than those shown in the preceding chapters, and that if a word begins with 'ex', we use the letter X, usually blended with the next character.

Armed with all this knowledge, let us now look to the future. Teeline is a system of fast *writing*, but it is not a bit of good writing quickly if, in the end, you cannot read what you have written. Anyone can put a lot of squiggles on a piece of paper, but they are useless unless they can be read back. That is the acid test. Speed in writing means nothing if what has been written cannot be read.

Return now to Chapter 9 and work through all the exercises up to Chapter 16 again, this time using the key and checking with the exercise. This may seem a tall order, but by doing this revision conscientiously your future progress will be greater and more satisfactory than if the work is neglected. Learning shorthand depends more on perspiration than inspiration, and Teeline is no exception, but it has the advantage of being easier to learn, and there isn't so much perspiration!

You have no doubt noticed when taking the dictation passages that your outlines become rather distorted and perhaps some of them were difficult to read. This is to be expected, because the outlines of even the the neatest writers lose their precision when written quickly. But this distortion is also a warning that pen control is both necessary and important. Try to keep your outlines the size of your normal longhand writing, which is your 'natural' size, but avoid any tendency to sprawl them. Keep all your outlines as neat as possible, no matter whether you write a small, cramped style or a large flowing hand.

Neatness, however, needs pen control. There are two ways this can be cultivated. One is by taking every care when copying the outlines in the exercises. Aim at perfect uniformity: ensure that M and W are always the same length, whether written normally or lengthened for R, and that B, H and L are the same height, and so on.

Let the Teeline follow the slope of your longhand. If you usually write with a backslope, then all your Teeline characters will tend to slope to the left as well. This is quite all right as long as the slope is consistent. Let the strokes follow the style of your longhand, but make sure they are written as neatly as possible and that you always have your pen under control.

The second way to make sure you exercise good pen control is rather more difficult. It is to write the alphabet as far as W without lifting the pen and without pausing:

.... *abcdefghijklmnopqrstuvw* ....

Try it a few times, writing as quickly as you can and without lifting the pen—not even to cross the T. This is more difficult than you may think, but as an exercise in pen control it is excellent. If you can persuade others to try it, alphabet writing soon becomes a party game!

By returning to Chapter 9 as mentioned above and working through the exercises from the keys, you will have plenty of opportunity to cultivate neater outlines and better pen control. In addition, this work will serve to give you practice in outline recognition and an even better appreciation of the logic behind the system.

A thorough mastery of all the special forms will help considerably in building up speed. They should be learned so thoroughly that they flow off the tip of the pen without your having to think about them. If at any time you have to stop and think of a special form, it is a warning that you do not know it as well as you should. Learning them can be deceptive. You may think you know them, but when it comes to writing them in a split second it can be a different story. Try recording some of the special forms on tape at 30 w.a.m., or get someone to read them to you at that speed, and when doing your daily practice spend three or four minutes taking them down. This will help your progress a lot.

18

WAYS WITH 'N': I
Adding N to T, D and P

We have already seen that when N follows the letter O, the two are blended by omitting the hook at the beginning of N in this fashion: ....ꟼ............... It is also possible to blend N with T and D, and it is done like this: .... TN, ...ꓕ...............

DN. Any vowel can be read between the two consonants, as with the CN and CM blends:

tan	ten	tonne or tone	tin or Tyne
Dan or Dane	dine	den	Denis
heighten	hidden	madden	lighten
laden	patent	written	ridden
garden	pardon	diffident	identity
heartening	hardens	dinner	tendency
fortunate	maintain	tannery	attend
attendance	stunt	sudden	certain or curtain

141

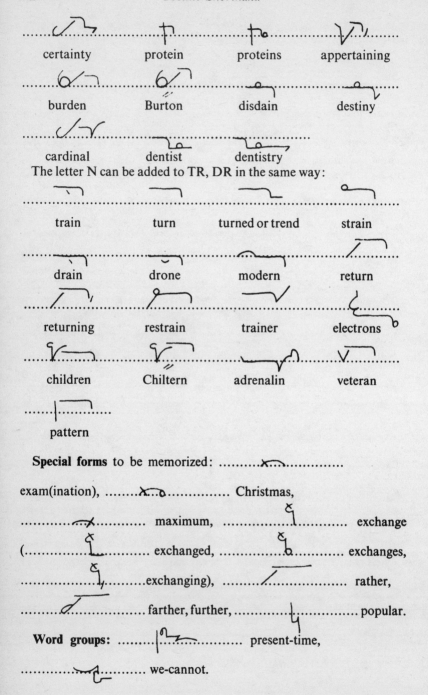

certainty   protein   proteins   appertaining

burden   Burton   disdain   destiny

cardinal   dentist   dentistry

The letter N can be added to TR, DR in the same way:

train   turn   turned or trend   strain

drain   drone   modern   return

returning   restrain   trainer   electrons

children   Chiltern   adrenalin   veteran

pattern

Special forms to be memorized: .... exam(ination), ... Christmas,

.... maximum, ... exchange

(.......... exchanged, ... exchanges,

.... exchanging), ... rather,

.... farther, further, ... popular.

Word groups: .... present-time,

.... we-cannot.

Exercise 39

Cover the key and read the sentences. Then copy and transcribe.

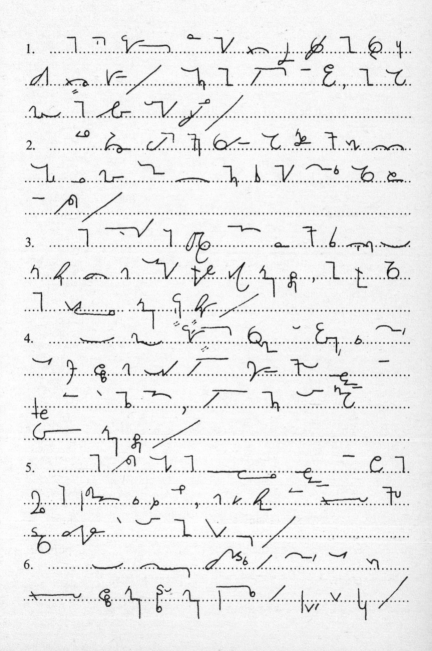

7.

8.

9.

10.

11.

12.

Key

1. The ten children sat their examination just before they broke up for-the Christmas holiday. When they return to school, they will know the result of-their efforts.

2. It-is almost certain that-the board will insist that any member who does not attend more than half their meetings will-be asked to resign.

3. The trainer of-the football team said that his men were in fine form and with-their experience earlier in-the season, they expected to-be the victors in-the Cup Final.

4. Our new Chiltern brand of clothing is meeting with great success and we-are rather glad that-we decided to produce it at this time, rather than wait until later in-the season.

5. The reason why the directors decided to sell the goods at-the present-time is easy to see, and I find it extraordinary that-you should-be surprised at what they have done.

6. Our modern furnishings are meeting with an extraordinary success in-the shops and the patterns are proving very popular.

7. We-cannot go any further in-the matter because the children concerned are on holiday with-their parents in-the Chilterns.

8. It-is heartening to know that-you-have-been able-to accept our offer and we-are quite certain that-you-have done right.

9. We wish to exchange our tickets for the concert on Monday, as-we-shall require an extra seat. We-have already written to-you once about this exchange, but so-far we-have not had an answer.

10. The extra issue of-the newspaper has proved very popular with its readers and it-is to-be hoped that-there-will-be more of-them in-the future, as I-am-sure they will-be received with approval.

11. The maximum number we-can accommodate in-the hall is 500. If-you-wish to reserve the hall for-your meeting just after Christmas I advise you to book immediately, as-the hall is very popular at that-time of year and there-is-a-great demand for it.

12. I-am rather sorry that we-cannot inquire further into the affair, because I-am quite sure that if-we had enough time we could solve the problem in a manner satisfactory to all concerned.

Figures can be written in Arabic numerals as in paragraph 11 of the above exercise. In Chapter 23 (p. 196) information is given on figure writing.

N Added to P. In addition to the TN, DN blends, we also have an NP blend which, in fact, is hardly a blend at all for it is simply a P following an N. It is, however, classed as a blend since the strokes are written in the

N position: .... Examples:

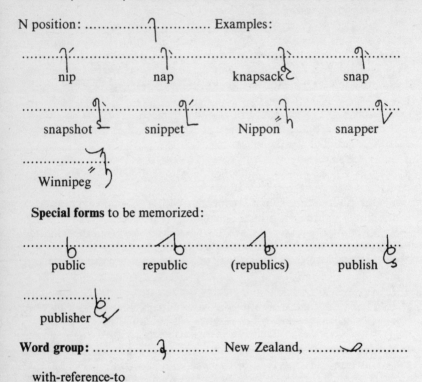

nip   nap   knapsack   snap

snapshot   snippet   Nippon   snapper

Winnipeg

Special forms to be memorized:

public   republic   (republics)   publish

publisher

Word group: .... New Zealand, ...

with-reference-to

Exercise 40
Cover the key and read the sentences. Then copy and transcribe them.

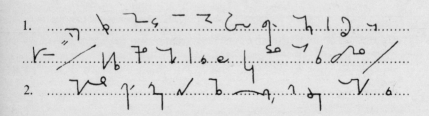

1.

2.

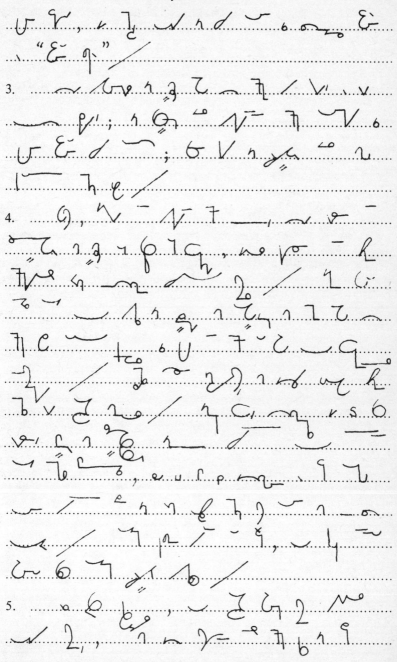

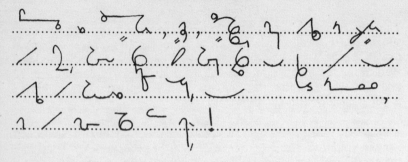

Key

1. Dan has-a tendency to take a-lot-of snapshots when he goes on holiday. Perhaps that-is why he is so popular with his friends.

2. There-was-a nip in-the air this morning and as-the weather is quite chilly, I think we-are in for what is sometimes called a 'cold snap'.

3. My relatives in New Zealand tell me that-they are having a very warm spring; in Britain it-is reported that-the weather is quite cold for autumn; but here in Africa it-is no hotter than usual.

4. Ladies and gentlemen, I-have to report that during my visit to Australia and New Zealand on behalf of-the company, I-was pleased to find that-there-was-a keen demand for-our goods. I-had long talks with our representatives in Sydney and Wellington, and they tell me that-the sale of-our products is equal to that of all our competitors together. This-is most encouraging and I-am-sure you-will find this very welcome news. In-the coming months I shall be visiting Canada and Zimbabwe in-order-to further our trade with those countries, so-you can see I-am-not a chairman who would rather sit in an office than go out and do some work. With-the present rate of exchange, we hope to-do a-lot-of business with the African republics.

5. As book publishers, we welcome all-the good reviews we-are getting, and I-am glad to-say that-the public in such countries as Australia, New Zealand, Zimbabwe and-the republics in Africa are getting a-lot-of benefit from all-the books we publish. Our representatives are always watching our interests, and are not to-be caught napping!

'Australia' is given in full in this exercise, but those who have to write the word frequently can abbreviate it to

......................., and 'Zimbabwe' can be cut to

....

Speed Building

Take the following passage at 40 words a minute and when you have succeeded, try it at 50 w.a.m. Just a reminder: 40 w.a.m. is 10 words (watch for the '/' mark) in 15 seconds. At 50 w.a.m., 12 words should be read in the first quarter minute and 13 in the second quarter; then 12 and 13 to the end of the passage. It may help your reader if a pencil mark is put at each twelfth and thirteenth word.

Dear Sir, With reference to your letter of yesterday's date, / for which I thank you, it would seem that there / has been some delay in sending the goods from our / warehouse and for this I offer my apologies. This laxity / is to be regretted and I will personally see that / it does not happen again. May I also say that / we value your custom and I appreciate the inconvenience you / have been caused and for which I can only offer / my apologies again. Yours truly (85)

Words you may care to check:

thank-you	warehouse	offer	laxity
regretted	personally	custom	appreciate
inconvenience			

19

WAYS WITH 'N': II
Blends with V, W and X

There are three more N blends which help considerably when writing
Teeline at speed and, as you will quickly realize, they are simple and
logical—so simple, in fact, that you may have already discovered them
(but if not, it does not matter because they are set out below).

When N is followed by V, we slope the N and blend it with the V:

.... never .... nave,

.... novel, ... Nov(ember).

With VN, we blend the two letters like this: ....,
as in

van or vane or vain   vanish   vanished

Venice   Vancouver   vainly   vanguard

vanity   Vincent   vend   vendor

ventilate   veneer   advantage   vanquish

vandal   vandalism   vinyl   vineyard

advent   venue

The letter N is added to W in the same way we add F (remember

.... FW and .... WF?)—simply

150

by turning the N on its side and merging the two: ....

NW, ... WN. Examples:

now (but new, for distinction)   nawab   nowadays

nowhere   win or wine   wand   wander

found   founder   wind   window

winter   wanderlust   wanderer   wane or wain

Wainwright   went or want   wonder   windmill

own   owner   town   gown

When the syllable **un-** precedes a W, the U indicator is added to the NW blend:

unwelcome   unwanted   unwind   unwittingly

unwarranted   unwary   unwell   unwilling

unwillingly   unwise   unworldly   unwashed

unwavering   unwholesome

We blend N to X in the same way as it was blended with V—by the simple expedient of sloping the N sign: ....X..... as in ....X..... next

annexe	annexing	annexes	annexed
anxious	anxiety	nix	noxious
obnoxious	inexpert	anxiously	nexus
inexpressive	inexact	inexpensive	

Special forms to be memorized:

inexperience(-d)	unexpected	owing

circumstance (circumstances)

Word groups:

next-week	next-month	next-time	next-day

now-and-then

Exercise 41

Cover the key and read the sentences. Then copy and transcribe them.

1.

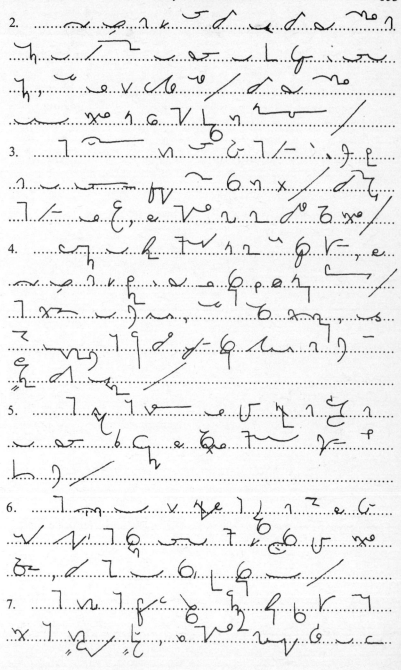

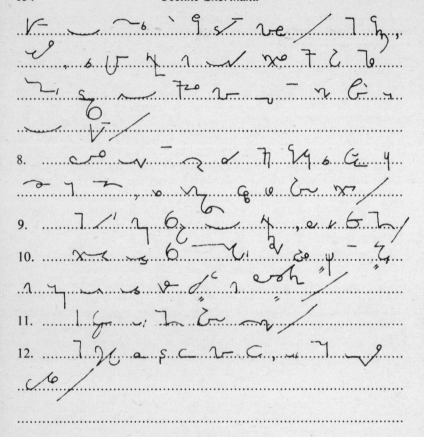

Key

1. The girl vanished from her home in London, taking her passport and some money. Interpol were alerted and she was found in Venice the next-day.

2. My wife and I went for-a walk for-a few minutes and when we returned we found we had left a window open, which was very careless of-us. For-a few minutes we-were anxious in case there had-been an intruder.

3. The motor van went along the road at a great speed and we wondered if-there might be an accident. Fortunately the road was clear, so there-was no need for-us to-be anxious.

4. Now-and-then we find that-we-are in need of-a brief holiday, so my wife and I spend a few days by-the sea or in-the country. The next-time we go away, which will-be next-month, we-shall take advantage of-the cheap fares offered by-the railway and go to Scotland for-the weekend.

5. The arrival of-the visitor was quite unexpected and unwelcome and we found his company so obnoxious that-we-were glad to-see him go.

6. The men were very inexperienced at-the job and took so long over repairing the broken window that I became quite anxious about-it, for they were being paid by-the hour.

7. The venue of-the conference has-been changed from-the public hall to-the annexe of-the Vancouver Hotel, as there-was nowhere else we could hold our meetings at such short notice. The change, of course, is quite unexpected and we-are anxious that all those attending should be aware that-it-is not due to any fault on our part.

8. Nowadays we-have to make sure that-the church is locked up most of-the time, as vandalism causes us a-lot of anxiety.

9. The ring and-the bangle were inexpensive, so I bought them.

10. Next-week we-shall be travelling across Europe to Italy and on-the way we-shall visit France and Switzerland. Then we-shall return to New Zealand by air from Rome.

11. He left owing them a-lot-of money.

12. The girl said she could not come, owing to-the adverse circumstances.

In such words as transmit, transaction, transfer, transparent—in fact, in all words beginning with the prefix **trans-**—the N is only sounded very lightly, so we omit it altogether and for 'trans-' we write

.... 'Trans-' is the first of several prefixes to which

you will be introduced. It is very easy to use:

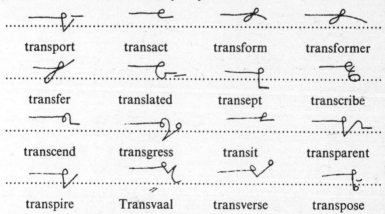

transport	transact	transform	transformer
transfer	translated	transept	transcribe
transcend	transgress	transit	transparent
transpire	Transvaal	transverse	transpose

In Chapter 21 (see p. 170) you will be introduced to several other prefixes which will enable a whole series of letters to be written in one quick, distinctive stroke.

Special forms to be memorized:

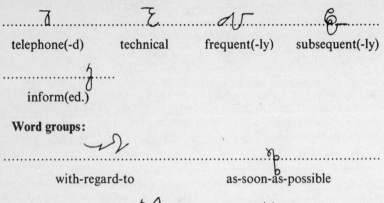

telephone(-d)   technical   frequent(-ly)   subsequent(-ly)

inform(ed.)

Word groups:

with-regard-to   as-soon-as-possible

in-reply-to-your-letter   your-order

Exercise 42

Cover the key and read the sentences. Then copy and transcribe them.

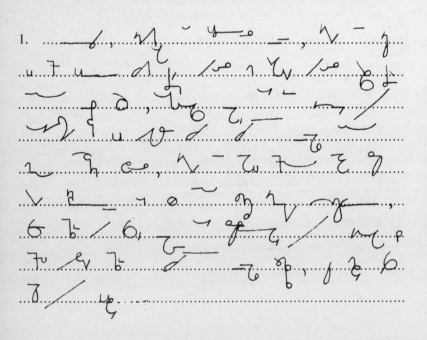

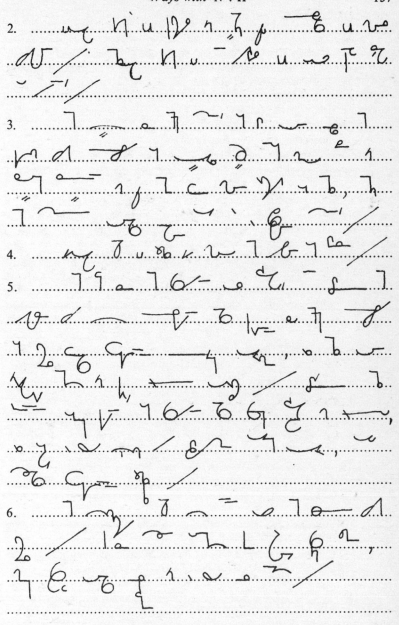

Key

1. Dear-Sir, In-reply-to-your-letter of yesterday's date, I-have to inform you that your-order for-the piston rods and valve rods has-been passed to-our despatch department, who-will-be dealing with it immediately. With-regard-to your request for further details of-our new machine screws, I-have to tell-you that-our technical staff have encountered one or two snags in-their manufacture, but these are being dealt with satisfactorily. I-will see that-you receive these further details as-soon-as-possible, if necessary by telephone. Yours-truly

2. You-will help your progress in Teeline if-you transcribe your notes frequently. This-will help you to recognize your own particular style of writing.

3. The Mayor said that-the meeting of-the council would discuss the plan for-the transfer of-the Works Department to-the new site in South Street and if they could not agree on this, then the matter would-be dealt with at a subsequent meeting.

4. I-will telephone you as-soon-as I know the result of-the contest.

5. The chairman said the board was unwilling to consider the request for more transport to-be provided so that-the transfer of-the goods could-be completed during-the weekend, as this would involve them in paying extra wages. I-consider this attitude on-the part of-the board to-be both unwelcome and extraordinary, as only a few men are concerned with-the work, which must-be completed as-soon-as-possible.

6. The manager telephoned me today with-reference-to the order for-the goods. He said most of-them had already been sent, and the balance would-be despatched in a few days' time.

Exercise 43

Write this exercise in Teeline. Make your outlines as neatly as possible, remembering that if you cultivate a legible style now, your shorthand will be much more legible when written at speed. Try to make your Teeline as neat as that in this book, where every outline has been written by hand and reproduced to size.

1. The south transept of-the church is in need of repair and a bazaar is to-be held next-month to raise funds for it.

2. The woman who vanished from her home on Wednesday was found wandering in-the town the next-day.

3. I found the old lady rather unwell. This made me anxious and I suggested that I telephone the doctor, but she was unwilling for me to-do-so.

4. The arrival of-the party of children at-the game was quite unexpected and we had nowhere to sit them, although we searched vainly for vacant seats.

5. We considered the manageress was quite incompetent, so we dis-

missed her and appointed a younger person, a lady with a-lot-of charm as-well-as-a good head for business. We-are now confident that-the takings will increase.

6. We found several old sets of games at-the back of-the shop which will only be a nuisance to-us, so we-shall throw them away and put the space to better use.

7. The new president unwittingly caused a surprise when he gave his opening address at-the conference because he knocked over the microphone, which fell with a deafening crash. However, his subsequent speech was well received and there-were frequent bursts of applause, particularly when he spoke with regard-to the need for more public transport in-the town.

Key

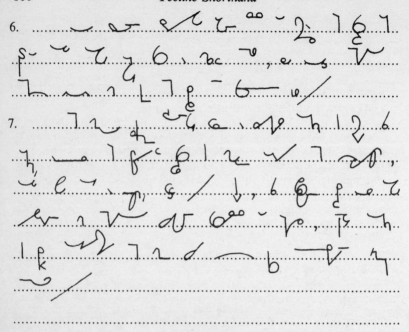

6. ...

7. ...

Speed Building

Take the following passage at 40 w.a.m. and when you have succeeded, transcribe it and check with the longhand. Then take it at 50 w.a.m. and transcribe.

Mr Chairman, It gives me great pleasure to come here / tonight to speak to you on the subject of wine / making. Next time any of you pass through France, I / suggest you visit a few of the vineyards, for you / will learn much more there than I can tell you. / However, I am anxious to tell you in the hour / or so at my disposal, as much as I can / about wine and particularly about what happens to the grape / after the *vendange*, or harvest, for that is when the / wine making takes place. (94)

Words you may care to check:

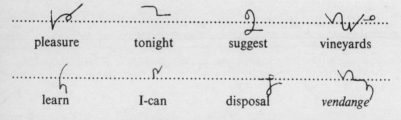

| pleasure | tonight | suggest | vineyards |

| learn | I-can | disposal | *vendange* |

harvest place

When you have taken the preceding passage to your satisfaction, try this one at 40 w.a.m. and then at 50:

Dear Sir, I have pleasure in enclosing with this letter / copies of our new technical catalogue, as you requested on / the telephone today. You will see that all the details / have been translated into French and German, so your customers / will be able to read the details in their own / language. We frequently have requests for copies in Italian and / Spanish, and details in these languages are being prepared for / subsequent issues of the catalogue. I hope you will find / this new catalogue satisfactory. Yours truly (86)

Outlines you may care to check:

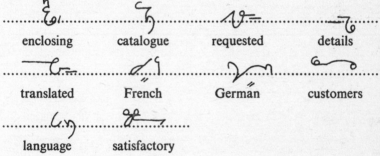

enclosing catalogue requested details

translated French German customers

language satisfactory

These passages may have seemed a little more difficult than those in earlier chapters. That is because you are constantly enlarging your vocabulary and at first it is necessary to think of the outlines for 'new' words in a short space of time. One reason why you should have complete mastery of the special forms is that you write them very quickly and this gives you a little more time to think out the symbols for the new words.

When two or three 'new' words come together and you feel you are dropping behind, don't panic. Force yourself to write a little faster and then afterwards check the outlines; if necessary, practise by writing them several times, remembering to say them to yourself as you do so.

20

HOW TO WRITE '-TION'

Many years ago when journalists and authors wrote their copy by hand, they saved time by abbreviating words. An 'o' stood for 'of', 'w' for 'with', 'wt' for 'without' or 'weight' or 'wait', and a 'g' was used for '-ing' as in 'wtg' (waiting), 'hvg' (having) and so on. Even after the introduction of typewriters, many reporters continued to write their copy by hand and these printers' abbreviations remained in use. At one time they were so wellknown that reference books gave lists of them.

One of those abbreviations was the use of the letter N for the syllables -tion, -sion, -cean, -xion, -cian, -shion, etc. In fact, whenever there was an ending which sounded like -tion, or nearly like it, the N was used, including the words 'question' and 'suggestion'.

In Teeline we do the same thing. Wherever we get -tion or one of its near relatives, we use the N sign, disjoined and written just above the rest of the outline, in the same way old-time reporters and authors used to do it:

tension	mention	mentioned	conclusion
ocean	emotion	ancient	patient
patience	expansion	notion	commotion
auctioneer	convention	affectionate	suggestion
suggestions	question	questioned	questions
cushion			

If an 'a', an 'i' or a 'u' immediately precede the -tion, then it is usual to add those letters to the disjoined N:

162

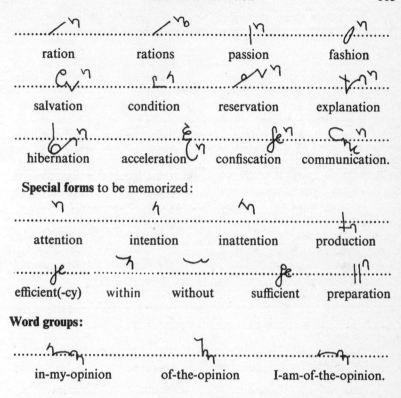

ration   rations   passion   fashion

salvation   condition   reservation   explanation

hibernation   acceleration confiscation communication.

Special forms to be memorized:

attention   intention   inattention   production

efficient(-cy)   within   without   sufficient   preparation

Word groups:

in-my-opinion   of-the-opinion   I-am-of-the-opinion.

Exercise 44

Write the following in neat Teeline, then check with the key below. Please bear in mind that an outline in the key may not be the only way in which a word can be written, and therefore it is not necessarily 'wrong' if your outline is different. Those used in the key are the more acceptable outlines when writing at speed.

1. In-my-opinion the scientist did not pay sufficient attention to-the preparation of-the work being done in his laboratory.

2. The society made a donation of rare books to-the library in re-cognition of-the work done by their late president. They were books which he had collected in his lifetime and had originally presented them to-the society, which was now being wound up. I-am-of-the-opinion that-their action in making the gift was the proper one.

3. The chairman mentioned that-the committee had some reserva-tions about-the intentions of-the company in approaching them with-he suggestion that-they sell the land in-order-to raise funds.

4. There-was some confusion over the communication they had received from-the national committee, as it did not clearly indicate their intentions.

5. Some indignation was expressed at-the suggestion that-the production had not-been done efficiently and that-it did not bear comparison with-the show put on last-year.

6. The farm is now in a good condition and in-my-opinion, with hard work and a little patience, it-will-be one of-the best in-the district.

7. I-can-say without fear of contradiction that-the preservation of-the ancient buildings in-the borough is of prime importance to-us and we pay a-lot-of attention to them.

8. I-have come to-the conclusion that-there should-be some explanation given us with-reference-to the sudden resignation of-the chairman.

9. I-am-of-the-opinion that-the committee of the amateur dramatic society did not allow sufficient time for-the efficient preparation of-the production. There-was a-lot-of inattention to detail and-the musicians had not-been sufficiently rehearsed.

10. There-was-a great deal of commotion when the auctioneer announced that-the picture had-been withdrawn from-the sale.

Key

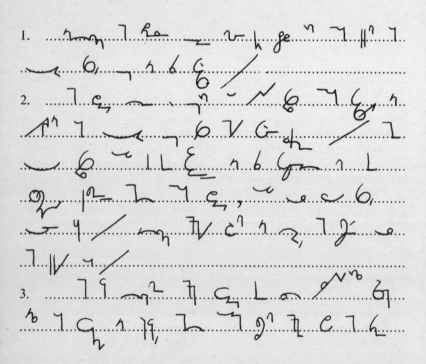

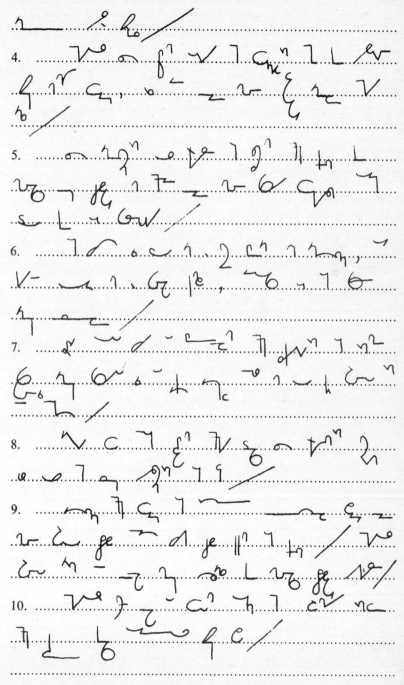

The common endings -tation, -dation, -diation, -tition, -dition,

-tuition and -tuation are represented by .... ⌐⌐ .... written
in either the T or D positions:

station	situation	erudition	affectation
elucidation	intuition	accommodation	inundation
fluoridation	foundation	rendition	sedition
radiation	partition	fluctuation	emendation

Special forms to be memorized: .... recommend-

ation ....expectation.

Exercise 45

Cover the key and read the following sentences. Then copy them and
transcribe.

1. ....

2. ....

3. ....

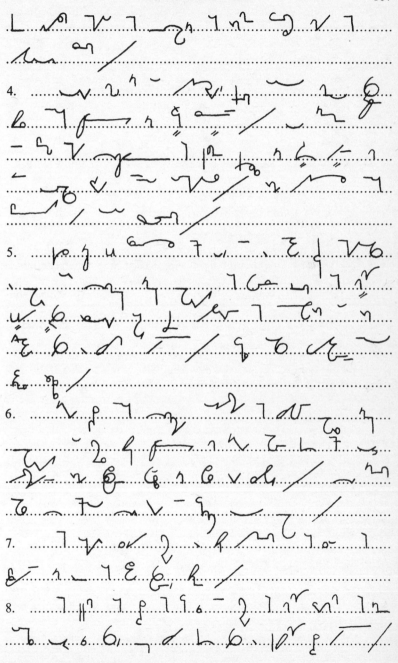

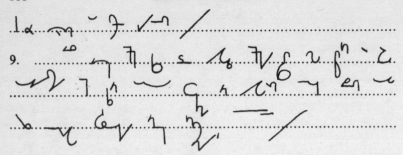

Key

1. When we arrived, we found the accommodation much better than we had expected and we-were glad that-we-had accepted the recommendation to stay there.

2. The sale of-the recently published book has come up to expectations and the suggestion that-it-is not selling well in some towns is without foundation.

3. I-had a-long telephone conversation with her with-reference-to the situation which had arisen through the demolition of-the ancient cottages near the railway station.

4. We-have no intention of removing production of-our new breakfast foods to-the factory in Exchange Street. We intend to continue their manufacture at-the present premises in Elm Road and it would-be inconvenient to-do otherwise. Any rumours to-the contrary are without foundation.

5. Please inform your customers that owing to a technical hitch there-will-be a delay of-a month in-the delivery of-the latest edition of-the National Year Book as-we-have only just received the translation of an article by a foreign writer. Copies will-be circulated to-our clients as-soon-as-possible.

6. I-have spoken to-the manager with-regard-to the frequent delays in-the delivery of goods from-the factory and I-have told him that we-shall regard any subsequent losses in sales very seriously. My intuition tells me that-we may have to change our dealer.

7. The opera singer gave a fine rendition of-the song at-the concert in aid of-the school building fund.

8. The preparation of-the speech the chairman is to give at-the national convention at-the end of-this week is being done for him by a professional speech writer. He is-a man of great erudition.

9. It-is important that-the public should realize that-there can-be no confusion at all with-regard-to the position of-our company in relation to-the situation which has developed elsewhere in the engineering trade.

Speed Building

Take the following at 40 w.a.m. and then at 50, as you did at the end of
the last chapter.

Dear Sir, Thank you for your letter in which you / inquire whether we
have any interest in property schemes in / the city centre. I am sure you
would like to / know that we have recently purchased a site comprising
fifty thousand / square feet of offices, shops and space for parking cars. /
If you are interested in taking any of this property / on short lease, we
shall be pleased to hear from / you, either by letter or telephone. We find
there is / quite a brisk demand and therefore we suggest that you / contact
us as soon as possible. Yours truly (98)

Outlines you may care to check:

inquire	property	schemes	city
purchased	thousand	parking	short
brisk	contact.		

Now try this short passage at 60 w.a.m. (each '/' indicates 10 seconds).

The chairman said the board would be represented at the / convention
later this month, but he had no intention of / going himself, as he thought
the deputation they were sending / would be sufficient. (33)

Words you may care to check:

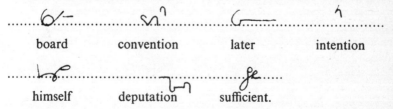

board	convention	later	intention
himself	deputation	sufficient.	

21

COMMON PREFIXES

There are thousands of words which begin with one of several very common prefixes. These include the word-beginnings under-, over-, self-, auto-, etc. Many others begin with trans- and this prefix you have already met (see p. 155). For these word-beginnings we have simple, easy-to-remember signs.

Under. Use .... ⌐......... either joined or disjoined:

| understand | understood | undertake | undertaking |

| undertaken | underhand | undercarriage | underline |

| undersigned | understudy | underdog | undercurrent |

| underfoot | undercharge | underestimate | underexpose |

| undergo | understaffed | undermentioned. |

Over. Use .... written above the rest of the outline:

| overcome | overcame | overcast | overhead |

| overhaul | overestimated | overland | overhanging |

| overtime | overtake | overtaken | overpower |

170

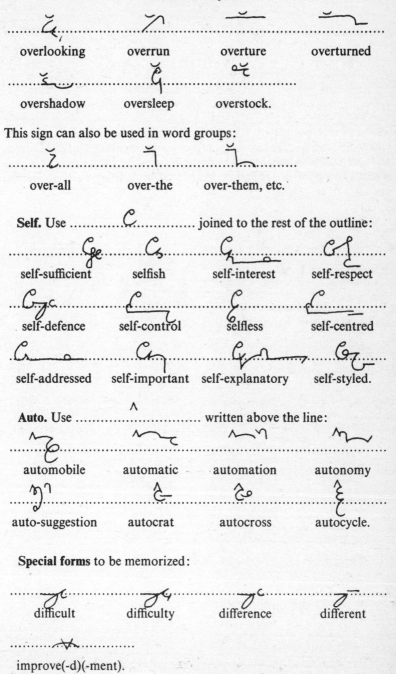

overlooking overrun overture overturned

overshadow oversleep overstock.

This sign can also be used in word groups:

over-all over-the over-them, etc.

Self. Use .... joined to the rest of the outline:

self-sufficient selfish self-interest self-respect

self-defence self-control selfless self-centred

self-addressed self-important self-explanatory self-styled.

Auto. Use .... written above the line:

automobile automatic automation autonomy

auto-suggestion autocrat autocross autocycle.

Special forms to be memorized:

difficult difficulty difference different

improve(-d)(-ment).

Exercise 46

Cover the key and read the sentences. Then copy and transcribe.

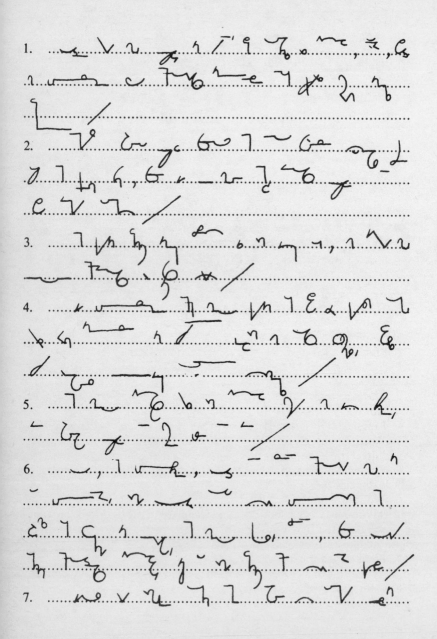

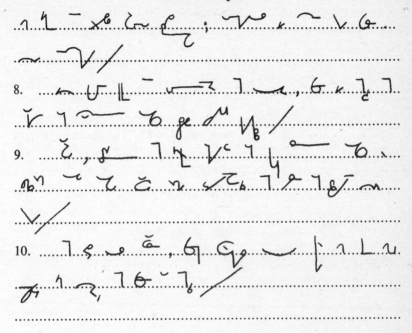

Key

1. We-should have no difficulty in writing such outlines as automatic, overtake, selfish and understand now that-we-have-been introduced to-the prefixes given in-this chapter.

2. There-is a-lot-of difference between the two latest models just off the production line, but I do not think it-will-be difficult to sell either of-them.

3. The principal change in-the system is an important one, and I-have no doubt that-it-will-be a big improvement.

4. I understand that-the new principal of-the school is-a person who has-a keen interest in further education and will-be organizing classes for adults during-the winter months.

5. The new automobile has an automatic gear and I-am finding it a-little difficult to get used to it.

6. We, the undersigned, wish to state that-we-have no intention of undertaking any work which may undermine the actions of-the company in developing the new housing estate, but we-are of-the-opinion that-we-should-be automatically informed of any charge that may take place.

7. I-was very annoyed when they told me of-their decision and I-had to exercise a-lot-of self-control: otherwise I might have lost my temper.

8. I-am quite prepared to undertake the work, but I think the overhaul of-the motor will be sufficient for-your purposes.

9. Over-all, I-consider the unexpected appearance of-the pop star will-be a sensation which will overcome any shortcomings the rest of-the concert may have.

10. The sky was overcast, but-the campers were happy and had no difficulty in making the best of things.

Always take care to write the prefixes in their correct positions: 'under-' is on the line of writing; 'over-' and 'auto-' are above the line.

Ev. For 'ev-' at the beginning of a word, we blend the V with the vertical E indicator: ....✓.............., and use this instead of ....✓.............. for EV, as in:

ever	every	even	evening

event	eventual	eventually	everlasting

everloving	evangelist	evaporate	evasion

eviction	evil	evergreen	everybody

everyone.

After. Although 'after' standing alone is written

..........⌐.............., when used as a prefix it can be abbreviated to a

full A ....∧.............. This is written *on the line* so that it does not clash with 'auto-', which, as you have already learned, is a full A *above* the line. Here are some examples of the 'after-' prefix:

..............⌒......... aftermath, ...⌒......... afternoon,

.... ⌇ .... afterglow, ... ⌇ .... after-thought.

It can also be used for the word 'after' in word groups and some examples of this are:

after-all   after-this   after-that   after-some

after-several   after-(a)-number-of.

Super. Use ...., written above the line, as in:

supertanker   superimpose   superman   supervise

supervision   superstructure   supersede   supernatural

superhuman   supernumerary   superpower   supersonic.

Circum. Use .... Examples:

circumference   circumvent   circumflex   circumspect.

Magna/Magne/Magni. For these we use a disjoined

...................., as in:

magnetize   magnitude   magnificent   magnetism

magnanimous   magnify   magnification

Special forms to be memorized:

super, superintendent   supermarket   superb.

Exercise 47

Cover the key and read the sentences. Then copy them and transcribe.

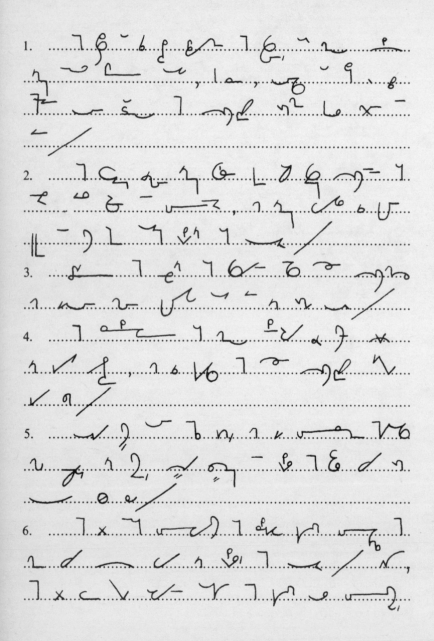

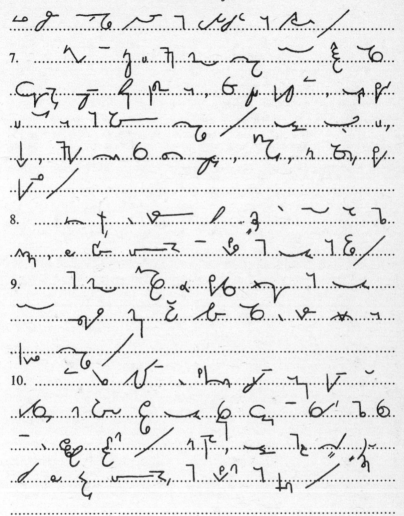

Key

1. The subject of his speech concerned the building of-a new supermarket in-the town centre which, he said, would be of such a size that-it would overshadow the magnificent ancient house next to it.

2. The committee is-not in-the least put off by-the magnitude of-the task it-is about to undertake, and in-the circumstances is quite prepared to go ahead with-the supervision of-the work

3. I-consider the decision of-the board to-be most magnanimous and I-would not quarrel with it in any way.

4. The superstructure of-the new supertanker is-a great improvement in every respect, and is probably the most magnificent I-have ever seen.

5. We-are going out this evening and I understand there-will-be no difficulty in getting Mr Smith to supervise the class for an hour or so.

6. The accident to-the undercarriage of-the supersonic plane underlines the need for more care in supervising the work. After-all, this accident could have occurred while the plane was undergoing its first trials round the circumference of-the runway.

7. I-have to inform you that-the new model of-our autocycle will-be completely different from-the present one, but if-you prefer it, we-can supply you with one of-the older models. We-should warn you, however, that-there may be some difficulty, eventually, in obtaining spare parts.

8. I-am expecting a visitor from New Zealand at two o'clock this afternoon, so I-cannot undertake to supervise the work of-the class.

9. The new automobile is-a superb example of-the work of-our designers and-the over-all result will-be a vast improvement on previous models.

10. It has required a superhuman effort on-the part of everybody and a-lot-of selfless work by-the committee to bring this business to a successful conclusion. In particular, we-should thank Mr Johnson for so kindly undertaking the supervision of-the production.

Speed Building

Take the following passage at 40 w.a.m. and then at 50 w.a.m. as before; but do not attempt it at 50 until you can get it all down at 40.

I am sorry to have to tell you that, having / regard to all the circumstances, we cannot see our way / to admit the public to the premises except during the / present permitted hours. This is because it is difficult to / arrange adequate supervision. I understand that a number of volunteers / have offered their services, but this is not sufficient for / our needs. We should require trained guards for the job, / and I regret we cannot afford them. (77)

Outlines you may care to check:

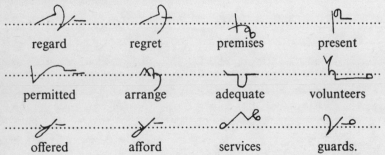

regard	regret	premises	present
permitted	arrange	adequate	volunteers
offered	afford	services	guards.

22

COMMON SUFFIXES

There are many words which have similar word-endings, or suffixes. For instance, '-ing' is the most common suffix in the English language and you have for long known how easily it is written in Teeline. There are many other frequently-used suffixes, such as '-able', '-ible', '-cial', '-ment', '-ology'. All of which can be represented at a stroke, thus saving time and many letters. Here are some examples:

-able. For this suffix we use a full A written at the end of an outline. Since this sign has been used for the word 'able' or for 'able-to' for some time, it will come as nothing new:

lovable	likeable	table	moveable
babble	cable	Mabel	remarkable
syllable	indictable	changeable	profitable
passable	adaptable	answerable	valuable
invaluable	desirable	capable	dependable
durable	suitable	endurable	fashionable
accountable	rabble	sable	saleable
unthinkable	commensurable		

-ability is shown by adding a small I indicator to the disjoined A:

likeability   moveability   capability   changeability

accountability   suitability   endurability   dependability

desirability   comparability, etc.

In word groups, the word 'ability' may be shown in the same way:

his-ability   their-ability   our-ability   no-ability

her-ability   best-(of)-our ability   best-(of)-my-ability

best-(of)-your-ability

-eble/-ebel is a disjoined full E:

treble   pebble   rebel   Kebble

-ible/-ibly, frequent suffixes, are shown by a full I, disjoined:

possible, possibly   terrible, terribly   horrible, horribly

tangible   intangible   credible   gullible

legible   edible   defensible   sensible

risible   negligible   visible

(or '-ly' in all these cases, according to context).

-ibility is shown by adding a small I indicator:

possibility   credibility   legibility   sensibility

visibility   gullibility

-oble/-obly/-ouble are represented by a full .... O ....,

disjoined and written on the line:

noble or nobly   double or doubly   doubled

trouble   troubled.

-obility is the same sign with an I indicator added:

.... nobility.

-ology/-alogy are shown by writing the normal O above the line:

biology   genealogy   psychology   sociology

zoology   meteorology   phrenology   numerology

graphology   mineralogy   physiology

-ological/-alogical are shown by adding an L:

biological	genealogical	psychological	sociological

zoological	meteorological	phrenological	graphological

numerological	physiological	mineralogical

For **-ologist** or **-alogist**, just add an ST to the O:

sociologist	mineralogist	meteorologist	zoologist

-ubble/-ubly, as you have no doubt guessed, is a disjoined

:

bubble	stubble	soluble	volubly.

Special forms to be memorized:

information	unfortunate	unfortunately	income.

Word groups:

United Kingdom	United States	United States of America

income-tax	trade union	per cent(-age)

in our

Exercise 48

Cover the key and read the sentences. Then copy in neat Teeline and transcribe.

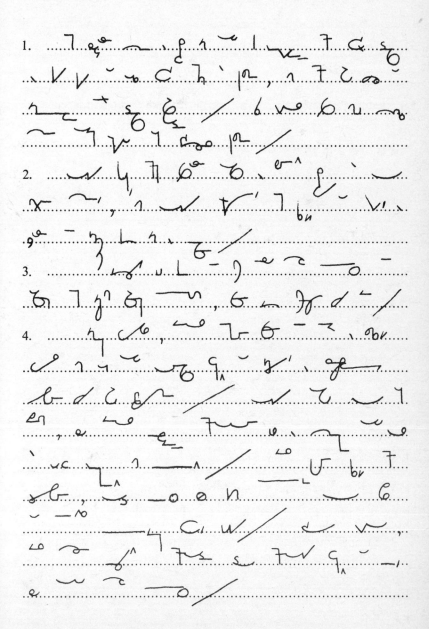

1.

2.

3.

4.

5.

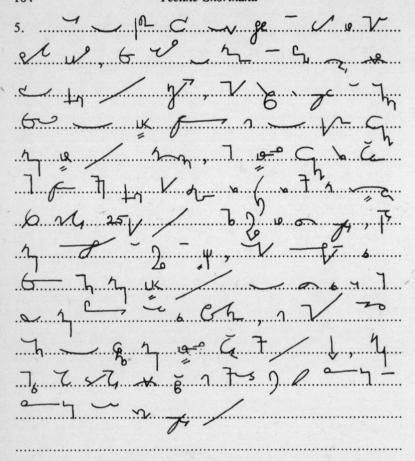

Key

1. The sociologist made a speech in which he advocated that income-tax should-be a higher percentage of one's income than at present, and that all forms of indirect tax should-be abolished. His views by no means met with-the approval of-the economists present.

2. We-are hoping that-the biologist will be a suitable speaker at our next meeting, and we-are exploring the possibility of having a zoologist to engage him in a debate.

3. I-am-sorry you had to go to-so much trouble to obtain the information about-the-trade-union, but I-am grateful for it.

4. In-the circumstances, it-was thought best to take a sensible course and one which would-be capable of ensuring a satisfactory result for all concerned. We-are well aware of-the situation, so it-was decided that-

we-would use a method which was at once adaptable and durable. It-is quite possible that as-a-result, we-shall double or even treble our sales of tables during-the coming year. In-our view, it-is most desirable that-we-should show that-we-are capable of doing so without much trouble.

5. With our present income we-have sufficient to carry us through several years, but of-course we intend to continue making improvements in-our production. Unfortunately, there has-been a difference of opinion between our United-Kingdom factory and our parent company in-the United-States-of-America. In-my-opinion, the United-States company has overlooked the fact that-the production here is-not as large as that in America by nearly 25 per cent. This gives us some difficulty, particularly in-the transfer of goods to Europe, where transport is better than in-the United-Kingdom. Our firm is one of-the few in-the country which is self-reliant, and there-are times when our cousins in-the United-States overlook that. However, I-hope things will shortly improve overseas and that-we-shall go from strength to strength without any difficulty.

Make sure you know the prefixes and suffixes thoroughly. By using them, it is possible to represent long words by short outlines.

Exercise 49
Write the following sentences in Teeline and then check with the key.

1. According to information reaching us, the biologist we-have engaged will join the firm as-soon-as-possible, and will not wait until the end of-the month.

2. It-will-be necessary for-us to take 25 per cent of-the shares if-we-are to obtain control of-the company, and I think the sensible thing to-do is to make overtures to some of-the small shareholders.

3. The trouble with-the trade-union has now been resolved and there-is-a strong possibility that-the staff will-be back at work tomorrow.

4. I-was questioned very closely for half-an-hour on-the suitability of my proposals for improving our output. Unfortunately the members of-the board did not agree with-me and said they did not consider the present system to-be capable of improvement.

5. There-is no doubt but that-the man is both dependable and capable as-well-as likeable, and I think that in-the office he will-be adaptable and a valuable addition to-our staff.

6. There-is no tangible evidence, so-far-as I-can-see, to show that-the proposal has any merit. In-fact, I find it a rather risible suggestion.

7. The meteorologist has gone to-the United-States to lecture at a-number-of universities.

8. I-am pleased to have your report on-the credibility of-the company and I-can assure you that I-have no doubt that-you-have prepared it to-the best-of-your-ability.

9. The witness was rather voluble when giving evidence, and it-was evident that he was very nervous.

10. Although we-have doubled our efforts, we-have-had no success in getting to-the bottom of-the matter, and we-are-sorry that-you-have-been troubled.

Key

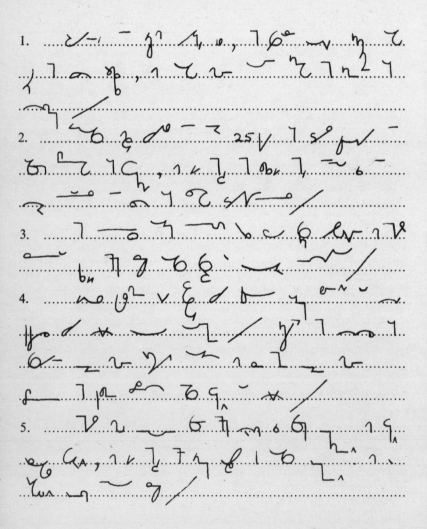

6.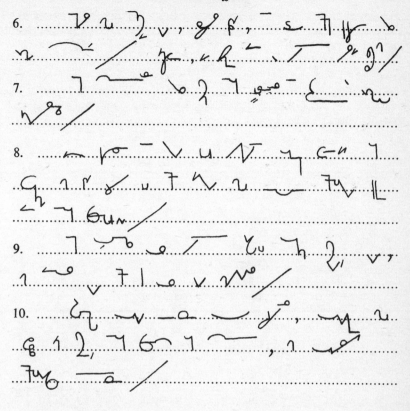

7.

8.

9.

10.

The endings **-tial, -cial, -shal** are all represented by a disjoined SH written at the end of the outline:

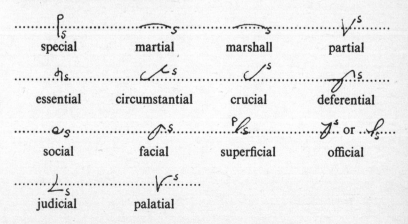

special   martial   marshall   partial

essential   circumstantial   crucial   deferential

social   facial   superficial   official

judicial   palatial

For **-cially** add an I:

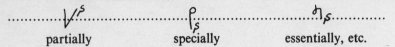

partially   specially   essentially, etc.

-ward/-word/-wood/-wide are shown by writing a disjoined W below the first part of the outline. In practice, writers tend to make a W slightly smaller than a normal one, and this adds to legibility:

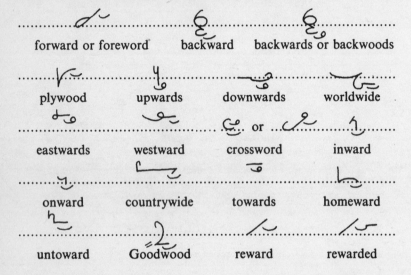

forward or foreword   backward   backwards or backwoods

plywood   upwards   downwards   worldwide

eastwards   westward   crossword   or   inward

onward   countrywide   towards   homeward

untoward   Goodwood   reward   rewarded

The disjoined W can also be used in word groups for 'would' if it is written like this:

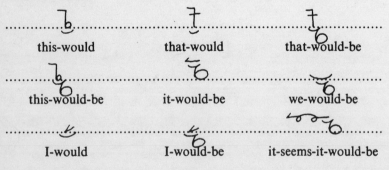

this-would   that-would   that-would-be

this-would-be   it-would-be   we-would-be

I-would   I-would-be   it-seems-it-would-be

we-would-be-able-to, etc.

Special forms to be memorized:

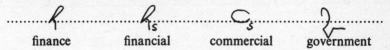

| finance | financial | commercial | government |

Exercise 50

Cover the key and read the sentences. Then copy and transcribe.

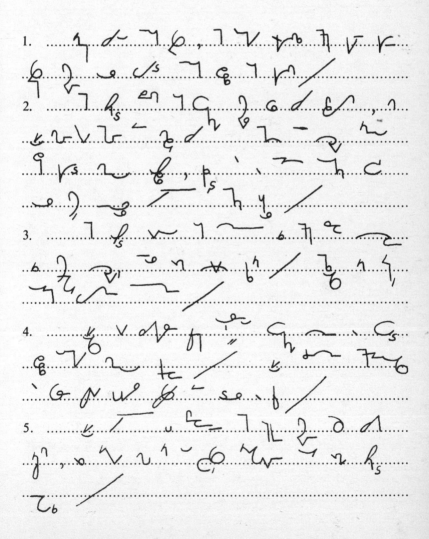

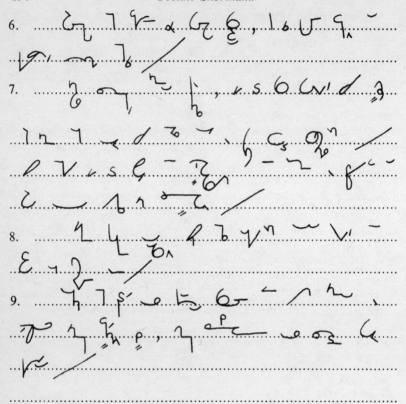

6.

7.

8.

9.

Key

1. In-the foreword to-the book, the author explains that-the part played by-the government was crucial to-the success of-the plan.

2. The financial situation of-the company gives cause for concern, and I-would not have thought it necessary for them to move into such palatial new offices, especially at a time when income was going downwards rather than upwards.

3. The official view of-the matter is that-the stock market is gradually moving towards an improved position. This-would-be in keeping with-the current trend.

4. I-would-be very surprised if-the Westwood company made a commercial success of-their new product. I-would estimate that-it-will-be at least five years before it shows a profit.

5. I-would rather you contacted the appropriate government department for-the information, as I-have no intention of becoming involved with any financial dealings.

6. Although the child is-a little backward, he is quite capable of per-forming many things.

7. Unless something untoward happens, I shall be leaving for New Zealand at-the end of-the week for talks with a large commercial organ-ization. From there I shall fly to Melbourne to attend a conference of all our representatives in Australia.

8. I-had hoped we-would-be-able-to finance this operation without having to call on government aid.

9. When the ship was homeward bound it ran into a typhoon in-the China Sea, and the superstructure was smashed like plywood.

The small W for -ward, -word, -wood, -wide is used only as a suffix. 'Ward', 'word', 'wide', etc., on their own are written fully.

A frequent word ending is **-ment**. Just as for 'ward', etc., we used a small W below the outline, so for '-ment' we employ a small M *above* the outline:

element	sediment	statement	fundament
experiment	experiments	payment	payments
excitement	temperament	supplement	detriment
instalment	instalments		

For **-mental** we add an upward L to the small M:

fundamental	fundamentally	experimental	experimentally
sentimental	detrimental	temperamental, etc.	

In the same way, for **-mentary** we add R to the '-ment' symbol. There is no need to add the final I indicator in this case:

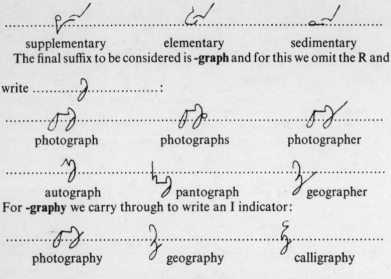

supplementary elementary sedimentary

The final suffix to be considered is **-graph** and for this we omit the R and

write .... :

photograph photographs photographer

autograph pantograph geographer

For **-graphy** we carry through to write an I indicator:

photography geography calligraphy

Exercise 51

Cover the key on the opposite page and read the sentences. Then copy
and transcribe.

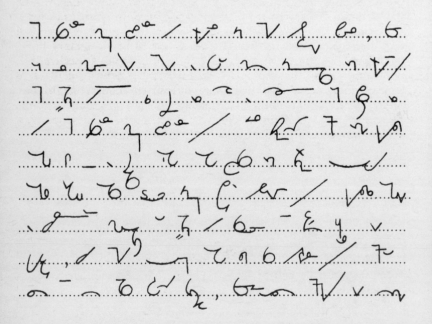

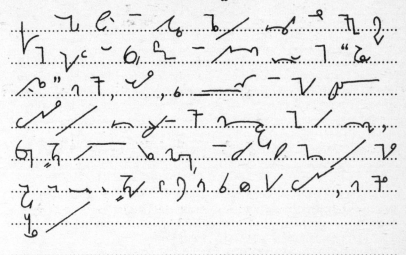

Key

The biologist and-the psychologist are experts in their respective fields, but one does not have to-have a long name in-order-to-be an expert. The Teeline writer is just as much a master of-the subject as are the biologist and-the psychologist. It-is fundamental that any person who can do a job well will become an excellent worker whose value will-be shown in-the salary received. Persons who-have a first-rate knowledge of Teeline are bound to climb upwards very quickly, for their worth will soon be recognized. That-would seem to me to-be elementary logic, but-it-would-seem that-there-are many people who fail to realize this. I-am-sorry to-say that-they give the appearance of being content to remain among the 'also rans' and that, of-course, is detrimental to their future careers. I-am afraid that numerically they are many, but-the Teeline writer has nothing to fear from them. There-is only one way a Teeliner can go in his or her career, and that-is upwards.

Although a small M is used for the suffix -ment, the word 'meant' must be written fully: .... The same applies to 'graph' standing on its own: ....

Exercise 52

Write the following in your neatest Teeline:

Dear-Sir, Thank-you-for-your-letter. I-am-sorry I shall be unable-to come to-the dinner next-week, but my deputy will-be-able-to attend on my behalf. With-regard-to the other matter you mention, we-are-able-to let-you-have-the goods you require, and my deputy will-be-able-to let-you-have all-the details, as he is an expert in photography and will-be-able-to explain all-the details of-the experiment to-you. I-am unable-to do-so because I do not know enough about-it. We-are very much in an experimental stage with our new work, so to speak, and to me it-is all very technical. I suppose that-is to-be expected, since my main interest is with-the commercial and financial side of-the firm. All-the same, it-is work which is full of excitement and I-am-sure it-will-be quite a step forward in-the realm of biology and in years to come it-will-be appreciated world-wide. Yours-truly

Key

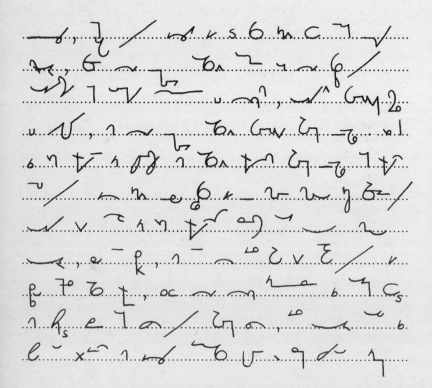

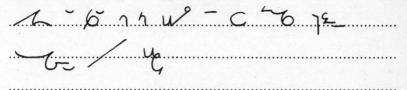

Speed Building

Take the following passage at 50 w.a.m. When you have succeeded in doing so, try it at 60:

Ladies and gentlemen, I have to inform you today that / our experimental work aimed at obtaining improved production in our / factory is proving very useful. We cannot yet say that / it is a success, but judging by the way we / are going, success cannot be very far off. During the / past few weeks, we have been encouraged by the amount / of progress that has been made and the work is / now entering a crucial stage. However, we are quite confident / that our technical staff will achieve what we want, and / we look forward to the day in the near future / when our efforts will be rewarded. (106)

Outlines you may care to check:

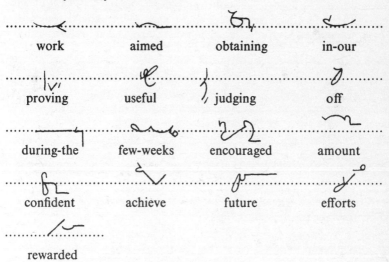

work	aimed	obtaining	in-our
proving	useful	judging	off
during-the	few-weeks	encouraged	amount
confident	achieve	future	efforts
rewarded			

When did you last revise the special forms? It will assist you greatly if you make a regular habit of doing so. You can't know them too well!

23

A NEW WAY WITH FIGURES

The accurate representation of figures is of great importance to a short-hand writer, for the transposition of two figures, or the dropping of a nought, could have serious repercussions. Sometimes these errors have led to legal proceedings and even court reporters and official shorthand writers have to be particularly careful when recording statistics. Some years ago there was a court case over a reporter's note in which there was confusion between the figure 6 and a shorthand outline. In legal work, the omission of a nought in a contract could lead to an enormous loss by one of the signatories.

You have only to look at the symbols in any shorthand system to realize that an isolated figure could be mistaken for a word. The figure might not make sense when read as a word, but the attempt to turn the figure into something else results in a pause in transcribing and therefore wastes time. The delay might only be momentary but even so it results in a loss of time; in fact, I can recall one instance when a shorthand student failed to complete a transcript in a speed examination because so much

time was lost through reading a '...............⌐...............' as a 'the' and trying to make sense of the following words.

The only figure which can safely be written in isolation is '8'. All others, when standing alone, should be written in Teeline:

| 1 | 2 | 3 | 4 | 5 | 6 | 7 | 8 | 9 | 10 |

It is also safer, when writing double figures, to put a ring round them, so as to make assurance doubly sure:

etc. If there are three or more figures in a row, they will be instantly recognizable provided they are not spaced too far apart.

All figures should be written clearly and simply. Speed is the essence in shorthand and there is no time to be fussy. If you write

...............2............... or ....4............... or

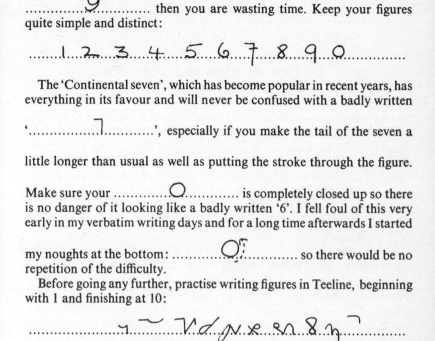

.... *9* .... then you are wasting time. Keep your figures quite simple and distinct:

.....1...2...3...4....5...6...7...8...9...0.............

The 'Continental seven', which has become popular in recent years, has everything in its favour and will never be confused with a badly written

'.............. *7* ....', especially if you make the tail of the seven a little longer than usual as well as putting the stroke through the figure.

Make sure your .... *O* .... is completely closed up so there is no danger of it looking like a badly written '6'. I fell foul of this very early in my verbatim writing days and for a long time afterwards I started

my noughts at the bottom: .... *O* .... so there would be no repetition of the difficulty.

Before going any further, practise writing figures in Teeline, beginning with 1 and finishing at 10:

Write them until they flow from the pen quite quickly. One of the difficulties with writing arises from the fact that when taking dictation, one naturally drops a few words behind the speaker. This helps in following the sense of what is being said, but it is of no use when recording a series of figures, since they generally do not follow any regular word pattern. With such phrases as 'one or two', 'three or four', there is a word pattern and as soon as 'one or — ' is heard, common sense dictates that the next word will be 'two', but when a speaker says 'one thousand two hundred and fifty-four' there is no word pattern, and if the writer is too far behind a transposition often occurs and the figures may well come out as 'one thousand two hundred and forty-five'. There is a danger of this happening when a series of figure groups is given in rapid succession.

Further, figure groups read out in this fashion are sometimes difficult to follow, since a slowness in writing causes a psychological block to build up. This can only be overcome by practice, practice, practice until a string of figures can be written as rapidly as they are spoken. So write your Teeline outlines for figures dozens of times:

This done, practise the writing of ordinary figures, making them simple but clear:

............1. 2. 3. 4. 5. 6. 7. 8. 9. 0.....................

Write a page of them in your notebook. Then try writing them in groups:

...1234.........2345....3456......4567.....5678...

and so on, and before very long the writing of groups will cease to have any difficulty.

One method of writing figures greatly favoured by high-speed and verbatim writers is easily mastered and is instantly recognizable. It is this:

Hundreds: use a short dash after the figure: ....4—.....................

400; ....8—........... 800; ....12—........... 1,200.

Thousands: use a long upward dash after the figure, but close to it so that it cannot be mistaken for a fullstop: ....2/.................

2,000; ....90/........... 90,000; ....212/.........
212,000.

Millions: use M below the figure: ....6........... 6,000,000;

.............47........... 47,000,000.

For **pounds** (money or weight) place a dot next to the line:

.............2—.........., £200 or 200 lb.; ....8/........,
£8,000 or 8,000 lb.

Combinations of these signs can also be used:

.............7—/........ 700,000

.............9—/26.... 900,026

.............5—.......... £500,000,000

.............2—/.......... £200,000

It is possible to show fractions just as rapidly and clearly. The most frequently used is 'half', which is represented by a short dash above the figure: .... $\overline{2}$ .... 2½; .... $\overline{24}$ 24½;

.... $\overline{10}$ .... 10½. A quarter is shown by using the same dash, but with a tick at the beginning: .... $\overset{\leftarrow}{3}$ 3¼;

.... $\overset{\leftarrow}{8}$ .... 8¼; .... $\overset{\leftarrow}{11}$ .... 11¼. For three-quarters, put the tick at the end of the dash: .... $\overset{\rightarrow}{4}$ 4¾;

.... $\overset{\rightarrow}{7}$ .... 7¾; .... $\overset{\rightarrow}{12}$ .... 12¾. Remember that a dot represents 'pounds' money or weight: .... 44. .... £44 or 44 lb; .... $\overset{\rightarrow}{4}.$ .... 4¾ lb.; .... $\overline{16}.$ .... 16½ lb., etc.

Other fractions are represented by writing the figures in the normal way but without the dividing line: .... $\overset{2}{3}$ .... ⅔,

.... $\overset{4}{5}$ .... ⅘, ... $\overset{7}{8}$ .... ⅞,

.... $\overset{9}{10}$ .... 9/10, ... $\overset{11}{16}$ .... 11/16, etc.

Years. A quick way of indicating years *of the present century* is to omit the '19' and write the last two figures so that they hang from the line of writing: .... 78 .... 1978; .... 82 .... 1982; .... 15 .... 1915; .... 86 .... 1986, etc. The position of the figures tells you to read '19' in front of them. All other years must be written in full: .... 1897 .... but

.... 97 .... (1997), ... 1650 .... but

.... 50 .... (1950), etc.

In different countries varying signs will be needed for **currency figures.** In addition to the dot for £, others are:

.... ℓ .... S .... $<$ .... $\frown$ ....

| | | | |
| francs | schillings | kronur | deutschemark |

..............———............ ....)........... ....(¸........... ....u........

drachmas　　　　guilders　　　　lire　　　　yen

........ȼ........ ....↶........ ....9........ ....b........

escudos　　　　rands　　　　rupees　　　　pesetas

........ʔ........ ....b........ ....⌐○........

dollars　　　　dinars　　　　roubles

Measurements. For weights: ....↶........... ounce,

................▲........... lb., ...⌐........... cwt,

................⌐........... tonne, ...)........... gram,

................ꜱ)........... kilogram. You will notice that the G for 'gram' is

a small one: ....*4.9*)........... 49 grams; ....*5.8*)...........

58 grams; and so is the 'G' for 'kilogram'; ....*4.*ꜱ)........... 4

kilograms.

For capacity: ....ʰ........... pint, ...⟩...........

gallon, ...(........... litre (LR written downwards),

..........↗........... millilitre (M and LR written upwards):

..........*5*ʰ........... 5 pints, ...*3.*⟩........... 3 gallons,

..........*3.*(........... 3½ litres, ...*26*↗○........... 26 millilitres.

For length: ....ꜰ|........... inch, ...ſ........... feet,

................ʟʟ........... yard, ...⌒........... metre (MR in the

T position), ...⌐........... centimetre, ...⌒...........

millimetre, ...<........... kilometre: ....*5*ſ *3*ꜰb...........

5 feet 3 inches; ....8........... 8 centimetres;

...........8.6........... 8 kilometres, etc.

Per cent: You already have the special form ....|........... for

per cent or percentage, and this is written after the figure:

...........5.|........ 5%; ....2.5.|........ 25%. For 'per cent

per annum' use ....‖...........: ....10.‖........... 10%

per annum; ....5.0.‖........... 50% per annum.

Word groups: ....Cu........... as-compared-with,

..........Ox........... ordinary-shares, ...ʔ.............. as-you-
know.

Another way of writing figures:

For 'quarter', use a small Q like this: ....2ᵛ........... 2¼;

...........6ᵛ........... 6¼; ....9ᵛ........... 9¾;

...........5ᵛ........... 5¾. For 'half' add an F to the figure:

...........4f........... 4½; ....5f........... 5½.

The DR blend is used for 'hundred': ....2........... 200;

...........6........... 600. Thousand: ....2b...........

2,000; ....10b........... 10,000. Hundred-thousand:

...........5b........... 500,000.

Exercise 53

Write the following in Teeline:

1. Dear-Sir, Thank-you-for-your-letter of-the 5th and for-your order for 4½ tonnes of best coal. We-shall be pleased to give you a discount of 2½% for cash. Yours-truly

2. Dear-Sir, Thank-you-for-your-letter of yesterday. We-have pleasure in informing you that-we-have today sent you the five metres of material you ordered and we trust it-will meet with your satisfaction. Thank-you for-your esteemed order, and we hope to-be of service to-you again in-the future. Yours-truly

3. You-will notice that in-the balance sheet, our capital now stands at £4,000,000 as compared with £3,500,000 last-year. During-the-year, as-you-know, we-have-had an issue of 100,000 ordinary-shares. We now have a reserve fund of £55,000 and it-is-our intention to add a further £5,600 to this.

4. You-will note that-we-have a net profit for-the year of £92,876 as-compared-with £64,253 for-the previous year and after-payment of-a dividend of 4% to holders of ordinary-shares, the remainder will-be carried forward.

5. A full year's interest on-the old 6½% debenture stock-would-have amounted to £24,000. Interest on-the new 8% debentures for-the-period covered by-the accounts amounted to £43,570. After-paying the fixed dividend of 4% per annum on the preference shares and transferring £42,800 to reserve, we propose payment of-a dividend of 5½% on the 250,000 ordinary-shares.

6. Our income from sales abroad has-been considerable this-year. From Sweden we received more than 1,500,000 kronur and from France we had 132,150,000 francs. Australia was responsible for an income of 8,700,000 dollars and Canada for another 4,500,000 dollars. Western Germany is-a new market for-us, but-it brought in 500,000 DM, which we consider to-be a good start. Even trade with Russia brought in 251,600 roubles.

Key

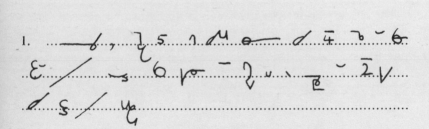

1.

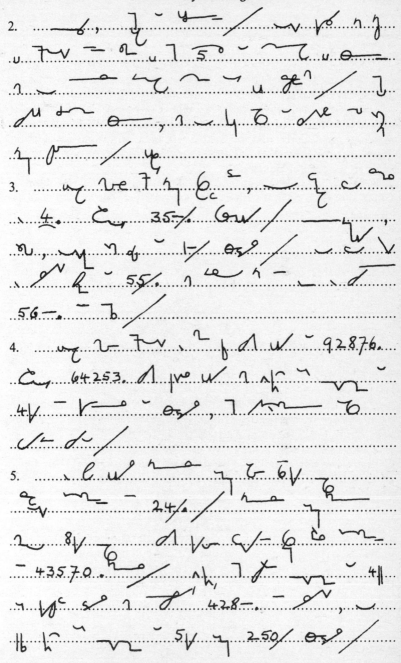

6.

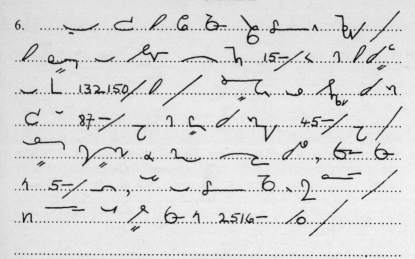

24

THE POLISHING TOUCH

With the previous chapter, you concluded your course in basic Teeline, but for the person who wishes to become more proficient in a particular field of work, there is still more that can be usefully learned. The knowledge so far acquired is sufficient, with speed practice, to make anyone a useful Teeline writer. With regular daily practice, the chances are that you have reached a state of proficiency in far less time than would have been taken with other symbol systems.

One of the secrets of success lies in the first four words of the preceding sentence: 'With regular daily practice.' You probably realized early in this course that what you have been doing is to learn to write all over again, but this time in a way which enables you to take notes much more quickly and just as efficiently. While doing so, there have probably been days when it has not been convenient to do any study, or when it has been necessary to put the book aside for several days. And what has happened when you have resumed? In all probability there have been some things that have been forgotten, or you have had to refer back to check on a special form, or on the writing of a blend. The reason for this is that the longer the interval since the last period of study, the more likely are you to forget what you have learned.

A study of shorthand is much more academic than most academics realize; it is the actual writing of the forms and symbols which makes it a skill. Like any other skill, such as playing a musical instrument or driving a car, proficiency only comes with constant repetition. A simple example can be drawn from your first steps with Teeline. At the beginning, you had to make a conscious effort to write every stroke of the alphabet. Although the letters are easy to recognize, since they are derived from the longhand equivalents, nonetheless it is a common experience with most Teeliners that they occasionally have to refer back in order to check a symbol. Within a short time, however, this is no longer the case, because the strokes have become so familiar that they can be written without thinking. But if there is a long interval between each practice period—say, three or four days—then this process will take longer, because although the symbol has been learned and recognized, the memory of it will not have been retained. With regular daily practice, however, the interval between each period is shorter and the ability to recall an outline or a principle does not require as much effort.

That is why regular daily practice is one of the secrets of success.

Indeed, fifteen minutes a day is more beneficial than one hour twice a week.

There is one other way in which greater proficiency will come more quickly, and that is by cultivating mental alertness. The person who thinks quickly will soon learn to read quickly, and with that will develop speed in writing. There is a correlation between reading shorthand and writing it, and this applies just as much to Teeline as to more traditional systems.

As Teeline is such an open-ended method, with as many distinctive ways of writing as ordinary longhand, it is sometimes considered that reading printed shorthand is not as necessary as it is with other systems. It is true that writers of Teeline can work out their own particular ways of getting down a word, yet there are times when guidance is not only sought but is downright necessary. Especially is this the case in the learning stages, when the sight of the outline for 'consult', for example, will serve as a reminder of the CN blend, which might have been forgotten after an interval of several days away from the book. Little reminders like this are both necessary and useful. In addition, the use of shorthand-into-longhand exercises serves to give valuable practice in outline recognition, even though you may prefer to write a word in a way different from that given in the text.

Further, the regular reading of shorthand serves to increase one's mental alertness and therefore cuts down the time-lag between hearing a word and recording it in a notebook. There is always a time-lag, even though it be but a fraction of a second, but when the outline for a word has to be thought out, that hiatus can become an entire second, or even longer.

There will be further reference to mental alertness in Chapter 30 but in the meantime this can be easily cultivated by spending a few minutes every day in reading a Teeline exercise two or three times and endeavouring to do so more quickly on each occasion.

Of course, there will be times when it will be necessary for you to pause and quickly think how to write an outline for a word, especially if it is a new one. There has already been some practice in this with each dictation passage. At first it was probably an effort to write each outline in the time allowed, and there were perhaps many occasions when a piece had to be attempted several times before it could be taken successfully. This is by no means unusual. Taking these passages meant that you were learning to familiarize yourself with thinking quickly and coping with unexpected words, which is what a shorthand writer is always having to do. For this reason, the outline checks were given *after* the passage had been taken. If they had been placed before the dictation passage then the element of unexpectedness would have been lost. It might have made the dictation easier, but it would not have been so beneficial.

At this point it will be well worth your while to go back to Chapter 18 and work through all the exercises again, but this time working from the keys and checking the sentences with the exercises. This will add a polishing touch to your Teeline ability. When doing so, please remember that your checking is not to see that your outlines are exactly like those given, but that you are putting the principles of Teeline to the most advantageous use.

Looking back at what you have learned of Teeline so far, the simplicity and logic of the system will become readily apparent, as will its glorious freedom in writing outlines in your own individual way without fear of them being 'wrong'.

25

TEELINE IN THE OFFICE

There will always be a need for Teeline in an office as well as elsewhere, in spite of the development of new technological devices. This statement is not made through a blind disregard of all that modern science can do, but from experience. A quarter of a century ago, there were prophecies that shorthand would be made redundant by the introduction of magnetic recording. Fascinating little machines which recorded speech on disc, on wire and later on narrow bands of tape would result, it was claimed, in 'old-fashioned' shorthand being thrown out of the window.

Nothing of the sort happened. Recording machines ceased to be playthings after a few years and took their rightful places in the realms of commerce and industry—and the shorthand writer was still needed. The same can be said of word processing, which is probably one of the biggest advances of the century. Every modern development has its uses, but there are still many examples of the individual being superior to the machine. In an office, the Teeliner has the great advantage of being able to take notes quickly and reliably, and a notebook is still very portable and cannot go wrong.

As has been mentioned in Chapter 23, words fall into patterns and the ability to record them quickly is a considerable asset. The word group 'thank you for your letter' is a good example of this, and in every office the secretary will find many word patterns which are peculiar to one particular field of commerce or industry. Those which are met with in legal work, for example, could well be quite different from those in the engineering or textile industries.

The following list of word groups is by no means exhaustive and it is emphasized that these are merely examples. No doubt some will be of immediate use, but others will need adapting to meet the needs of the writer. Some of the examples will seem rather unusual, since they include some intersections which do not appear to follow any known principle, such as 'early reply' and 'I have pleasure'. This is because they happen to be 'anticipations'—that is, they are governed by a principle which will be given later (see Chapter 29, p. 237).

So in this chapter a number of general commercial words groups are given. It is not suggested that all of them should be committed to memory; rather should they be regarded as examples of what can be done, and the office secretary should adapt and invent according to requirements. The following are for you to experiment with:

according-to   according-to-the   at-the-moment   as-requested

as-requested-in-your-letter   as-a-result   as-soon-as

as-soon-as-possible   above-mentioned

board-of-directors   balance-of-your-order   Bank-of-England

brought-forward   before-mentioned   by-return-of-post

best-attention   bank-rate   best-terms

can-you-quote   can-you-say   can-quote-you

careful-consideration   could-have-been   could-not-have-been

Chamber-of-Commerce   chairman-and-managing-director

company-limited   cash-discount   public limited company (plc)

discount-for-cash   delivery-instructions   delivered-to-you

draft-agreement

early-reply   earliest-convenience   early-consideration

estimated-expenditure   estimated-receipts

free-of-charge

in-reply   in-reply-to-your-letter   in-reply-to-our-letter

I-have-pleasure   I-now-have-pleasure   in-payment-of-account

I-am-obliged   I-am-much-obliged   in-accordance-with

in-our-experience   in-our-opinion   in-the-circumstances

increased-prices   in-the-same-manner   in-the-same-way

lowest-terms   let-us-know   let-me-know

net-cash,   net-weight

owing-to-the,   owing-to-our

please-send   please-acknowledge   please-forward

please-let-us-have   please-quote   prompt-attention

rate-of-exchange   reduced-cost   referring-to-your-letter

referring-to-the enclosed   regret-to-state   regret-to-inform-you

should-be-pleased   should-you-consider   should-we-consider

should-I-consider

telephone conversation   telex message

under-separate-cover   urgently-require   unless-we

unless-we-have

we-have-received   we-are-sending-you   we-are-glad-to-state

we-may-say   we-are-pleased-to-tell-you   we have-pleasure

Further Reading

First Teeline Workbook, by I .C. Hill; *Second Teeline Workbook*, by I. C. Hill (Heinemann Educational Books).

Specimen Examination Papers

These papers have been recounted in 10's for convenience of those who wish to use them at varying speeds from 30 w.a.m. upwards, but the speed for which each passage was originally set is given at the head of each piece, together with the name of the examining body, whose address will be found under 'Acknowledgements' on p. vii and from whom details of the examinations can be obtained. The quarter-minute markings are those of the examining body.

50 words a minute for four minutes (London Chamber of Commerce and Industry, Winter examination, 1981):

A LETTER CONCERNING THE OPENING OF AN OFFICE SERVICES BUREAU

Dear Sirs,

We have pleasure in introducing ourselves to you. / On nineteenth ($\frac{1}{4}$) July next we are opening an office services / bureau in town, in the ($\frac{1}{2}$) High Street. We propose to / cater for all your typewriting and copying ($\frac{3}{4}$) requirements.

Our agency / will enable you to bring us work, which we will / (1) then type to a first-class standard using good quality / stationery and, ($\frac{1}{4}$) where possible, we will return the completed work / to your office the same ($\frac{1}{2}$) day. We shall also install / a number of different types of copying machines ($\frac{3}{4}$) which are / now available and we shall be pleased to advise you / about copying (2) any documents.

We give a quick service and / our work is superior. ($\frac{1}{4}$) We think you will agree, from / our charges outlined on the attached sheet, ($\frac{1}{2}$) that our rates / are extremely reasonable and we feel they are ($\frac{3}{4}$) the / cheapest in town.

We are also able to provide excellent / temporary office (3) staff to help you during your problem times, / such as holidays. We ($\frac{1}{4}$) would be very glad to give / you full details, including our charges, for ($\frac{1}{2}$) this additional service. /

We would be happy to give you more detailed ($\frac{3}{4}$) information, / and, if you wish, samples of our work.

Yours faithfully. / (4)

60 w.a.m. for four minutes (London Chamber of Commerce and Industry, Winter examination, 1981):

A LETTER CONCERNING A DINNER SERVICE ORDERED FROM
AN OUT-OF-DATE CATALOGUE

Dear Mrs Jones,

We acknowledge with thanks your order dated / first January for a twenty-($\frac{1}{4}$) four piece dinner service priced / at fifteen pounds, ninety-nine.

Firstly, may we apologize for / ($\frac{1}{2}$) the apparent delay in despatching your goods. We are rather / puzzled as to why we ($\frac{3}{4}$) only received your order this / morning, and we can only assume that it was delayed / (1) in the post for some reason.

Secondly, we notice that / you have used catalogue number ($\frac{1}{4}$) two six nine two for / this particular dinner service and we are of the opinion, / ($\frac{1}{2}$) therefore, that you have consulted an out-of-date catalogue. / This opinion is confirmed by ($\frac{3}{4}$) the fact that the price / you have quoted is incorrect, as we have, unfortunately, been / (2) forced to increase the cost of this item to seventeen / pounds, ninety-nine. Nevertheless, we ($\frac{1}{4}$) hope you will agree that / even at this increased price, the dinner service is excellent / ($\frac{1}{2}$) value. In fact, we believe you would not find any / of equal quality anywhere at ($\frac{3}{4}$) the price we are charging.

We hope, however, that the dinner service arrives in plenty / (3) of time for your daughter's wedding, in spite of the / delay, and that the inconvenience ($\frac{1}{4}$) you have suffered on this / occasion will not stop you ordering from our company again / ($\frac{1}{2}$) in the future as we would like our long association / to continue. We assure you ($\frac{3}{4}$) that any orders you send / us will receive our careful and prompt attention.

Yours truly, / (4)

90 w.a.m. for four minutes (London Chamber of Commerce and Industry, Winter examination, 1981):

A SECRETARY'S DUTIES IN CONNECTION WITH MEETINGS

A capable secretary may sometimes be asked to make all / the arrangements for meetings in the company for which she / works. Quite ($\frac{1}{4}$) often these will be meetings of the Board / of Directors. Firstly, it will be necessary to send out / a notice to every member ($\frac{1}{2}$) of the Board, notifying the / date, time and venue of the meeting. The agenda is / frequently added onto this notice, or can ($\frac{3}{4}$) be on another / page, and the minutes of the previous meeting are often / included.

The agenda is just a list of all the / (1) items which are to be considered at the meeting, and / the secretary will prepare this with the assistance of the / Chairman or ($\frac{1}{4}$) the Company Secretary.

On the day of the / meeting, the secretary will make sure that the board room / has been prepared, that any ($\frac{1}{2}$) necessary stationery is there, and / spare copies of the agenda and minutes are provided. She / will have to take detailed notes of ($\frac{3}{4}$) all that is / discussed at the meeting, and must be careful to ensure / that the words of the speakers are correctly recorded. Afterwards, / (2) she will compose, from her notes, draft minutes for approval / before they are ready for duplication and forwarding to members / of the ($\frac{1}{4}$) Board.

The secretary may have to deal with / all the correspondence in connection with the meeting, and see / that the required action is ($\frac{1}{2}$) taken.

The Chairman is responsible / for controlling the progress of the meeting and the speakers / must address all their remarks through him. ($\frac{3}{4}$)

There are many / rules and regulations for the conduct of such meetings, and / secretaries must be aware of these. For instance, the notice / (3) of a meeting should usually be issued a certain number / of days before the meeting is due to take place. / Also, most ($\frac{1}{4}$) of the items in an agenda will be / in a special order.

Until the secretary is able to / do the work required for ($\frac{1}{2}$) the easy running of such / meetings, it may perhaps be sensible to assemble a list / of items so that nothing essential is ($\frac{3}{4}$) overlooked. This kind / of work is, of course, highly confidential and the secretary / will often find that it is most interesting. (4)

100 w.a.m. for $3\frac{3}{4}$ minutes (Royal Society of Arts, Winter examination, 1981):

APPLYING FOR YOUR FIRST JOB

Soon you will be leaving school or college and applying / for your first job. You will probably consult your local / careers officer, who will advise ($\frac{1}{4}$) you on the vacancies in / your area. You should also look through the advertisements in / the press. Many colleges and schools advertise one or two / ($\frac{1}{2}$) positions on the official notice board. If you are required / to apply by letter you should decide whether you are / going to type or write ($\frac{3}{4}$) your letter. Some employers will / request all applicants to apply in their own handwriting. You / must therefore comply with this, and your writing must be / (1) legible. If your letter of application is typed, it should / be well displayed, and, of course, accurate. Always remember that / your letter gives the first ($\frac{1}{4}$) impression, and it should be / clear and concise and without any errors. Employers first sort / through the letters, discarding any which are poor. Those candidates / ($\frac{1}{2}$) are rejected. Most firms send out application forms and these / should be completed carefully, as you will only receive one / copy. It is probably a ($\frac{3}{4}$) good idea to complete this / very lightly in pencil before either typing or writing it. / Should the employer think that you may be suitable, the / (2) next step will be your interview.

You should wear appropriate / clothing. Some employers, for example the clearing banks, do not / allow women to wear jeans ($\frac{1}{4}$) or other trousers. Hair should / be well-groomed and excessive make-up should be avoided. / You should present yourself for interview in plenty of time, / ($\frac{1}{2}$) bringing with you any certificates and school reports you think / may be needed. It would be a good idea when / you are interviewed for a ($\frac{3}{4}$) secretarial post to take a / dictionary, pen and eraser, in case a test piece is / dictated to you. It is worth thinking about likely questions / (3) and preparing your answers to these before attending the interview. /

At any interview you should speak plainly, and give clear / answers to questions. If your ($\frac{1}{4}$) promotion prospects are not mentioned / at the interview, you should be prepared to ask about / these and any other matters. It is your future and / ($\frac{1}{4}$) you should be concerned about it. Some teachers arrange trial / interviews in class during the last term by splitting the / group into pairs for practice. ($\frac{3}{4}$)

26

THE MEDICAL SECRETARY

Few people occupy as responsible a position as the medical secretary and few shorthand systems can be as suitable as Teeline for the work. The responsibilities of a medical secretary may vary from that of an executive in charge of one or more medical shorthand typists, to the person who does secretarial work for a local doctor and sometimes acts as receptionist.

For the position of medical secretary training is generally full-time and is spread over a four-term (sometimes six-term) course and at the end, if qualified, the candidate earns the recognition of the Association of Medical Secretaries. The examination requirements are exacting and are as follows. For the certificate, a pass in Papers I to IV and, in addition, an endorsement in either the RSA Stage II Medical Shorthand-typist's Certificate or Medical Audio-typist's Certificate. For the Diploma, a pass in papers I to IV with an endorsement both in the RSA Stage II Medical Shorthand-typist's Certificate and 100 w.a.m. Medical Stenography.

The realm of medicine has broadened enormously in its scope and there is no sign yet of its ceasing to do so. The field is now so great that the nomenclature used by one group of experts is often only vaguely understood by others who, in turn, may well be familiar with other medical terms which are 'foreign' to someone else. Today the advances in medical science are such that no medico, let alone the secretary, can ever know all the terms.

New sections of medicine are opening up all the time, and with each comes a new vocabulary. Long words are sometimes referred to only by initials, of which ACTH (adrenocorticotropic hormone) is perhaps the best known outside medical circles but there are others, such as MCV (mean corpuscular volume) and THA (tetrahydroaminacrine), and the medical secretary must be familiar with them even if reference books have to be consulted for the definitions.

To the newcomer medical terms may seem long and tongue-twisting but after a little while it becomes obvious that this is not necessarily true. A few minutes' study will show that the majority of the compound words in medicine are made up of prefixes or suffixes which are combined in order to make these 'long' words, the meaning of which then becomes apparent. To know that 'derma' or 'dermat' means 'skin' immediately gives a meaning to specialist words beginning with those syllables, and to learn that '-itis' means 'inflammation of' helps in the recognition of other words, some of which are known to the layman, such as tonsillitis, appendicitis, and dermatitis.

To give a long list of outlines for words to be committed to memory would be useless but a list of these prefixes and suffixes is invaluable, so it is given here. The Teeline writer wishing to become a medical secretary or a medical shorthand typist starts with the advantage of having a system in which ordinary spelling is followed and it is therefore possible to record these syllables with great accuracy, as it is essential to show the differences between some of them. 'Micro' and 'macro', for instance, are opposites, and 'sapro' and 'supra' mean two different things. Distinctive ways of writing them are therefore required and these are given in the following list. It is not exhaustive by any means, but it gives the principal prefixes and suffixes.

Prefixes

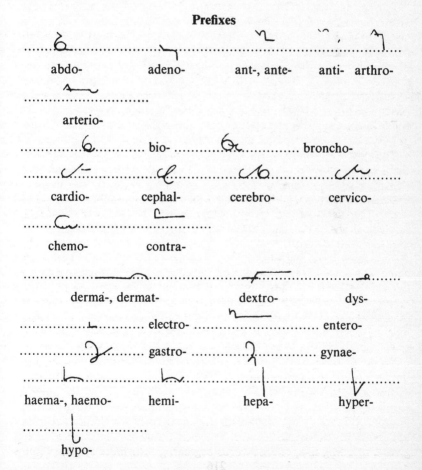

abdo-   adeno-   ant-, ante-   anti- arthro-

arterio-

bio-   broncho-

cardio-   cephal-   cerebro-   cervico-

chemo-   contra-

dermá-, dermat-   dextro-   dys-

electro-   entero-

gastro-   gynae-

haema-, haemo-   hemi-   hepa-   hyper-

hypo-

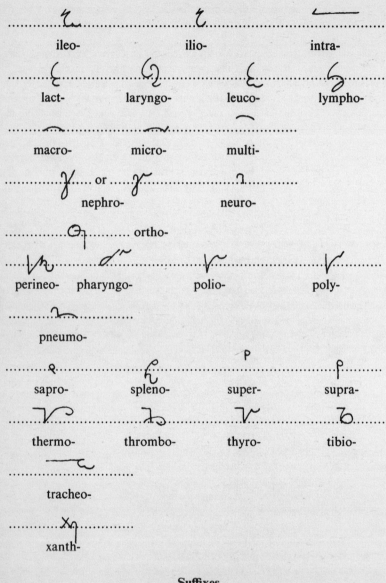

ileo-   ilio-   intra-

lact-   laryngo-   leuco-   lympho-

macro-   micro-   multi-

or   nephro-   neuro-

ortho-

perineo-   pharyngo-   polio-   poly-

pneumo-

sapro-   spleno-   super-   supra-

thermo-   thrombo-   thyro-   tibio-

tracheo-

xanth-

Suffixes

(For the use of the disjoined S, see p. 245.)

-aemia   -aesthesia

-clysis   -coccus

.... -desis

.... -ectasis .... -ectomy

.... -genesis

.... -iasis   -iatric   -itis

.... -kinesis

.... -lith   -lysis   -lytic

.... -malacia

.... -ology   -ologist   -ological   -osis

.... -ostomy   -otomy

.... -pathy   -penia   -pexy   -pelvic

.... -phage   -phobia

.... -rhaphy .... -rhythmia

.... -stasis .... -stomy

.... -taxia   -tomy   -tosis

.... -uria

Many other medical terms are easily represented in Teeline, such as 'cysto' and 'graph', etc., without any special forms being given to them and it may be that writers will devise their own prefixes and suffixes. Those given above are for guidance and for building upon, but here are some examples of their use:

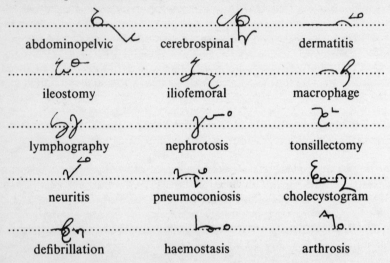

abdominopelvic	cerebrospinal	dermatitis
ileostomy	iliofemoral	macrophage
lymphography	nephrotosis	tonsillectomy
neuritis	pneumoconiosis	cholecystogram
defibrillation	haemostasis	arthrosis

With such a specialized subject it is not possible to do more than explore the fringes in a general textbook, and the person who wishes to train as a medical secretary is advised to enrol for one of the many courses that are held in schools and colleges.

Specimen Examination Papers

128 syllables a minute dictated in three minutes (80 w.a.m.), Royal Society of Arts Spring examination, 1980, passage 3 (counted in 10's):

AN ORTHOPAEDIC REPORT

About four months ago, during the football season, this patient / began to get swelling and pain in the right knee / joint and this was followed by some pain in the / left knee joint around the area of the patella. This / has gradually become much worse when he bends his knee / and now both knees tend to swell, the left more / than the right. When he wakes in the morning his knees are stiff for about half an hour. He has / no other joint swellings. He has had no skin troubles / and his eyes are normal. There seems to be no / family history. On examination he looked a fit boy. In / the locomotor system there was a full range of painless / movement of the lumbar spine and there was no pain / in the sacroiliac joints. Hips were normal. Both knees had / cold boggy effusions and were stable. There was a full / range of movement in both. There was no other joint / abnormality. I aspirated twenty cubic centimetres of clear fluid from / the left knee joint but did not inject anything. I / thought it best to try to exclude any inflammatory arthropathy. / There were no crystals in the synovial fluid. As you / know, diseases such as ankylosing spondylitis and gut disorders such / as Crohn's disease and ulcerative colitis can be present with / these sorts of knee effusions and I shall be following / him regularly to await any changes that may indicate this. / Meanwhile, he is on soluble aspirin tablets, two three times / a day, and I shall see him again shortly.

400 syllables dictated in 2½ minutes (100 w.a.m.), Royal Society of Arts Summer examination, 1980, passage 2 (counted in 10's):

LETTER FROM A CONSULTANT PHYSICIAN TO A G.P.

Dear Dr Fletcher,

Mrs Margaret Johnson—date of birth twenty- / three—four—twenty-nine.

Thank you for your letter concerning / this patient who, for eight years, has been experiencing attacks / of palpitation in which her heart beats rapidly and also, / she thinks, irregularly for several days. Subsequently, she may enjoy / up to two months without trouble. She has been somewhat / short of breath for approximately twenty years but she attributes / this to her nerves and says that when she is / breathless she cannot inhale deeply. You have treated her with / Digoxin and Propanolol but she felt sick and stopped taking / the tablets. There is also a history of hypertension and / she was given Navidrex but she only took this for / seven days, too. On examination she was flushed, pulse ninety / per minute, blood pressure one hundred and ninety over one / hundred. She had a pulmonary systolic murmur and an accentuated / pulmonary second sound. X-ray of her chest showed a well / marked cardiac enlargement. She had a normal blood count, / Sedimentation Rate thirty millimetres in one hour. The electrocardiogram showed / a prominent P-wave in lead two. This lady is / very resistant to tablets but I have asked that she / tries taking Digoxin nought point two five milligrammes daily. It / is hard to be sure just what happens during her / attacks of palpitation without an electrocardiogram at the time. However, / she does appear to have pulmonary as well as systemic / hypertension. Yours sincerely, Consultant Physician.

384 syllables dictated in two minutes (120 w.a.m.), Royal Society of Arts Summer examination, 1980, passage 1 (counted in 10's):

CASE NOTES OF A CHILD WITH APPENDICITIS

The seven-year-old child was admitted to the hospital / at 11.30 a.m. in severe pain, which he / indicated as being in the central region of his abdomen. / He was vomiting. Under examination his temperature was found to / be one hundred and one degrees and there was extreme / tenderness in the right iliac fossa. There were clear signs / that the child had appendicitis. The intensity of the pain, / together with foetid breath and furred tongue, showed that peritonitis / could be developing. It was decided that the child should / be operated on without delay. Post-operative care included the / use of a nasogastric tube passed through the nose into / the stomach in order to aspirate the contents hour by / hour. The fluid intake was maintained intravenously and specimens of / urine were obtained each day as long as the intravenous / therapy continued. Twice in each of the twenty-four hour / periods penicillin was administered. Recovery proceeded normally for five days. / On the sixth day, however, the child began to show / signs of pain and it was clear that there was / inflammation caused by another infection. A large abscess was found / to have developed. Every attempt was made to drain the / abscess but a further operation had to be performed. This / was completely successful and the child began to recover after / forty-eight hours of intensive care. The child was soon / able to go for several weeks of convalescence.

Further Reading

The student beginning a medical secretary's course will find it useful to have: *Livingstone's Pocket Medical Dictionary*, edited by Nancy Roper (Churchill Livingstone), *The Penguin Medical Encyclopedia*, by Peter Wingate (Penguin Books), Baillière's *Atlas of Female Anatomy* (Baillière, Tindall and Cassell), *Second Teeline Workbook*, by I. C. Hill (Heinemann Educational Books). Others may be recommended by course lectures.

27

THE BILINGUAL SECRETARY

With the extension of trade and commerce throughout the world and particularly in Europe and the Far East, there is an increasing demand for secretaries who can not only speak a second language but can write Teeline in it. Because Teeline follows normal spelling, it is easily adapted to other languages and the change can be made almost automatically, depending on the writer's proficiency.

There are adaptations of Teeline into French, German and Spanish, and an Italian one is in course of preparation. The structure of the system is such that there are no basic changes and in some colleges it is usual, when a class has reached 60 w.a.m. in Teeline, to introduce the second language at 50 w.a.m. and take it from there. No long textbooks are required and the Teeline adaptations consist mainly of exercises in the other languages. As an example of the ease with which the switch can be made, the author was writing and transcribing Teeline in French before ever seeing the book containing the adaptation.

In the sphere of bilingual shorthand, Teeline has been notably successful and in examinations of both the London Chamber of Commerce and Industry and the Royal Society of Arts there have been many prize winners at speeds up to 140 w.a.m. in a second language.

Specimen Examination Papers

French

60 w.a.m. for four minutes: London Chamber of Commerce and Industry, Spring examination, 1980 (counted in 10's):

LIVRAISON ENDOMMAGÉE

Monsieur,

Votre envoi de verres de cristal annoncé par lettre / du 3 courant m'est ($\frac{1}{4}$) parvenu ce matin. Je me vois / obligé, à mon grand regret, de vous faire part ($\frac{1}{2}$) de / la casse de plusieurs pièces.

A première vue la caisse / paraissait intacte ($\frac{3}{4}$) et étant donné qu'à la manutention aucun bruit / ne permettait de déceder (1) quoi que ce soit, la livraison / fut acceptée et une décharge donnée à la ($\frac{1}{4}$) Compagnie des / Chemins de Fer. C'est en procédant au déballage que les / dégâts ($\frac{1}{2}$) furent révélés.

En l'absence de trace de manutention négligente, je suis ($\frac{3}{4}$) porté à croire que la casse résulte d'un / emballage défectueux. J'étais (2) en effet étonné de constater que la / couche supérieure touchait presque ($\frac{1}{4}$) le couvercle et que, à mon / avis, il n'y avait pas assez de frisons pour amortir / ($\frac{1}{2}$) le moindre choc.

Je regrette beaucoup d'avoir à vous signaler / cet incident, le ($\frac{3}{4}$) premier de son espèce depuis que je / traite avec vous, et je garde l'envoi à (3) votre disposition / pour vous permettre de vérifier mes dires.

J'aimerais ($\frac{1}{4}$) naturellement qu'il / soit possible d'arriver à une rapide solution et que ($\frac{1}{2}$) vous / me fassiez parvenir, sans plus de délai et à votre / charge, un second envoi de ($\frac{3}{4}$) remplacement.

Agréez, Monsieur, mes salutations / les plus empressées. (4)

80 w.a.m. for four minutes: London Chamber of Commerce and Industry, Spring examination, 1980 (counted in 10's):

SICOB—SALON INTERNATIONAL DE L'INFORMATIQUE, DE LA COMMUNICATION ET DE L'ORGANISATION DU BUREAU

Monsieur le Directeur,

Après un premier entretien au Salon International / de l'Informatique, de la ($\frac{1}{4}$) Communication et de l'Organisation du Bureau, / une étude minutieuse avec l'un de ($\frac{1}{2}$) vos représentants, nous a conduit à l'achat de l'un de vos matériels: le duplicateur / K 480. ($\frac{3}{4}$) Cet appareil nous a été livré / par vos soins le 2 juin; il porte le numéro / de série 17528. (1) Le / contrat de vente nous assurait l'assistance d'un technicien et d'un / formateur chargés de ($\frac{1}{4}$) l'après-vente.

Le 3 juin le technicien / a procédé à la mise en place, au réglage et / aux essais de ($\frac{1}{2}$) l'appareil. Nous avons attendu huit jours la / venue du formateur devant mettre au courant le personnel de / ($\frac{3}{4}$) notre entreprise responsable de son fonctionnement. Il n'a été présent / que deux heures, ce qui nous a paru (2) insuffisant.

Ce / duplicateur ne nous donne pas, pour l'instant, satisfaction: il est / peu utilisé. C'est une ($\frac{1}{4}$) gêne au fonctionnement des Services Administratifs / de notre entreprise. Nous ne mettons en cause ni ($\frac{1}{2}$) les / qualités de votre appareil, ni notre personnel chargé de son / usage.

En exécution des ($\frac{3}{4}$) conditions du contrat de vente, nous / vous prions de remédier dans les plus brefs délais à / cette situation.

Nous (3) suggérons un stage immédiat de formation, à / vos frais, et d'une durée de huit jours, soit une / journée entière ($\frac{1}{4}$) pour chacune des huit personnes appelées à manipuler / ce duplicateur.

Nous avons tout lieu de croire que ($\frac{1}{2}$) vous / comprendrez notre grief. Il est aussi fort probable que nous / soyons appelés à vous acheter ($\frac{3}{4}$) d'autres machines. Nous voudrions donc / garder nos relations d'affaires amicales et espérons vous lire bientôt. / (4)

German

50 w.a.m. for four minutes: London Chamber of Commerce and Industry, Spring examination, 1980 (for language reasons, this passage has not been recounted):

Es ist selbstverständlich, dass Sie gut verdienen wollen, und das sollen Sie ($\frac{1}{4}$) auch. Es ist heute sicher nicht leicht, bei den hohen Kosten, den vielen Steuern ($\frac{1}{2}$) und den besonderen Wünschen Ihrer Kunden einen angemessenen ($\frac{3}{4}$) Verdienst zu erzielen. Die Wünsche Ihrer Kunden können Sie dabei (1) noch am einfachsten erfüllen. Wenn Sie wirklich gute Arbeit liefern, ($\frac{1}{4}$) dann sind auch Ihre Kunden zufrieden. Man wird Sie dann auch im Bekanntenkreis ($\frac{1}{2}$) weiterempfehlen. Dies gibt wieder neue Aufträge, und damit steigt ($\frac{3}{4}$) auch Ihr Umsatz.

Ich sehe meine wesentliche Aufgabe darin, (2) Ihnen hochwertiges Material für Ihre Arbeit zu liefern. Ich ($\frac{1}{4}$) liefere selbstverständlich alle Artikel, die Sie in Ihrem Betrieb ($\frac{1}{2}$) benötigen. Sonderwünsche werden ebenfalls erfüllt. Damit Sie auch ($\frac{3}{4}$) wirklich etwas verdienen können, habe ich meine Preise sehr genau (3) errechnet. Am besten unterhalten wir uns persönlich über Ihre ($\frac{1}{4}$) Wünsche. Ich werde Sie in Zukunft regelmässig besuchen, um alle ($\frac{1}{2}$) geschäftlichen Fragen mit Ihnen zu besprechen. Als Fachmann verfüge ($\frac{3}{4}$) ich über langjährige Erfahrungen auf unserem Gebiet. (4)

60 w.a.m. for four minutes: London Chamber of Commerce and Industry, Spring examination, 1980 (for language reasons, this passage has not been recounted):

Einige meiner besten Kunden haben die Zahlungen eingestellt. Dadurch habe ich ($\frac{1}{4}$) in letzter Zeit grosse Verluste erlitten. In zwei Fällen verlor ich kurz nacheinander ($\frac{1}{2}$) sechzig Prozent meines Guthabens und hatte einen Schaden von 6 000 ($\frac{3}{4}$) D-Mark. Diese Verluste hätte ich aber noch tragen können, wenn mein Umsatz eini(1)germassen befriedigend gewesen wäre. Wegen der scharfen Konkurrenz auf dem ($\frac{1}{4}$) Auslandsmarkt konnte ich nur noch Geschäfte zu Preisen abschliessen, die kaum einen Gewinn ($\frac{1}{2}$) brachten. Dadurch wurden auch meine Rückstellungen aufgebraucht, die ich für Notzeiten ($\frac{3}{4}$) gemacht hatte.

Durch diese Entwicklung ist es mir leider nicht mehr möglich, meine Gläubiger (2) zu befriedigen. Diesem Schreiben füge ich meine letzte Bilanz bei. Sie gibt ($\frac{1}{4}$) Ihnen eine Uebersicht über meinen Vermögensstand. Meine Geschäftsbücher können ($\frac{1}{2}$) Sie jederzeit einsehen. Die Bilanz zeigt, dass ich meinen Gläubigern einen Vergleich von ($\frac{3}{4}$) höchstens fünfzig Prozent anbieten kann. Ich bitte Sie daher, mit meinem Vorschlag (3) einverstanden zu sein. Sollten Sie mein Angebot ablehnen, muss ich einen Antrag auf ($\frac{1}{4}$) Eröffnung des Konkursverfahrens stellen. Dann würden allerdings den Gläubigern noch ($\frac{1}{2}$) grössere Verluste entstehen. Ich hoffe jedoch, dass ich mich mit allen Lieferern ($\frac{3}{4}$) einigen kann.

Indem ich Ihrer Antwort gern entgegensehe, verbleibe ich freundlichst. (4)

Spanish
50 w.a.m. for four minutes: London Chamber of Commerce and Industry, Spring examination, 1980 (not recounted):

Muy señores nuestros:
Acusamos recibo de su carta del ($\frac{1}{4}$) nueve del corriente en la que nos comunican que están ustedes ($\frac{1}{2}$) interesados en la adquisición de doce máquinas de ($\frac{3}{4}$) escribir.

Adjuntamos varios folletos de los distintos modelos (1) que tenemos en almacén, así como una lista con los ($\frac{1}{4}$) precios al día.

Aunque nos piden un número elevado de ($\frac{1}{2}$) máquinas, podremos entregarlas tan pronto como recibamos ($\frac{3}{4}$) su pedido oficial.

Dado que son ustedes clientes regulares (2) y después de considerar la importancia de los pedidos ($\frac{1}{4}$) que recibimos, estamos dispuestos a concederles un ($\frac{1}{2}$) descuento del diez por ciento.

Aprovechamos esta ocasión ($\frac{3}{4}$) para incluir folletos de los nuevos modelos de muebles de (3) oficina que vamos a recibir a finales del mes en ($\frac{1}{4}$) curso.

Verán que las mesas y sillas son de madera de roble ($\frac{1}{2}$) y de construcción muy sólida.

Quedamos pendientes de sus noticias ($\frac{3}{4}$) sobre el particular y les saludamos muy atentamente. (4)

70 w.a.m. for four minutes: London Chamber of Commerce and Industry, Spring examination, 1980 (not recounted):

Muy señores nuestros:
La Sección Comercial de la Embajada Española en Londres nos ($\frac{1}{4}$) ha dado su nombre, mencionando que son ustedes los exportadores de máquinas de ($\frac{1}{2}$) coser más importantes de España.

Desde hace algún tiempo, hemos encontrado ($\frac{3}{4}$) dificultades en obtener todas las máquinas que necesitamos para el mercado (1) inglés. Importamos máquinas japonesas desde hace varios años y en vista de la ($\frac{1}{4}$) gran demanda que tenemos para este artículo, hemos decidido introducir ($\frac{1}{2}$) máquinas españolas en nuestras importaciones. Les rogamos nos envien folletos ($\frac{3}{4}$) y cotización de sus máquinas de coser así como condiciones de entrega de (2) puerto a puerto incluyendo flete y seguro.

Si su oferta fuera favorable ($\frac{1}{4}$) nos interesaría obtener la agencia en exclusiva para todo el Reino Unido. ($\frac{1}{2}$) Con objeto de discutir las condiciones de este contrato de representación, ($\frac{3}{4}$) estaríamos dispuestos a enviar a nuestro Director Financiero a esa ciudad (3) durante el próximo mes de abril. Este señor desearía en el curso de su ($\frac{1}{4}$) viaje visitar los talleres donde se producen las máquinas y conocer a los ($\frac{1}{2}$) ingenieros que los dirigen.

Confiando poder llegar a un acuerdo con ustedes, ($\frac{3}{4}$) quedamos a la espera de sus gratas noticias saludándoles muy atentamente. (4)

Further Reading

French Teeline by Ann Harvey and Germaine Kemble (Teeline Education Ltd, Haywood, Queen Street, Helensburgh, Dunbartonshire, G84 9QQ); *German Teeline* by Frances J. Burton and Germa Meder (Teeline Education Ltd); *Spanish Teeline* by Joan McClung and Robert Orr (Mr R. Orr, Department of Modern Languages, College of Business Studies, Brunswick Street, Belfast BT2 7GX). Tapes for the French and German courses are available from Teeline Education Ltd, and for the Spanish course from Mr Orr.

28

TEELINE FOR REPORTERS

In the world of journalism, shorthand is a basic necessity. One of the things a trainee journalist has to do before qualifying to sit the Proficiency Test of the National Council for the Training of Journalists (NCTJ) is to pass a test of shorthand writing at a speed of 100 words a minute or more. There are some reporters—mostly specialists—who get by with an abbreviated, scribbled longhand, but they are few in comparison with the thousands working on newspapers and magazines. In a survey carried out on behalf of the Printing and Publishing Industry Training Board, it was established that 'there has been a significant trend towards the study of Teeline' and that of those who had recently entered journalism no fewer than 43 per cent wrote Teeline, which is also one of the systems approved by the NCTJ. The same survey said that in the regional Press (by far the largest proportion of journalists) 47 per cent of those questioned said shorthand was essential and a further 34 per cent said it was desirable.

The first person to use shorthand in newspaper work is believed to have been Thomas Lechford, publisher of a London newspaper called *Plain Dealing, or Newes from New England's Present Government*, which had a short life in 1642. He used a system invented by John Willis in 1602. Through the centuries more and more newspapers came to rely on reporting by those who knew shorthand. At first, they were people who took down sermons and published them in pamphlet form. The first of these appears to have been as early as 1589, a year after the publication of the first British system, Timothy Bright's 'Characterie'. The sermon was registered at Stationers' Hall as: 'An Ordinary Lectvre, Preached at the Blacke-Friers, by M. Egerton. And taken as it was vttered by Characterie.' The shorthand was written by a gentleman known today only by his initials: A.S. In a preface, he said he had learned Bright's system and 'I hauing learned, haue put in practice, in writing sermons thereby to preserue (as it were) the life of much memorable doctrine. . . .'

From reporting sermons to recording plays was but a short step, and it is suggested that some of the 'bad' quartos of Shakespeare's plays were the result of this habit, which was widespread in the first half of the seventeenth century. This would account for some passages in Shakespeare appearing as prose in some editions and blank verse in others, for the shorthand writer would not be able to distinguish the two.

It was but another step to the recording of speeches on important occasions and it is thought that shorthand was used in the courts and Parliament about the same time. The Old Bailey trial of a republican agitator, John Lilburn, on 24, 25 and 26 October, 1649, was taken by an unknown writer and published with a comment on the title pages saying that it was 'exactly as pen'd and taken in shorthand as it was possible to be done in such Croud and Noise, and transcribed with Indifferent and Even-hand both in reference to the Court and the Prisoner'.

An early use of shorthand in Parliament (but not the first) was by John Rushworth, an assistant to the Clerk to the House. He reported the speech of Charles I when that monarch went to the House of Commons to demand that five Members accused of high treason should be delivered up to him. Rushworth then found himself working against the clock, as the modern journalist frequently does, for it is recorded that the speech was 'taken down as uttered and the same evening Rushworth . . . took it to the King, who corrected it, and it was published the following morning'.

Before long, shorthand was in regular use among those working on newspapers, where the reporter was often the editor and printer as well. Even at the beginning of the present century, when some provincial newspapers were still being set by hand, the reporter would return from a meeting, don a printer's apron and set up the type from his notes.

In the last few decades it has become usual to report speeches with greater brevity but the need for shorthand has never diminished, for it is only with its aid that accurate reporting is possible. There are, however, indications today that the pendulum is swinging the other way and there is a tendency among some provincial newspapers to give longer reports to compete with local radio. In this way, newspapers are able to go into greater detail than is possible in a brief spoken news bulletin. This means that fast, accurate shorthand writing is just as necessary as ever it was and today more than half the trainee journalists in Great Britain are learning Teeline as their system. In addition it is used widely by reporters in other parts of the world, particularly in New Zealand, Australia, Singapore and Zimbabwe. All British trainee journalists joining Reuter, the international news agency, are taught Teeline and so are any non-shorthand journalists who join the BBC.

A reporter, unlike an office worker, is likely to be sent anywhere: one day to a police court, another to a council meeting or a noisy demonstration, or on a third to interview an important person. This means that the journalist must be able to cope with a variety of subjects and therefore needs a greater number of word groups and advanced writing methods than the majority of Teeliners. To this end, the trainee journalist will find Chapter 29 of special interest, but below are appended a number of outlines which apply particularly to newspaper work. They should be practised thoroughly, as they are all in frequent use.

Public Administration

county council   district council   town council   parish council

metropolitan borough   town clerk

town clerk's department   public health department

borough surveyor   county surveyor   education officer

medical officer   parks superintendent   local authority

town planning committee   the committee   this committee

housing scheme   product of a penny rate

rateable value   rating and valuation   I propose

I second   I move   I move the reference back

development plan   city.

In word groups, 'committee' can be shown by ....,

as in examples given above, and in .... that com-

mittee, ... any committee, ...

housing committee, etc.

Magistrates' and Coroners' Courts

police station   police constable   detective constable

police sergeant   taken into consideration

house-breaking   breaking and entering

evidence of the defence   evidence of the defendant

witness   defend   defendant   prosecute

prosecution   guilty   not guilty

cross-examination   charged with   evidence in chief

from the evidence   made a statement   make a statement

without due care and attention   taking and driving away

drinking and driving   drunk driving

according to the witness   witness for the prosecution

witness for the defence

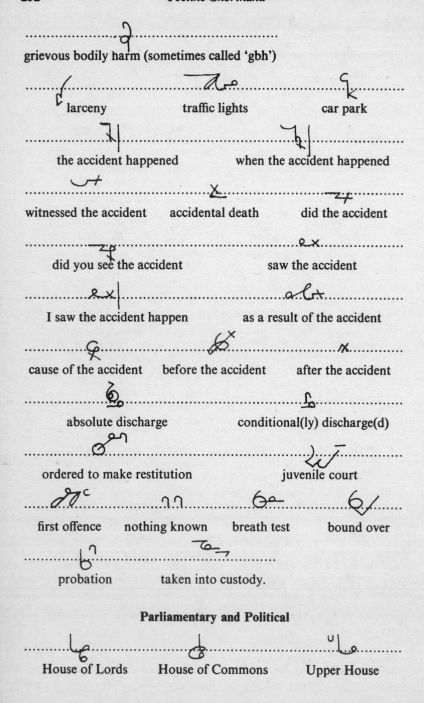

grievous bodily harm (sometimes called 'gbh')

larceny   traffic lights   car park

the accident happened   when the accident happened

witnessed the accident   accidental death   did the accident

did you see the accident   saw the accident

I saw the accident happen   as a result of the accident

cause of the accident   before the accident   after the accident

absolute discharge   conditional(ly) discharge(d)

ordered to make restitution   juvenile court

first offence   nothing known   breath test   bound over

probation   taken into custody.

Parliamentary and Political

House of Lords   House of Commons   Upper House

Lower House　　　Parliament　　　Houses of Parliament

Member of Parliament　　　M.P.　　　Prime Minister

Chancellor of the Exchequer　　　Secretary of State

Home Office　　　Foreign Office　　　Home Secretary

Foreign Secretary　　　Leader of the Opposition

Labour Party　　　Conservative Party　　　Liberal Party

Social Democratic Party　　　Ulster Unionist

members of the Cabinet　　　cost of living

unemployment　　　unemployment figures　　　junior minister

honourable Member　　　constituency　　　constituent

Minister of Housing　　　Housing Minister

Lord President of the Council　　　Minister of Agriculture

....
Secretary of State for Trade

....
Secretary of State for Social Services

....
Minister of Transport　　　　Ministry of Agriculture

....
his Ministry　　　Foreign Ministry　　　Department of Industry

....
Department of the Environment

....
Department of Education and Science

....
Department of Employment　　　　　Scottish Office

....
Department of Energy　　　　　　　Treasury

....
Under Secretary of State　　　　government whips

Specimen Examination Papers

When trainee journalists take their qualifying speed in shorthand, only
the official test of the NCTJ is recognized by the Training Council.
These tests are for four minutes. The minimum speed is 100 w.a.m., but
higher speeds can be taken if desired. The following papers are reprinted
with the permission of the NCTJ. In each case the original speed is
indicated, but the passages have been recounted in 10's so that they may
be taken at a lower or higher speed for practice.

100 w.a.m. for four minutes.
PROSECUTION'S CASE IN CARELESS DRIVING OFFENCE

Your Worships, at half past three on the afternoon of / January the twelfth the defendant was driving a car along / the High Street. She had pulled up correctly at the / traffic lights and when they changed to green she proceeded / on her way. Then, for some reason to which she / refers later on in a statement made to the police, / she suddenly pulled up and then started to reverse her / car. Traffic was moderately heavy at this time and this / sudden braking put a driver who was following in a / Ford Escort car in some difficulty. He braked violently and / pulled up with the front bumper of his car practically / touching the rear bumper of the defendant's car. However, a / man who had been following the Ford Escort in line / was also placed in a position of some difficulty and / he, too, had to pull up sharply. He was not / so fortunate in avoiding the car in front of him / as the driver of the Ford Escort had been. He / drove straight into the back of the Ford, which, in / turn, was shunted into the defendant's car. Fortunately, there were / no personal injuries but there was a considerable amount of / damage to all the three cars involved. Police were called / and Police Constable Smith arrived at the scene of the / accident just a few minutes after it had occurred. He / spoke to the defendant and asked her if she could / explain what had happened. After he had taken the necessary / particulars from the other two drivers, the defendant went by / appointment to the police station and there she made a / statement which, after the customary caution had been given, was / taken down in writing. It was read over to her / and she signed it. I now produce the statement. It / states: I was proceeding along the High Street at a / comparatively low speed, having just started away from the traffic / lights. As I was doing so I spotted a man / leaning against a shop doorway. This man was known to / me through my voluntary work as a social helper. He / had recently been discharged from hospital where he had been / having psychiatric treatment. I could see that there was something / wrong with him and knowing that he was in need / of attention I just put my brakes on and then / started to reverse. I realize now that this was inexcusable. /

100 w.a.m. for four minutes.
INQUEST ON A PEDESTRIAN

This is an inquest on a man who walked along / a dark country road with his back to the traffic / and he died because he did not obey the rules / laid down for everybody's protection. He was Mr James Smith, / a thirty-year-old married man, and he was walking / along the road with his wife when he was hit / by a motor cycle. He was injured and died in / hospital two days later. We have heard evidence from the / widow that they were walking along the road because their / car had broken down and they were trying to get / help from a nearby garage. She said they were walking / towards the garage, alongside each other, with their backs to / the traffic. Her husband was next to the road. The / night was very wet and windy and Mrs Smith said / she did not hear the motor cycle until it had / gone past and, at the same time, realized that her / husband was no longer walking with her. There has also / been evidence from a passing motorist who said that he / saw a single headlamp coming towards him. According to his / evidence, the light suddenly disappeared and the motor cycle went / over the bank. He stopped his car, got out and / then saw a man lying by the side of the / road. It was obvious that the man was badly injured / and the driver covered him with a rug and hurried / off to call an ambulance. Mr John Brown, the motor / cyclist, said he realized he had hit someone and went / back to the scene of the accident. Just before the / accident he had been driving along at about fifty miles / an hour when he was dazzled by the lights of / an approaching car. As the car got nearer he saw / two people on his side of the road walking side / by side. Suddenly he found himself going over the bank / and knew that he had hit the person walking on / the outside. We have also heard police evidence that the / motor cycle was found to be in excellent condition when / they examined it and there were no mechanical defects which / might have contributed to the accident. It was very unfortunate / that the motor cyclist did not see the two people / in the light of his headlamp and, from the evidence / we have heard, I record a verdict of accidental death. /

29

ADVANCED TEELINE

It will by now have become obvious that Teeline is no more than a streamlined longhand and that writing it depends very much on the individual. In practice, you have no doubt found that many long words can easily be abbreviated without any danger to the accuracy of the transcript. Notice how easy this is:

> He promised his full *co-op* in the matter.
> He said he would *co-op* in every way.
> It is *poss* to *abb* as much as you like.
> Credit cards can be used for *purch* goods from any *org* accepting them.
> The mayor talked about the new *mun* offices they were building.

There is no difficulty in completing the words printed in italics, for they can be recognized immediately—and they can in Teeline, too. But for increasing speed there are additional ways in which it possible to abbreviate, and they are dealt with in this chapter.

It must be emphasized that all these principles are entirely optional. Teeline is such an open-ended system that you can become competent without them, but at least some of them will prove useful. This is not a chapter to be learned, but rather one to be delved into, and you can adapt and adopt just as the fancy takes you. The beauty of Teeline—to use the word 'beauty' in a colloquial sense—is that the writer is not bound by rigid rules. In the following pages you can pick and choose as you wish, selecting this or discarding that, safe in the knowledge that you can still be a good Teeliner even if you decide to ignore everything.

The 'PL' Principle

This is perhaps one of the most popular principles of advanced Teeline because it enables the letters PL to be represented by one stroke. This is done by writing a downward L through the line, or through a preceding stroke, to represent the letters PL when they come together, as they so often do. Until now, the word 'play' has been written with a P and an

upward L: .... ⎸⎺............. play. Now, if you wish, you may write

it .... ⎧............. play. The P has been ignored and it is shown by writing the downward L through the line. This device can be used whenever PL come together:

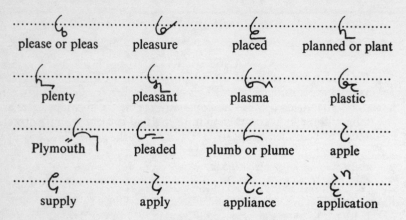

please or pleas	pleasure	placed	planned or plant
plenty	pleasant	plasma	plastic
Plymouth	pleaded	plumb or plume	apple
supply	apply	appliance	application

It can also show PL by writing the downward L through a preceding stroke:

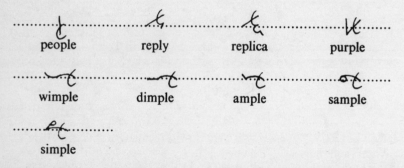

people	reply	replica	purple
wimple	dimple	ample	sample
simple			

You should bear in mind that this principle cannot be used when a vowel comes between the P and the L: .... place but .... palace, ... apply but .... appal, ... plea but .... appeal, ... ample but .... impale. It is only when PL come together that this form can be used. It is also advisable not to use it when intersecting for R: .... is cruel, not cripple, which would be written either .... ⟨outline⟩ .... or .... ⟨outline⟩ ....; and

.... ⟨outline⟩ .... is grill, not grapple, which would be

.... ⟨outline⟩ .... or .... ⟨outline⟩ ...., according to whether

or not you choose to intersect for R.

This advanced principle for PL is worth trying, especially if you intend to write at speeds above 120 w.a.m. Practise the above outlines a few times and see how you take to it. If you find it useful and it comes easily to your pen, then adopt it.

Extended Use of 'TR'

The use of the TR blend can be extended to include -THR, but *not* when THR begins a word. As far as possible, the blend is written in the T position:

another	author	mother	together

gather	bother	smothering	dither

weather, etc.

It will be found that there is no risk of confusion between, for example, 'matter' and 'mother', or 'better' and 'bother'.

Although the TR blend should never be used for THR at the beginning of a word, it is convenient to use it for 'there' or 'their' at the start

of word groups: .... ⟨outline⟩ .... there-is-a,

.... ⟨outline⟩ .... there-is-no, ... ⟨outline⟩ .... there-will-

be, ... ⟨outline⟩ .... there-was-a .... ⟨outline⟩ ...., there-

could-be, etc. As with all other aids to advanced writing, this extended use of the TR blend is entirely optional.

Lightly Sounded 'N'

You will recall that when writing the prefix 'trans-' the lightly-sounded N is omitted, so that we in fact write 'trasmit', 'trasfer', 'trasparent' and so on. The loss of the N in no way impairs the reading of the outline and some time is saved in writing. You will no doubt have noticed the same thing with the special form of 'income': that even without the N, the word cannot be mistaken.

The omission of the lightly sounded N is adopted enthusiastically by a majority of students, although some prefer not to use it, or to use it in some cases and not in others—it is all a matter of individual choice. Here are instances where N can be left out:

When IN is followed by T or D:

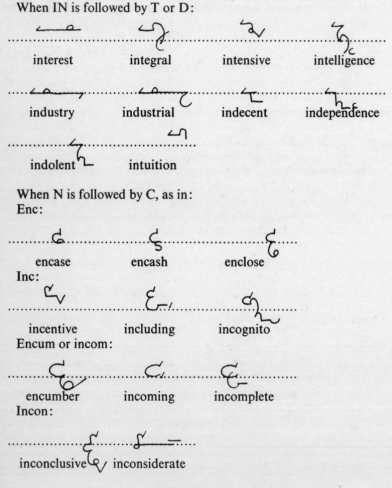

interest   integral   intensive   intelligence

industry   industrial   indecent   independence

indolent   intuition

When N is followed by C, as in:
Enc:

encase   encash   enclose

Inc:

incentive   including   incognito

Encum or incom:

encumber   incoming   incomplete

Incon:

inconclusive   inconsiderate

Exercise 54

Write the Teeline for the following words (no key is provided as the words can easily be checked by reference to the preceding paragraphs):

incommensurate include encumbrance interesting enclosure intercede increase incoherent intake incorrect encumbered inconsistent introduce intuition ploy father arthritis platinum inclement pleasure incompletely ripple pliable player dithering plug tether sapling

An '-NTH' Blend

An aid to faster writing is to blend N and H to represent NTH, thus:

.... Whenever possible this is written on the line to avoid being mistaken for the NP blend, but in outlines where NTH falls into a different position in a word it is still safe to use:

in-the	month	anthrax	anthracite

enthrone	enthuse	anthropologist

or

anthology	enthralling	unthinking	tenth

plinth

Special forms:

enthusiasm	enthusiastic	north

A 'B' Blend

The sign .... has been introduced as a special form

for 'public', and it also seen in .... republic and

.... publish. If desired, this sign can be used in any

word where PB come together, even when a vowel intervenes:

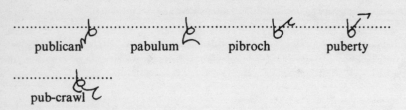

publican   pabulum   pibroch   puberty

pub-crawl

If you wish, the special form for 'public' can also be used in other words beginning with those two syllables, even when the 'C' has a 'soft' sound:

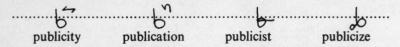

publicity   publication   publicist   publicize

In words which might otherwise take the hand a long way below the line of writing, the B can be abbreviated to the large circle:

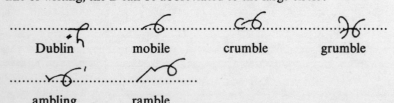

Dublin   mobile   crumble   grumble

ambling   ramble

The L follows the motion of the B circle and sometimes goes upwards.

If desired, B may always be cut to the circle when it comes before or after M:

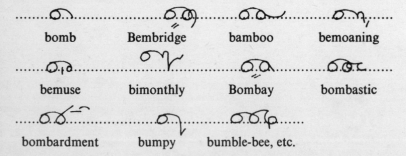

bomb   Bembridge   bamboo   bemoaning

bemuse   bimonthly   Bombay   bombastic

bombardment   bumpy   bumble-bee, etc.

This affects only a limited number of words, and for the more common ones many Teeliners prefer to stick to .... bomb,

.... bump, etc.—but the BM blend is there to use if you like it.

Exercise 55

Write the following words in Teeline (no key):

northwards publications northern bemoan rambling mobbed
enthronement another bumble rumbled bombast bombarded
enthralled publicized Hamble preamble bumper ambition symbol
jumble tumble humble

Additional Suffixes

-ly. In some outlines, the L can be omitted from -LY:

clearly	formerly	firmly	variously

eventually	fearlessly	quickly

This suffix should be used with care until experience shows when it can be used. It would be unwise to use it in 'mainly' or 'unlikely', because the resulting outlines could be read as 'many' or 'unlucky'. In fast writing this suffix has its uses since it saves the writing of a stroke, but caution is advised until you have fully explored the possibilities.

-ality, -elity, -ility, -olity. For these word-endings, use a disjoined L, generally written upwards:

morality	legality	finality	senility

debility	personality	fidelity	formality

frivolity	eventuality	agility	jollity

-arity, -erity, -ority. Use a disjoined R:

hilarity	barbarity	sincerity	minority

authorities   temerity   seniority   inferiority

similarity   severity

-fulness is contracted to a disjoined FLS:

cheerfulness   helpfulness   artfulness   usefulness

spitefulness   thoughtfulness   sinfulness

-lessness becomes a disjoined LS:

thoughtlessness   cheerlessness   harmlessness   hopelessness

carelessness

-self as a suffix is different from 'self-' as a prefix, for the final F is added and can be written upwards or downwards:

herself,   himself,

yourself, and the plural '-selves' is shown by

adding an S: ourselves,

themselves.

-ship. A joined SH is used for this suffix:

membership   friendship   championship   craftsmanship

There is no danger of confusion with the suffix '-cial', which is represented by a *disjoined* SH.

-avity, -evity, -ivity are shown by a disjoined V written in the T position at the end of a word:

gravity	levity	cavity	brevity

longevity	depravity.

-tivity is a disjoined TV:

productivity	activity	sensitivity	relativity

-ses, -sis can be shown by a disjoined S:

houses	premises	this-is	raises or rises

Nemesis	heresies	senses	paralysis

This suffix is very useful for medical secretaries.

Additional Prefixes

above-. Use a V above the outline which follows:

.... or .... above-mentioned,

.... above-named, ... above-all.

Special word group: .... over-and-above.

semi-. Use a disjoined S:

semi-darkness	semicolon	seminar	semi-detached

semicircle	semiquaver	semibreve	semi-official

semi-final semitone semi-tropical semiprecious

anta-, ante-, anti-. For these prefixes, it is useful to use

.... in the T position:

antagonism antagonist antechamber or

antenna ante-room antecedents antiquated

antimony antipasto antifreeze antidote

antisocial antithesis antibiotic

electric, electro- is shown by a full E:

electricity electroscope electronic electric blanket

electrical electrotherapy

multi- becomes a disjoined M:

multistorey multilateral multipurpose multifarious

'Nation' Words

A number of words contain the syllable 'nation' and for these some writers

use an enlarged N .... as in

nation nations national international

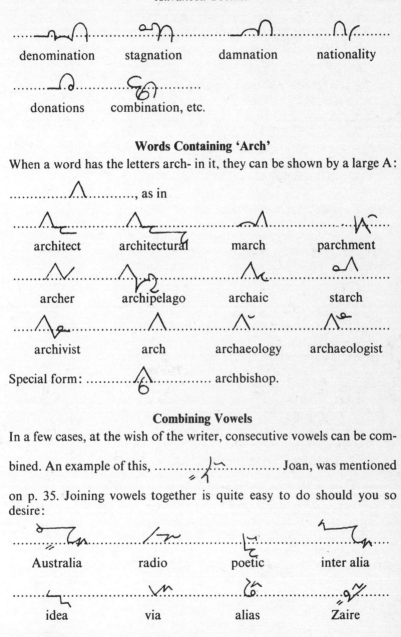

denomination stagnation damnation nationality

donations combination, etc.

Words Containing 'Arch'

When a word has the letters arch- in it, they can be shown by a large A:

..............., as in

architect architectural march parchment

archer archipelago archaic starch

archivist arch archaeology archaeologist

Special form: .... archbishop.

Combining Vowels

In a few cases, at the wish of the writer, consecutive vowels can be combined. An example of this, ... Joan, was mentioned on p. 35. Joining vowels together is quite easy to do should you so desire:

Australia radio poetic inter alia

idea via alias Zaire

anaemia

The first of the two vowels should be shown by the full sign and the second by the indicator. If you wish, AU at the beginning of a word can be indicated by using a full A:

Australia   August   author   audience, etc.

Most writers, however, appear to be satisfied with the A indicator.

Exercise 56

Write the following words in Teeline (no key):

oneself fearlessness nativity hopefulness severity electric-light inferiority mentality quickly selectivity archer hardship semiquaver antirrhinum scholarship antipodes electrocuted nationalism thesis diagnosis succinctly brevity above-board querulously fearlessly hopelessly

Advanced Word Grouping

From time to time reference has been made to word patterns—that is, the order in which words fall. Our familiarity with the language plays an important part here, for it enables us to anticipate intelligently just what a sequence of words will be. So far, the word grouping given in this book has been of an elementary and exploratory nature; examples have been given and they have been extended in the text on those occasions when their use has been obvious. The word 'a' is an instance of this. After one or two examples such as 'is-a' and 'as-a' had been given, it was a logical step to proceed to 'of-a', 'was-a', 'there-is-a', 'it-is-a' and so on, which are readily recognizable.

Quite often a pattern of words can be anticipated without conscious effort. If you heard 'Time after —' and the next word went unheard owing to some extraneous noise, your common sense would tell you it was 'time' because 'time after time' is such a common word pattern that you are able to anticipate what is coming. Other examples are 'quicker and quicker', 'more or less', 'freedom of speech', 'heaven and earth', 'men and women', 'sums of money', 'sooner or later'—the list is almost endless. Obviously it is a waste of time to write each word separately, or even to write the entire outline. When writing at speed saving time is essential, for at 120 w.a.m. you are recording, on average, two words *every second*. Now it stands to reason that some outlines are going to take longer than half a second to write; therefore time must be saved in writing other words. Corners have to be cut and there must be economy in writing. This does not mean that you will save time by writing smaller outlines—the chances are that this will impede your speed (see Chapter 30). A famous shorthand writer of a century ago (Edward Pocknell, inventor of 'Legible Shorthand') said, quite rightly, 'Shorthand is found to depend, not upon a formidable array of marshalled hieroglyphics, but upon the active manoeuvring of a few selected signs.' And that is what one does in writing advanced word groups.

Generally speaking, words that make up a group are, when spoken, so combined with each other in grammatical relation and construction that they form a definite idea or mental picture. We have only to look at the examples given in the previous paragraph to realize this: 'sums of money', 'men and women', 'quicker and quicker', and so on. They all straight-away conjure up an idea with which we are readily familiar. You will find as you delve into the fascinating world of word grouping that it is difficult to formulate any hard and fast rules. This is perhaps as well, for what is a fluid, easy-to-write word group for one person may present difficulty to another. This can be due either to one's style of writing or to the extent of one's knowledge of word patterns. A Teeline writer in the civil courts of law would be familiar with the word pattern 'further and better particulars' and have an outline for it readily to hand; but the writer who was not used to court work would probably be stumped on first hearing the term. Mentally, the question would be asked: 'Further and *what*?', and a precious moment would be lost. So it must be understood that it is possible, with advanced word grouping, only to lay down guidelines.

A good word group will, in most cases, follow natural speech. Words which flow together as if they were syllables of a single word, and are therefore spoken with more than average rapidity, suggest a good group. Notice how people say 'Ithingtsa' for 'I think it is a' or 'on thutherand' for 'on the other hand'. These are instances of words being spoken with rapidity.

Short and common words constitute about nine tenths of good grouping, but this does not mean that it is wise to join a whole string of words together. A series of short strokes joined with obtuse angles will be found at speeds over 100 w.a.m. to take up more time than several longer signs. This is because extra careful pen control must be exercised in writing them, whereas longer strokes, or outlines containing sharp angles, can be recorded with greater facility.

There are two types of word groups. The first is the simple one, composed of two or more special forms with little or no modification:

.... it-will, ... I-am, etc. The

second type is the compound group in which there is some change in the form of one or more of the outlines. Under this heading comes

.... it-will-be, in which the 'be' is cut to the large circle so that it blends with the L in 'will' (some would say that it is the other way round, and the B takes the place of the L). Other examples

are ....⌐.............. at-the, ...⌐⌐.............. for-the,

................⌐⌐............ as-soon-as-possible, ...⌐⌐...............

this-thing, and so on.

There is another form of compound grouping which is perhaps the most important of all so far as time saving is concerned, and it might be called, for want of a better word, the 'elliptic' group. (Just a reminder: 'ellipsis' means the omission of a word or words which would logically be necessary to the sentence construction, but whose absence does not obscure the meaning.) Into this category come a number of word groups

with which you are familiar, such as ....⌐.............. thank-you-

for-your-letter, ...⌐............ with-reference-to,

..............................⌐ with-regard-to. Examples of elliptic groups will

spring readily to mind—face face; deaf dumb; Act Parliament—in each of which your knowledge of word patterns provides the missing words.

It might be as well to define here what does *not* make a useful word group. First, the mere stringing together of outlines willy-nilly; second, uncommon words or proper names; third, words which require long outlines or a succession of obtuse angles. Outside those limitations, the possibilities of grouping word patterns are endless. When writing at speed they are invaluable, but do not fall into the trap of making them too long. The words 'It is possible to make certain that the . . .', if you attempted to put them into one group when writing at 100 w.a.m. or more, would cause you to lose all pen control. It would be far better to write 'It is possible / to / make certain / that the . . .'. Compare the two:

..⌐..⌐....⌐⌐.......... and ..⌐......⌐..⌐.....⌐... There is no need to

tell you the first is difficult to write quickly, and that the second is not only more facile but easier to read.

One final point: grouping can be deceptive. What appears to be a useful word group when written slowly is not necessarily a good one when written at higher speeds (by 'higher speeds' is meant 120 w.a.m. or more, which is when advanced grouping is especially advantageous). In many cases it is for the writer to adapt to suit the individual style of writing. An instance of this is the student who could write ....

'with-regard-to' quite comfortably at 100 w.a.m., but who found it caused a loss of time at 120; so she adapted it by writing only

.... It is quite easy to dream up word groups for slow writing, but the acid test is: will they stand up to higher speeds? For that is when they are most needed.

Some Teeliners who already know the system may be rather surprised at several of the examples given below, but what one person prefers may not find favour with another, even among high speed writers. Just as there can be more than one way of writing a word, so is there more than one way of writing a group of words. There is no 'best' way: it depends entirely on the writer. It is not intended that these examples should be committed to memory, even though they have all been in use for some years. The groups are given as *ideas* for the writer to build upon or reject as thought fit.

Omission of 'and'.

hard (and) fast	or	qu(icker and) quicker
fast(er and) faster	h(igher and) higher	slower and slower
now and then	more and more	less and less
greater and greater	profit and loss	heaven and earth
men and women	man and woman	man, woman and child
men, women and children		part and parcel
first and foremost	trade and industry	half and half

again and again   read and write   hither and thither

large and small   life and death   over and over again

Omission of 'of' and 'of the'.

in respect (of)   sums (of) money   loss (of) revenue

latter part (of)   in the case of   out of the question

fact of the matter   on behalf of

Omission of 'a' and 'or'.

as a matter of   it is a matter of   in a matter of   sooner or later

one or two   five or six   day or two   in a moment

in a minute   in a minute or two   there is a limit to ... or ...

this is a matter   this is a motion   day or so   at or near

make or break   month or two   week or two   days or weeks

one or both   first or second   just a minute   up to a certain beyond a reasonable doubt   more or less

'Fact', 'fact that'.

it is (a f)act (that)   as (a) matter (of f)act

in fact   (note in effect)   accomplished fact (that)

aware of the fact that   are you aware of the fact that

in view of the fact that   is it a fact that   is it not a fact that

'Time'.

from time to time   first time   this time   at a time

in time   in due time   any time   another time

any other time   some other time at the same time   at some time

'Thing', 'Think'.

something   same thing   anything   another thing

any other thing   particular thing   I think   we think

we think that   I think the   people think   many things

many think	all things considered	few things
most things	a number of things	several things
several think		

'Than'.

better than	worse than	less than	more than
any more than	sooner than	later than	rather than
further than	more than necessary		firmer than
more than now	longer than	shorter than	greater than
nearer than	younger than	older than	other than
bigger than	harder than	better than ever	more than ever
worse than ever	later than ever	shorter than ever	

Use an end-opening notebook for your exercises. Write on one side of the paper only, and when you reach the end, turn your book round and write on the blank pages going back. This is the method used by all speed writers.

Miscellaneous groups.

on the other hand   on either hand   from one to the other

from one to another   between two stools   best yet

multi-storey car park   one-off   from beginning to end

hour by hour   hour after hour   minute by minute

day by day   day after day   night after night   week by week

week after week   month by month   month after month

year by year   year after year   standard of living

cost of living   last but not least   quarter of an hour

'G' and 'J'

As a conclusion to this chapter, here is a tip about the letters G and J. If G takes an outline a long way below the line of writing, it can be made smaller, as in

large   catalogue   Cambridge   delegate

pledge   deluge

After M and N, the letter G can be substituted for J to make a more facile joining, as in

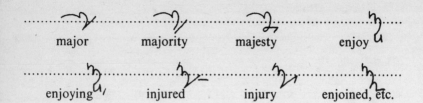

major   majority   majesty   enjoy

enjoying   injured   injury   enjoined, etc.

30

BUILDING TO HIGH SPEED

There is always a fascination about writing shorthand at speed, but you have to train like an athlete to do it properly. With the accomplishment of a high speed comes a great sense of achievement.

In the seats of government, in law courts, at the United Nations, and elsewhere, the shorthand writer is one of the most important people present. History depends on the accuracy of the shorthand writer. So does justice. So does the managing director in his office. Much of the administration of law and commerce and industry would grind to a halt without shorthand.

Being able to write Teeline quickly brings its rewards in every sphere of work. It is within the scope of everybody to write at speed, and the only ceiling upon that speed is the one imposed by the writer. No book can give you the necessary ability to write at speed. Neither can a teacher. A book or an instructor can guide and teach you, but in the end *it is the writer who counts*. That is something always to be borne in mind: nothing can stop you climbing the speed ladder except yourself. The more effort you put into your practice, the more frequently you take dictation, the higher will be your speed.

The first requisite of anyone trying to write at a high speed is *perseverance*. A famous French shorthand writer, the late Jean-Baptiste Estoup, official shorthand writer to the Chamber of Deputies, once said: 'One learns to write shorthand as one learns to sew, to saw, or to polish—by repeating and repeating indefinitely the same actions'—and by persevering with them, proficiency is achieved.

In order to write at a quick and useful speed there are several things to be considered. The first is your writing equipment. Teeline can be written equally well with a pen, pencil or ballpoint. The latter is recommended because a ballpoint will glide over the paper much more smoothly than a pen, and it offers less resistance than a pencil, which has a tendency to wear down quickly. Use a good make of ballpoint—one which has a long-lasting ink container. Although this type costs more, the point is better and the ink will neither clog nor flow too freely. In addition, this type does not crack or break when dropped and it is much more comfortable to hold.

The type of writing paper you use is a matter of personal preference. Some people use loose sheets; others clip them together in the top left-hand corner; but serious consideration should be given to using an end-opening notebook. For sustained work and general neatness, a notebook cannot be beaten and there is no danger of getting the pages out of order as there is when using loose sheets. Further, an end-opening notebook is much better than a side-opening one, since it is easier to turn the pages with rapidity.

If possible, use paper with a smooth surface on which the lines are approximately three eighths of an inch (1 cm) apart. If your lines are too narrow, you will probably find that your style is cramped and a lower speed results, but before making a final decision, you may care to experiment a little. Much depends on the size of your notes. If you normally write a small hand, then your notes are also likely to be small, in which case narrow lines may suit you. On the other hand, if your shorthand tends to sprawl when writing at your maximum speed, you may well prefer an even wider ruling.

When you have found the ideal notebook, stick to it. Always use notebooks of the same width, otherwise you could find that your speed is hampered by using a line which is longer or shorter than the one to which you are accustomed, as well as by a different width in line ruling. When choosing a notebook, make sure that when the pages are turned over they will lie flat. Nothing is more certain to affect your speed than a page which flops back and hides the outlines as you try to write. For this reason it is best to avoid notebooks which are held together with staples, and if selecting a notebook with a spiral binding, make certain the wire spiral is such that every page will turn freely. When starting a new book, flip through the pages three or four times to loosen them and to ensure that none stick together. When notebooks are cut to size by the printers' guillotine there is often a tendency for the edges to stick, and this riffling through is an easy way to prevent any difficulty when turning a page rapidly.

These may seem minor points, but the high-speed writer will be well aware that they are in fact quite important. More than one examination has been failed through pages sticking together at a crucial moment and quite recently a candidate failed a speed test because the cheap ballpoint she was using suddenly dried up.

By now you will not be surprised to learn that there is even a right way and a wrong way to sit. You will find that the best way is to have your notebook in front of your writing arm (the left arm if you are left-handed and the right if you are right-handed). This means that your head is turned slightly in the direction of your book. If you put the notebook immediately in front of your chest, you will soon experience discomfort and this will not happen if you put the book in front of your writing arm.

Sit in a relaxed position. Have both feet on the ground. If you cross your legs then sooner or later you will want to change your position and this will serve to remove your concentration from the job of writing to that of making your legs more comfortable. With both feet on the ground and the body relaxed, you are able to give your mind to the job of writing shorthand.

Your free arm should be extended so that it holds the edge of the page. The necessary concentration will not come if you use your arm for holding up your head. You have your neck for that, not your arm, and you will need that arm for moving up the page and turning it so that a minimum amount of time is lost. Of that, more in a moment.

When writing at speed, the bottom of your notebook should be about a couple of inches from the edge of the desk or table. Your writing arm should hold the pen so that the fleshy part of the forearm is resting on the edge of the desk and acts as a pivot, and your hand holding the pen can just reach from one side of the page to the other without having to move the arm other than on its pivot. As you proceed down the page, the other hand holding the edge of the book moves the bottom of the page upwards towards the pen, so that it is about halfway up the notebook by the time you reach the bottom line. Then with a flick of the hand, the page goes over almost effortlessly and your hand returns to the top of the next page. You will find that as your pen moves down the page, the rest of the page is slid up towards it.

This habit will not come all at once, but the more you practise it, the easier it will become and, consequently, the less interference there will be from having to spend precious portions of a second in turning a page. Try it a number of times. It will be worth your while doing so.

When you have done this, get into the habit of bringing the hand from the end of one line to the beginning of the next as quickly as you can. With the fleshy part of your writing arm as the pivot, this can be done very quickly. The return of the hand should be almost a snatch, quick as a cat pouncing on a mouse. Slow-motion studies on cinema film of high-speed writers doing this show that the hand can be returned to the beginning of the new line in three sixteenths of a second. You may not be able to do this right away, but with a little effort you can soon cut down on the time it takes. (Incidentally, the same slow-motion films show that it takes five sixteenths of a second to turn a page quickly.)

An increase in speed comes only with regular practice and 15 minutes every day is far better than half an hour every alternate day. A few days away from the notebook and the edge is soon taken off one's speed.

Do not be surprised if sometimes you seem to 'stick' at a speed. These plateaux, as they are called, affect every student at some time so do not be discouraged by them—it is the precise time, if anything, for putting in more effort, not less. How to do this will be described presently.

Another thing you will find is that the higher your speed, the longer it will take to reach the next stage. Getting from 30 to 40 w.a.m. is child's play, although it might not have seemed it at the time! Going from 70 to

80 takes longer, and from 110 to 120 takes longer still. You must be prepared for this.

In order to take dictation, if you do not have the services of a teacher, persuade a relative to read to you, or record passages on tape. First, search for suitable passages. Circular letters, business correspondence, speeches from newspapers—all is grist to the mill. If you work in an office, perhaps it will be possible to obtain some old commercial letters for use, or you can buy a book of dictation passages already counted for various speeds (see 'Further Reading' at the end of this chapter). Trainee journalists can use speeches from their own newspapers. Medical secretaries can also obtain old material. If possible, choose extracts which will last for four or five minutes each, so that you train yourself for longer periods than might be required in any examination you may take.

The next thing is to mark them for timed dictation. At low speeds—30 or 40 w.a.m.—it is best to mark off every 10 words. At 30 w.a.m., 10 words represents 20 seconds; at 40, 10 words equals a quarter of a minute; at 60, it is 10 seconds. With the aid of a stopwatch, or at least a watch with a second hand, record your pieces on tape. It is useful, five seconds before the dictation begins, to say 'Five seconds' and then two seconds before the start to say 'Ready'. This acts as a warning for you. This is far better than saying 'Right' or giving some similar warning. In one batch of examination papers sent to a marker the transcripts should have begun 'Mr Chairman . . .' but every paper in the batch began 'Now Mr Chairman . . .' because the reader had said 'Now!' to indicate that dictation was about to commence!

Each passage must be read at an even speed, with only a slightly longer pause after a fullstop. The fullstop is the only punctuation mark you indicate in dictation and you do so by pausing slightly longer. Never give any verbal indication of punctuation, such as 'comma' or 'semi-colon'. You must indicate such things by the tone of the voice, as a speaker usually does, and drop the voice slightly at the end of a sentence, pausing a fraction of a second longer. It will help if you put a little expression into the dictation and read with meaning. At the end of the recording, pause for five seconds and say 'End dictation'.

In the early stages—say, until 80 w.a.m.—repetition plays an important part, and especially repetition at an increasing speed. This helps the brain in the quick-thinking process. The words and phrases will spring to mind with greater alacrity and less time will be spent in thinking out the outlines.

Two words of caution: do not be satisfied when you can take just one piece at a given speed, because you cannot assess your progress on one take alone. Be fair to yourself—only acknowledge that you can do a given speed when you can take several passages at that rate. The other word of caution is this: do *not* attempt to take dictation from the radio or television, as the speed is much too fast for a beginner. News bulletins on the air are usually read at a speed of 180 w.a.m.—that is three words every second and at this stage you are not yet ready to try that!

It is important not to attempt taking Teeline at a speed well beyond your limit, as this would be a waste of time. It may sound rather paradoxical to say that in matters of speed you should take things slowly, but that really is the case. Any new speed is difficult at first. The voice says a word; you try to think of the outline in the given time; the voice goes inexorably on and you make a valiant attempt to keep up with it. Sometimes you succeed, at other times you don't; and as you progress from 60 to 70, 70 to 80, 80 to 90 you will find that more and more attempts have to be made before you achieve that extra coveted 10 words a minute.

It is at this stage that perseverance is necessary, and it is as well to remember Estoup's words that learning to write shorthand is like learning to sew, saw or polish—'by repeating and repeating indefinitely the same actions'. Many would-be capable shorthand writers give up at the 80 w.a.m. stage because they find it takes a bit longer to reach 90. They drop out of the race often when they have the next step within their scope. Few things can be more disappointing to a teacher than to see a student who, to the instructor's experienced eye, is on the verge of the next speed and decides to give up 'because I don't seem to be getting anywhere'. It is just at this point where stalemate seems to have crept in that a little extra effort is needed. If you persevere, success will come sooner than you think.

As each rung in the speed ladder is reached, so your vocabulary is widened and you encounter new words—new, that is, to your shorthand writing, although you may already be familiar with the words and their meanings (if you are not, then look them up in the dictionary and so add to your armoury of words, for words are the stock-in-trade of the writer). These 'new' words have outlines which have to be thought out quickly, and it is this part of speed building which causes difficulty. If you have properly mastered all the special forms then you will be able to write them faster than the voice dictates and this gives you a fraction of a second more in which to work out the outline of a new word.

Some people get the wrong idea about building up speed. They assume that 'speed' depends upon the rapidity with which the pen moves across the paper, whereas in fact 'speed' depends upon the rapidity with which you *think* of the outline. The better you know Teeline and the more mentally alert you are, the faster will your mind work out the outlines for 'new' or 'hard' words.

Generally a word is 'new' only because you have never written it before in Teeline, and a word is only 'hard' because it takes too long to work it out mentally. Sometimes a writer will panic whenever one or two of these words are encountered in quick succession and simply throw in the towel—or, rather, put down the pen. Not only does this show a lack of perseverance but there is no need for this feeling of panic. It can easily be overcome by reading a passage in a book or newspaper or magazine and mentally 'writing' the outline for each word as you read. Spend two or three minutes every day on this exercise and you will soon realize that, thanks to the ingenious Teeline blends, some quite long words have relatively short outlines. Do not try this exercise for more than two or three minutes at first because it can become mentally tiring, but after a while it will be found that this form of 'writing' can be kept up for longer periods. It is an exercise which quickly cultivates the very necessary mental alertness, so it should be done every day—if you wish, two or three times a day, but only for a few minutes at a time.

When you find yourself picturing an outline the very instant you hear someone say the word or when you see it in print, then you will know that you are really getting somewhere and that this exercise in mental alertness is beginning to pay dividends.

Like everything else, you have to put in a bit of effort if you are going to get anywhere. No matter how well you may have learned Teeline, your knowledge will never get you far unless you put in the effort to write it quickly. To do this it is necessary to embark on a training programme in the same way as sportsmen do. The footballer, the golfer, the swimmer, the runner all do a period of training two or three times a week. Physically your training will not be so strenuous but mentally it will be more exacting and it should be done every day. As your speed improves it is usually found that more time is voluntarily spent on speed training because it can become quite exhilarating. Reaching up to the next rung on the speed ladder presents itself as a challenge and there is a great feeling of achievement when it is attained.

At each stage pause deliberately for some consolidation work. It has been known for a writer at 80 w.a.m. suddenly to take a passage at 100 without ever succeeding in getting a 90. Then there may be a period when 100 is never obtained again until after the 90 has been reached. The 100 was just a flash in the pan and the writer is discouraged because this success cannot be immediately repeated.

This is the time consolidation work is needed. If 80 w.a.m. has been reached, then make a point of regularly taking a difficult piece at 60 in order to get used to meeting up with unusual words. Such dictation should be really difficult—extracts from Dickens (himself a Parliamentary shorthand writer in his early days) are ideal, or even a technical report. As you progress, always take difficult passages at 20 w.a.m. below your normal speed. Awkward or unusual words will then be taken in your stride instead of causing a temporary panic and possibly the loss of words. In this way your speed will steadily increase until you are writing at 120 w.a.m. or even higher.

In all speed training, being able to read what you have written is just as important as getting it all down. Transcribing your notes is the acid test of your ability to write at a given speed. That is why, in a speed examination, you have to transcribe a passage within a set time as well as get it down; and if you exceed the number of errors allowed, then you fail. Transcribing Teeline is easy. It only becomes difficult to those who skimp the work, or who are content to take down dictation without getting it back.

In the early stages everything taken down should either be read back or transcribed. When reading back, try to do it as quickly as possible and cultivate the habit of keeping the eye a little ahead of the outline being read. This is especially helpful if a word gives rise to uncertainty. Suppose the phrase being read is 'It is quite possible that the . . .' and then comes a word beginning with R which makes you pause because the outline has been slightly distorted. A glance at the following words shows that they are 'amount of money'. Look again at the distorted outline and by this time, armed with the knowledge that the following words are 'amount of money', your commonsense will come to the rescue and tell you whether the troublesome outline is 'required', 'requested' or 're-quisite', as the case may be.

Make a habit of looking forward in this way whenever a word gives rise to hesitation. More often than not your knowledge of what the outline looks like, plus your commonsense, will provide the answer.

Reading back or transcribing is quite straightforward but always keep the sense of the passage in your mind. The easy method of word-by-word transcription without looking ahead can lead to a lot of errors, whereas if you pay due regard to the sense of the passage pitfalls can be avoided. In this way you are not likely to write a lot of nonsense. One candidate in an examination took down 'The prison system is trapped in its own past' but transcribed it as 'The prison system has dropped unjustifiably fast'; and another transcribed 'transform the bleak marshland' as 'transform the blue marshland'.

Lack of transcription practice can lead to many similar misreadings if the custom of looking a few words ahead is not followed. It was obviously a word-by-word transcriber who made 'it looks as if it has turned sour' into 'it looks as if it has made swear', and 'they are unable to seek shelter in a sudden storm' became 'they are unable to safely shelter for a sandy stream'.

The end of a sentence must always be shown. It is not sufficient to indicate a fullstop by leaving more space after an outline or by starting a new line for each sentence, because this often leads to error. One candidate in an examination lost marks for transcribing '. . . has prevented telephones being installed. Now, I learn . . .' as '. . . has prevented telephones being installed now. I learn . . .'. Another example of a wrongly-placed fullstop was '. . . hardly anybody lived there. Apart from a lighthouse . . .', which became '. . . hardly anybody lived there apart from a lighthouse'. More than one candidate has failed an examination through a fullstop being put in the wrong place. In addition, of course, an omitted or misplaced fullstop can alter the sense of a passage.

It is essential to listen carefully for the end of a sentence by noting the drop in the voice and the slightly longer pause. Never fail to indicate a fullstop in the proper manner as described in this book, no matter how far you are behind the speaker, otherwise your transcript might become a complete muddle.

When the transcription has been completed, check it through. It can sometimes happen that identical outlines occur in close proximity and during transcription the eye jumps from one to the other, thus bringing about the omission of a number of words. There have been many examination failures due to this cause, whereas a few minutes spent in checking the transcript with the Teeline note might well have resulted in a pass. Use only one side of a sheet of paper and make any corrections distinctly. It is better to cross out a word or a figure than to write over it. If, for instance, a figure 5 is altered to a 3, it may not be clear to the examiner which was intended, and he or she may not be allowed by the marking rules to give the benefit of the doubt; but there would be no danger of losing marks if the figure or word was crossed out and the correct one written above it. All insertions, whether a single word or an entire phrase, should be indicated clearly so there can be no mistake where they come. Failure to do so could well entail a loss of marks.

As your speed increases, so the necessity for a lot of transcribing diminishes, but even at 150 w.a.m. at least one passage in three should be transcribed and the other two read through, even outside the class. Mark every error, no matter how small. At first there will probably be many mistakes. With each one refer to your Teeline note, asking yourself 'Now where did I go wrong? Which outline did I misread?', and make a note of it so that the error is not repeated. In this manner you will become familiar with your own way of writing Teeline. In any shorthand system, outlines written at the maximum speed do not have the same appearance as when they are written slowly. In the early stages of speed training some students write 'you' and 'we' so much alike—because they have not fully developed their pen control—that they misread them when transcribing. But they soon benefit from their mistake and learn to make 'you' deep and narrow so there can be no confusion with the shallow, broader curve of 'we'. By transcribing you learn rapidly from any such mistakes and come to recognize your own writing idiosyncracies.

Students sometimes ask: 'How large should my outlines be?' The only true answer to this question is: 'Write your outlines the size that comes naturally to you.' Some people write a large style of longhand; others write small letters, or with a backward slope (in which case the Teeline will also tend to slope backwards, but that doesn't matter because there will be a consistency in all the outlines). As you build up speed, you will naturally adjust your Teeline to the size most suited to your hand. In the formative lessons the outlines may have a clumsy appearance. When

80 w.a.m. is reached, they will begin to take on a style and size of their own without any conscious effort on your part and by the time 120 is within sight, your shorthand will be so distinctive that colleagues will recognize it readily, just as one person can recognize the longhand of another. Regardless of what you may be told, once you begin to write at speed do not deliberately try to control your style of writing. To do so will only hamper your speed. You will not write more quickly by trying to write smaller than you naturally do, although it is true to say that the neater your writing has been when working through the earlier chapters, the neater it will be at speed. Do remember to show the differences in the length of strokes and if necessary exaggerate those differences—make a 'T' short and a 'TR' very long, so there is no danger of misreading. *

From time to time there have been suggestions that left-handed writers cannot get up to a good shorthand speed. This is rubbish. There have been many official shorthand writers in the law courts and elsewhere who have been left-handed. It is the *thinking* part of the operation that counts and it does not matter whether you write with the right hand or the left. Unfortunately, many left-handed students think they are doomed as shorthand writers and once they start thinking that, they are halfway to failure. They can write just as fast as anyone else if they try.

Dictation Tapes

The lone worker who does not have a lot of time to put dictation material on tape for practice, or who cannot find a suitable reader, may care to know that dictation tapes are available for purchase or hire. These cover all speeds from 30 w.a.m. upwards. Details of such tapes are available from the following:

reach-a-teacha, 2 Hastings Court, Collingham, Wetherby, West Yorkshire, LS22 4AW, England, and The National Council for the Training of Journalists, Carlton House, Hemnall Street, Epping, Essex, CM16 4NL, England. French, German and Spanish tapes are available from Teeline Education Ltd, Ardentigh, Glenoran Road, Rhu, Helensburgh, Dunbartonshire G84 8JU, Scotland.

Details of Teeline speed examinations, which can be taken at any time, can be obtained from the publishers. Other speed examinations are held on fixed dates by the London Chamber of Commerce and Industry, the Royal Society of Arts and the National Council for the Training of Journalists, whose addresses will be found under 'Acknowledgements' at the front of this book.

Building up speed requires a certain amount of discipline on the part of the student but reaching the goal you have set yourself makes it all worth while and gives a sense of achievement rarely equalled in other spheres. Anyone can write Teeline, but it is the determined ones who reach their targets and become the cream of Teeliners. If you follow the advice in this book, you can be one of them.

Further Reading

Teeline Dictation and Drill Book, by I. C. and G. Hill (Heinemann Educational Books, 22 Bedford Square, London WC1B 3HH). Dictation passages are also given in *Teeline: the shorthand magazine*, the new monthly for students and teachers which is available on subscription from 35 Great Russell Street, London WC1B 3PP, or may be ordered through newsagents.

31

HOW TO TEACH TEELINE

One of the best ways to learn any subject is to teach it to someone else, whether it be a relative or a friend. This is equally true of Teeline. Teaching is itself a specialized subject on which many books are available, but Teeline can successfully be taught by those who know the system because it is so simple, but of course there are a few elementary rules to be followed.

First, the teacher must be patient with the pupil. Do not forget your own early efforts and that sometimes you forgot things and had to be reminded of them. Your pupil will be in the same position as you were at the beginning of this book. In some ways, you will see your own beginnings with Teeline reflected in the person you are teaching.

Second, make every lesson as interesting as possible. As early as you can, show how students can write their names in Teeline; then their addresses or the names of friends or of any other students there may be. If you have to use blends or principles still to come, tell them so and make it clear they will soon know how to use them.

Third, prepare every lesson in note form, and think of examples which are different from those given in this textbook. Never give a lesson without having first prepared it—and, if necessary, rehearsed it in an empty room. In this way you will learn to present a lesson with an economy of words. Make a point of seeing that one piece of information leads naturally to the next. Nothing can confuse a student so much as a lesson in which the teacher jumps from one thing to another and then goes back to the first. Make your progression natural and logical and the student will easily understand the principle as you develop it. Before giving a new lesson, spend a few minutes revising the previous one. This is especially necessary if there are only one or two lessons a week.

Do not talk too much. Most people can only concentrate properly for a few minutes at a time and if you go on for too long, students' minds will start to think of other things. Talk for 10 minutes then give a brief exercise on what has been learned. If possible include a joke or two in the exercise, because learning Teeline can be fun, and a good laugh can often help to put over a point.

Let the students do some of the work. Shorthand is a skill and they will learn more by doing than by passive listening. After demonstrating a few outlines, put a word on the board and ask what it is. Get them to say the word, and within a short time they will be saying them as you write without waiting to be asked. A word of advice here: the brighter pupils will always be the first and the loudest in saying the words, so after three or four examples, call on one of the quieter or more shy students to give the answer. Do not 'pick on' anyone who seems hesitant in giving an answer and above all do not be sarcastic with such a person. There could be several reasons for such apparent backwardness—perhaps a home problem which is uppermost in the mind, or a slight deafness. If it is obvious that for some reason the student has not grasped what has been said, be patient. Go over the principle again because if one person has not completely understood it there may be others as well. Or it may even be that your method of presentation is at fault.

Be comprehensive in your choice of examples and do not put them on the board too quickly. Pause after each one and give plurals and past tenses as well as the root word and any derivatives that can be covered. If you give 'seem' as an example, then follow with 'seems', 'seemed' and 'seeming'. If anyone asks for 'seemingly', show them how to write it *according to the stage they have reached*, but stress that later on they will be shown a quicker way of representing the word. Remember that Teeline is such a simple system that after the first few lessons a student can write any word in the language, albeit in a 'long' way, and that later lessons concern blends which enable words to be written more quickly and simply. With Teeline you can cut off anywhere you like in the theory and still have a usable shorthand.

Teeline is used in most cases for recording the spoken word, so from early in the course some dictation should be given in every lesson. It should be simple at first: sentences like 'Bake me a cake' or 'Take the book to the girl'. With repetition, such simple words can be written very quickly soon after the start of the course. There are plenty of these easy sentences that can be used in the early exercises. Go slowly so that the students have ample time to think of the outlines and correct any tendency they may have to write the first stroke of a word and then pause before writing the second. Encourage them to work out the entire outline mentally before putting pen to paper. With practice—and there should be twice as much practice as instruction in any lesson—the writing of known outlines will be done at an increasing speed.

The inventor of Teeline, the late James Hill, used to say that speed was 'seven-eighths above the collar and only one-eighth below the cuff'. In other words, the faster you think, the faster you will write. All teachers —especially those new to teaching—should recognize the importance of this, and it is as well that these eight points should be appreciated. They are:

1. **Stimulus**—the impact the spoken word makes on the ear. The more clearly the word is heard, the greater the stimulus.
2. **Transmission**—the ear transmits the word heard to the appropriate area of the brain.

3. **Perception**—the reception of the stimulus and its intuitive recognition.

4. **Apperception**—the interpretation of the stimulus which has just been received and its correlation with the hearer's understanding of what is being said.

5. **Translation**—mentally turning the word heard into Teeline.

6. **Recall**—the mental impulses necessary for the execution of the symbols; the instant recall of blends, prefixes or suffixes to be used.

7. **Impetus**—the transmission via the body's nervous system of the brain's message to the hand to write the outline.

8. **Reception**—the hand receives the message and physically writes the outline.

It will be seen that of the eight operations required to write an outline, seven are mental and only the eighth is physical. All these processes are going on simultaneously, even when writing from very slow dictation. At 30 w.a.m. they are happening once every two seconds; at 60, once a second; at 120, twice; and at 180 they are happening three times a second. It will therefore be obvious that, since the brain has to be trained to react very quickly (mental alertness again), the job has to be done slowly at first, gradually speeding up as the dictation practice continues with each lesson.

No group of students ever progresses at the same rate. Some are slow learners with the theory and faster at speed; others are quick all through the course; but no bright pupils should be favoured more than the plodders, or vice versa. Always ensure that there is something for everyone to do—a transcription exercise for the 'stars' of the class while you are explaining outlines to the less progressive ones, and some revision or additional study for the plodders while you turn your attention to the brighter ones. Never have anyone sitting still and doing nothing.

Why do people want to learn Teeline? In most cases it is because it will be useful in a career, or because a knowledge of shorthand will result in a better salary. Turn this to good use in your earliest lessons. Write the word 'pay' in Teeline and without saying what it is, remark 'There you are—one of the most important words in the language'. Someone will soon say 'Pay' and the ripple of laughter in the class will show that they are on your side!

This motivation in wanting to learn shorthand must be maintained from lesson to lesson and from week to week. It can be done by showing students how to write their names, as has been mentioned earlier, or by stressing how easy and logical Teeline is, or by substituting the names of local streets in dictation passages. Anything that will maintain interest should be used. Ask them how they would write the names of people and places currently in the news, taking them from either the national or your local papers. Do not show them how; just ask them to work out the outlines. Then you can put them on the board and perhaps discuss them, pointing out where someone might have gone wrong, or where another way of writing is more acceptable at speed. This need not be done frequently—just enough to keep their interest bubbling. In the majority of cases this will not be necessary because Teeline itself generates enthusiasm. One lady learning the system lost her textbook and later found it in her son's bedroom. Unbeknown to her, he was teaching himself and, she reported, was making a very good job of it! That is how Teeline can generate enthusiasm.

All teachers should insist that students write neatly from the first lesson. Because Teeline is a system in which it is almost impossible to write a 'wrong' outline (in that respect it differs radically from the traditional systems) there is not much correcting of exercises to be done, but it is advisable to watch students' writing very carefully. Make sure that there is consistency in the different lengths of strokes and that the hooks are kept narrow on G and N. See to it as well that the differences between O, U and W are shown with care (later this will become second nature to them) and that such strokes as M and W have the same length and degree of shallowness. Students can write the strokes any size they like, but there must be consistency at all times so that, for example, the circle on the B is kept large and that the S is kept small, especially when written on the end of an L.

Take your time over the early lessons and see that the students develop a good writing style: the neater, the better. Any untidiness in the formative stages will transmit itself to outlines written at speed and lead to difficulties in transcription.

An entire chapter need not be taken in one lesson. If you wish, a chapter can be spread over two or three lessons, according to its length and the learning ability of the students. Remember the maxim: a little learning, a lot of practice. If lessons are not being given daily, insist on home study being done every day and allocate work accordingly. As far as possible the exercises in this textbook should never be transcribed in class. They may be used for reading practice, but copying and transcribing should be done for homework.

See that the special forms are not neglected and that pupils are given class tests on them from dictation. Special forms have to be 'overlearned' until they come off the tip of the pen instantly, so tests on them should be given frequently.

When writing outlines on a board during instruction, always stand to the side so that the class can see your hand as you write. Use the board from top to bottom and from left to right, as you would a sheet of paper. When instruction has been completed it should be possible for a student to read it like the page of a book. It is a good idea, when preparing lesson notes, to write your examples in the order you intend to present them on the board. A class will only be confused if you start somewhere in the middle, then go to the top and then the bottom, and finally put some more examples in the middle. They are in class to receive orderly instruction, not to fit the pieces of a jigsaw puzzle together. Good board presentation is the sign of a good teacher.

In conclusion, a word to those who have been teaching other systems and are converting to Teeline. The principles of teaching are the same the world over for any subject, but the approach to teaching Teeline is different from that of other shorthand systems. It is sometimes difficult for teachers of a traditional shorthand system to accept the freedom of Teeline and they may think they are not doing the job properly because their marking load is so much lighter. From the beginning, Teeline offers a wide vocabulary which quickly becomes almost limitless, so what might be fairly advanced passages in another system can be dictated much sooner in Teeline. Most important, however, is to forget about writing by sound. There is no such thing as a 'shun' sign in Teeline (it is 'the disjoined N ending'); and there is no 'above the line' or 'on the line' —it is 'the T position' or 'the D position'. With the S symbol—in use in no fewer than 24 systems since 1654—it does not matter which side of a stroke it is written and rules applying to any other system should be ignored.

Further Reading

Handbook for Teeline Teachers, edited by Harry Butler (Heinemann Educational Books, London, 1983).

32

HOME CLASSES IN TEELINE

It is quite common for many Teeliners to learn their shorthand in private homes in areas away from schools or colleges and many prefer private tuition to sitting in a large evening class. There is quite a number of such home groups where, once or twice a week, people sit around the dining-room table and prepare themselves for a career. This chapter is for the guidance of writers who wish to start their own private classes.

For home tuition, the ideal is to have two classes a week. Two one-hour lessons will be better than one two-hour lesson. The students may be young people still at school with other subjects to study, or those who come after a tiring day at the office, or even housewives who are anxious to equip themselves for part-time secretarial work. If you decide to teach typewriting as well, an ideal book is *Practical Typewriting Made Simple* by Margaret Davis in the same series as this book.

If you decide to have your classes on Mondays and Thursdays, or Tuesdays and Fridays, bear in mind how many days there are in between when allocating homework. Each student should have two end-opening shorthand notebooks. The first lesson and the following homework will be done in notebook A. When they come for the second lesson, they will hand in notebook A for any marking and will work in notebook B. At the third lesson, book A will be exchanged for book B, and so on.

When going through the exercises, remember that it is almost impossible to write incorrect outlines. If a student has written an outline which is in accordance with the principles then it is correct, even if the 'S' is not on the side of the stroke on which you would yourself write it. After the first few lessons, it will only be necessary to check through the books to see that students have grasped the principles of the previous lesson. If this is not so, then go over it again. The fault may not be with the student—the new teacher often puts too much information into a lesson, and this must be avoided at all costs.

A problem which has to be overcome with home teaching is the lack of a board for writing upon. An excellent substitute is a large sheet of paper on which one can write with a felt-tipped pen. Use a large sheet of cardboard or a piece of three-ply wood for backing and clip the paper on to it with two or three bulldog clips. Put several sheets of paper on the board (a local printer will sell you some of the size you require quite cheaply, for it does not have to be good quality paper) and when one has been filled, turn it over to the blank one underneath. It is useful to have felt-tipped pens in several colours—one for drawing lines, one for writing the Teeline and a third for any longhand you may want to write.

Once the class has started the best publicity is the satisfied, successful student. There is nothing so good as word-of-mouth advertising, but an occasional newspaper advertisement does not come amiss, or even a card in a local shop window.

If you advertise in a newspaper, specify whether you want your announcement under 'Personal', 'Educational' or 'Tuition' (classifications vary from newspaper to newspaper). The 'Personal' column is possibly best because most people read those announcements. Here are some suggested wordings:

Teeline shorthand, easily and quickly learned. Small classes, individual tuition. (Add address and telephone number.)

Learn Teeline, the sure and certain shorthand, in a few weeks. (Address)

Classes in Teeline shorthand just beginning. Simple, certain, straightforward—such a change! (Address)

Teeline shorthand, the easy system that's sweeping the country. Individual tuition in small classes. (Address)

Best results are obtained at the time when other evening classes are enrolling, but regular announcements throughout the autumn and winter (say, once a week or once a month) serve to keep your classes before the public eye.

With small classes, much more personal attention can be given than in a large evening class and results will be better. In this respect, the home class can win hands down and from time to time your students can sit for the speed examinations of Teeline Education Ltd which can be held at any time to suit the teacher. Some of the best writers have come from such classes, but this does not mean that good students are not to be found in the schools and colleges, where the great advantages of Teeline are becoming more and more recognized. Some pupils prefer a school; others like to go to home classes because they are nearer to their places of residence and are therefore more convenient. It is all a matter of personal preference—like writing Teeline.

Appendix 1

ALPHABETICAL LIST OF SPECIAL FORMS

The figures after each outline indicate the chapter in which they are first given.

A	3	bring	15
able, able-to	6	business	7
accept	7	can	10
accident	6	chairman	4
and	4	Christmas	18
appropriate	15	circumstance	19
approval	15	come	11
approximate, -ly	15	commercial	22
archbishop	29	convenience	13
are	4	convenient	13
at	3	council	10
attention	20	county council	10
be	4	day	3
because	9	dear	14
become	11	department	7
before	14	develop, -ed	15
behalf	14	difference	21

274

different	....	21
difficult	....	21
difficulty	....	21
do	....	3
efficient, -cy	....	20
enthusiasm	....	29
enthusiastic	....	29
equal, -led	....	7
Europe	....	15
European	....	15
evidence	....	9
evident	....	9
exam(ination)	....	18
exchange	....	18
expect	....	11
expectation	....	20
expected	....	11
experience	....	11
extra	....	14
extraordinary	....	14
eye	....	3
farther	....	18

finance	....	22
financial	....	22
firm	....	14
for	....	13
form	....	14
frequent, -ly	....	19
from	....	4
further	....	18
general, -ly	....	6
gentleman	....	11
gentlemen	....	11
go	....	3
government	....	22
half	....	14
has	....	7
have	....	4
he	....	3
his	....	7
hour	....	16
however	....	7
I	....	3

immediate	16	* Mr	10
immediately	16	much	4
importance	16	my	3
important	16		
improve, -d, -ing, -ment	22	necessary	7
in	3	newspaper	15
inattention	20	nine	6
income	22	no	7
inconvenience	13	noon	6
inconvenient	13	north	29
inexperience, -d	19	number	7
inform, -ed	19	object	14
information	22	o'clock	9
intention	20	of	3
it	3	on	3
		one	5
kind	5	only	7
		or	5
letter	5	our	16
		owing	19
maximum	18		
mayor	16	particular	16
me	3	particularly	16
member	6		

* For 'Mrs', just add an S.

perhaps		15
popular, -ly		18
prefer		14
preparation		20
prepare		15
prepared		15
principle, -pal		15
probable, -ly		15
production		20
profit		14
public		18
publish		18
publisher		18
rather		18
recent		10
recently		10
recognize		10
recommend, -ed		11
recommendation		20
refer, -red reference		14
represent, -ative		7
represents, -atives		7
republic		18
shall		4
speech		15
subject		14
subsequent, -ly		19
success		10
sufficiently, -ly, -cy		20
super		21
superb		21
superintend		21
supermarket		21
technical		19
telephone		19
that		4
the		3
therefore		14
they		4
thought		7
to		3
today		3
to-do		3
too		5

trade union	....	22	what	....	4
two	....	5	which	....	4
			who	....	4
unexpected	....	19	why	....	4
unfortunate	....	22	with	....	3
unfortunately	....	22			
			within	....	20
very	....	4	without	....	20
we	....	3	you	....	3
were	....	16	your	....	4

Appendix 2

TOWNS IN THE UNITED KINGDOM AND EIRE

This list is only a selection, so that students can see how Teeline is applied in writing the names and can work out the outlines for any other places they may require. In this list, ... 🔾 .... has been used for towns ending in -bury, and .... 🔾 .... has been used for -borough, -brough, or -burgh.

The full outline has first been given under the column headed Full, and in the case of long outlines abbreviated forms appear under the column headed Abbreviated.

	Full	*Abbreviated*
Aberdeen		
Aberystwyth		
Abingdon		
Accrington		
Aldershot		
Ayr		
Banbury		
Barking		
Barnsley		
Barrow-in-Furness		
Basildon		
Basingstoke		

Teeline Shorthand

	Full	Abbreviated
Bath		
Bedford		
Beeston		
Belfast		
Berwick-upon-Tweed		
Bexhill		
Bexleyheath		
Birkenhead		
Birmingham		
Bishop's Stortford		
Blackburn		
Blackpool		
Bolton		
Boston		
Bournemouth		
Bracknell		
Bradford		
Braintree		
Brentwood		
Bridgend		
Bridlington		
Brighton		

	Full	*Abbreviated*
Bristol		
Bromley		
Bromsgrove		
Bude		
Burnley		
Bury		
Bury St Edmunds		
Camberley		
Cambridge		
Canterbury		
Cardiff		
Carlisle		
Chatham		
Chelmsford		
Cheltenham		
Chester		
Chesterfield		
Chichester		
Colchester		
Colwyn Bay		
Cork		

	Full	Abbreviated
Coventry		
Cromer		
Croydon		
Darlington		
Denby		
Derby		
Dornoch		
Douglas		
Dover		
Dublin		
Dundee		
Dungannon		
Dunstable		
Durham		
Eastbourne		
Edgware		
Edinburgh		
Ely		
Enfield		
Epsom		
Exeter		

	Full	Abbreviated
Fareham		
Farnborough		
Felixstowe		
Fife		
Folkestone		
Gairloch		
Galloway		
Galway		
Gateshead		
Glasgow		
Gloucester		
Gravesend		
Grays		
Great Yarmouth		
Greenford		
Grimsby		
Guildford		
Hanley		
Harlow		
Harrogate		
Harrow		

Teeline Shorthand

	Full	Abbreviated
Hastings		
Hemel Hempstead		
Hereford		
Hertford		
High Wycombe		
Holyhead		
Horsham		
Hounslow		
Hove		
Huddersfield		
Hull		
Huntingdon		
Ilford		
Ilfracombe		
Ipswich		
Jarrow		
Kettering		
Kidderminster		
King's Lynn		
Kingston-upon-Thames		

	Full	Abbreviated
Lancaster		
Leamington Spa		
Leatherhead		
Leeds		
Leicester		
Lichfield		
Limerick		
Lincoln		
Liverpool		
Llandudno		
London		
Londonderry		
Lowestoft		
Luton		
Lyme Regis		
Maidenhead		
Maidstone		
Malvern		
Manchester		
March		
Margate		

Teeline Shorthand

Full   *Abbreviated*

Middlesbrough		
Milton Keynes		
Monmouth		
Morecambe		
Motherwell		
Nelson		
Newbury		
Newcastle		
Newhaven		
Newport		
Newquay		
Northampton		
North Shields		
Norwich		
Nottingham		
Oadby		
Oban		
Oldham		
Oxford		
Paisley		
Penzance		

	Full	Abbreviated
Perth		
Peterborough		
Peterlee		
Plymouth		
Porthcawl		
Portsmouth		
Port Talbot		
Preston		
Pwllheli		
Ramsgate		
Reading		
Redcar		
Redhill		
Reigate		
Rhyl		
Richmond		
Ripon		
Rochester		
Romford		
Rugby		
Salford		

Teeline Shorthand

	Full	Abbreviated
Salisbury		
Scarborough		
Scunthorpe		
Sevenoaks		
Sheffield		
Shrewsbury		
Sittingbourne		
Skegness		
Slough		
Solihull		
Southampton		
Southend		
South Shields		
Southwell		
Stafford		
Staines		
Stamford		
Stevenage		
Stirling		
Stockport		
Stoke		
Stonehaven		

	Full	*Abbreviated*
Sunderland		
Swansea		
Swindon		
Taunton		
Tenby		
Thurso		
Tiverton		
Torquay		
Truro		
Ventnor		
Wakefield		
Wallasey		
Walsall		
Walton-on-Thames		
Warrington		
Watford		
Welling		
Wellingborough		
Wellington		
Welwyn		

Teeline Shorthand

	Full	Abbreviated
Wembley		
West Bromwich		
Westcliff		
Weston-super-Mare		
Wexford		
Weymouth		
Whitby		
Whitley Bay		
Wick		
Wimbourne		
Winchester		
Windsor		
Witney		
Woking		
Wolverhampton		
Worcester		
Worthing		
Yarmouth		
York		

Appendix 3

COUNTRIES OF THE WORLD AND THEIR CAPITALS

Country	*Capital*
Afghanistan	Kabul
Albania	Tirana
Algeria	Algiers
America (see also USA)	Washington
Andorra	Andorra la-Vella
Angola	Luanda
Antigua	St Johns
Argentina	Buenos Aires
Australia	Canberra
Austria	Vienna
Bahamas	Nassau
Bahrain	Manama

Country	Capital
Bangladesh	Dacca
Barbados	Bridgetown
Belgium	Brussels
Belize	Belmopan
Bermuda	Hamilton
Bolivia	La Paz
Botswana	Gaborone
Brazil	Brasilia
Bulgaria	Sofia
Burma	Rangoon
Cameroon	Yaoundé
Canada	Ottawa
Central African Republic	Bangui
Chad	Ndjamena

Country	*Capital*
Chile	Santiago
China	Peking
Colombia	Bogotá
Congo	Brazzaville
Costa Rica	San José
Cuba	Havana
Czechoslovakia	Prague
Denmark	Copenhagen
Djibouti	Djibouti
Dominica	Roseau
Ecuador	Quito
Egypt	Cairo
Eire	Dublin
El Salvador	San Salvador

Country		Capital	
Equatorial Guinea		Malabo	
Ethiopia		Addis Ababa	
Falkland Islands		Stanley	
Fiji		Suva	
Finland		Helsinki	
France		Paris	
Gambia		Banjul	
Germany (East)		Berlin	
Germany (West)		Bonn	
Ghana		Accra	
Gibraltar		Gibraltar	
Greece		Athens	
Greenland		Godthaab	
Grenada		St Georges	
Guatemala		Guatemala	

Country	Capital
Guernsey	St Peter Port
Guinea	Conakry
Guyana	Georgetown
Haiti	Port-au-Prince
Hong Kong	Hong Kong
Hungary	Budapest
Iceland	Reykjavik
India	New Delhi
Indonesia	Jakarta
Iran	Tehran
Iraq	Baghdad
Isle of Man	Douglas
Israel	Jerusalem
Italy	Rome

Country	Capital
Ivory Coast	Abidjan
Jamaica	Kingston
Japan	Tokyo
Jersey	St Helier
Jordan	Amman
Kampuchea	Phnom-Penh
Kenya	Nairobi
Kiribati	Tarawa
Korea	Seoul
Kuwait	Kuwait
Laos	Vientiane
Lebanon	Beirut
Lesotho	Maseru
Libya	Tripoli
Luxembourg	Luxembourg

Country		Capital	
Madagascar		Tananarive	
Malawi		Lilongwe	
Malaysia		Kuala Lumpur	
Mali		Bamako	
Malta		Valletta	
Mauritius		Port Louis	
Mexico		Mexico City	
Monaco		Monaco-Ville	
Mongolia		Ulan Bator	
Montserrat		Plymouth	
Mozambique		Maputo	
Namibia		Windhoek	
Nauru		Nauru	
Nepal		Katmandu	
Netherlands		Amsterdam	

Country	Capital
New Hebrides	Port Vila
New Zealand	Wellington
Nicaragua	Managua
Niger	Niamey
Nigeria	Lagos
Norway	Oslo
Pakistan	Islamabad
Panama	Panama
Papua New Guinea	Port Moresby
Paraguay	Asunción
Peru	Lima
Philippines	Manila
Poland	Warsaw
Portugal	Lisbon

Country	*Capital*
Romania	Bucharest
Russia	see USSR
St Christopher	Basseterre
St Helena	Jamestown
St Lucia	Castries
St Vincent	Kingstown
Saudi Arabia	Riyadh
Senegal	Dakar
Seychelles	Victoria
Sierra Leone	Freetown
Singapore	Singapore
Solomon Islands	Honiara
Somalia	Mogadishu
South Africa	Cape Town

Country		Capital	
Spain		Madrid	
Sri Lanka		Colombo	
Sudan		Khartoum	
Swaziland		Mbabane	
Sweden		Stockholm	
Switzerland		Berne	
Syria		Damascus	
Taiwan		Taipei	
Tanzania		Dar es Salaam	
Thailand		Bangkok	
Tonga		Nuku'alofa	
Trinidad		Port-of-Spain	
Tunisia		Tunis	
Turkey		Ankara	
Tuvalu		Funafuti	

Country	Capital
Uganda	Kampala
United Kingdom	London
Upper Volta	Ouagadougou
Uruguay	Montevideo
USA (see also America)	Washington
USSR (see also Russia)	Moscow
Vatican City	Vatican City
Venezuela	Caracas
Vietnam	Hanoi
Virgin Islands	Road Town
West Indies	(see Antigua and St Christopher)
Western Samoa	Apia
Yemen (North)	Sana'a

Country	Capital
Yemen (South)	Aden
Yugoslavia	Belgrade
Zaire	Kinshasa
Zambia	Lusaka
Zimbabwe	Harare

Index

A, 5
  after H, M, N, P, 24
  before R, 19
  indicator disjoined after upward L, 39
  indicator used for -ANG, 48
  indicator written upward before V, W, X, 21
  omission in word groups, 252
  writing -ANK, 58
Abbreviation of words, 237
Above as prefix, 245
-ability as suffix, 180
-able as suffix, 179
Advanced Teeline, 237
Advanced word groups, 248
After as prefix, 174
-ality as suffix, 243
-alogical as suffix, 182
-alogist as suffix, 182
-alogy as suffix, 181
Alphabet, 5
And, omission of, 251
Anta, ante, anti as prefix, 246
Arch words, 247
-arity as suffix, 245
Auto as prefix, 171

B, 5
  blended with M, 242
  blended with P, 241
Bilingual secretaries, 223

C, 6
  before T or D, 92, 137
  blended with V, 31
  CK, 6, 67, 92, 136
  soft C, 67, 136
  substituted for K, 58
  writing -NCE, 68, 137
  writing -NCH, 70, 137
Capitals of countries, 295
CH, 29
-cial as suffix, 187
-cially as suffix, 188

Circum as prefix, 175
Classes at home, 272
CM blend, 79, 137
CN blend, 73, 92, 137
CN blend distorted, 93
CNV blend, 89
Combined consonants, 29
Combined vowels, 247
Commercial word groups, 209
Countries of the world, 295
Currency, how to write, 199

D, 6
  after R, 12
  after upward L, 39, 64
  before and after F, 12
  before and after T, 12
  position, 9, 63
D-tion, 166
Days of the week, 103
Dictation, 84, 139, 260
  tapes, 265
DN blend, 141
Double vowels, 36
DR blend, 108, 138
DRN blend, 142

E, 6
  indicator disjoined after upward L, 39
  indicator used for -ENG, 48
  indicator written horizontally, 21
  writing -ENK, 58
-eble as suffix, 180
Eire, towns in, 284
Electric, electro as prefix, 246
-elity as suffix, 243
Ellipsis in word groups, 250
-erity as suffix, 243
Estoup, Jean-Baptiste, 257, 261
Ev as prefix, 174
-evity as suffix, 245
Examinations, specimen papers, 211, 220, 223, 234

F, 6
  as substitute for PH and GH, 6
  before and after T or D, 12
  blended with M, 138
  blended with R, 97, 138
  blended with W, 138
  not blended with R, 98
Fact, fact-that omitted in word groups, 253
Figures, 196
-fulness as suffix, 244

G, 6
  made smaller, 255
  substituted for J, 255, 256
  used for DG, 3
-graph, -graphy, as suffix, 192
Grouping of words, 42, 248

H, 6
  blended with V, 30
High speed, 257
Hill, James, 1, 3, 62, 66, 268
Home classes, 272

I, 6
  before L and V, 24
  indicator used for -ING, 48
  indicator used for Y, 4
  writing -INGLE and -INGLY, 54
  writing -INK, 58
-ibility as suffix, 181
-ible, -ibly as suffix, 180
-ility as suffix, 243
Indicators, medial, 25
Indicators, vowel, 16, 48
Intersecting for R, 114

J, 6
  made smaller, 255
  substituted by G, 255, 256
Journalism, 228
Journalists' word groups, 230

K, 7
  before T or D, 92
  joined to H, J, P, 15
  substituted by C, 6, 58, 92

L, 7
  after M, 64
  after N, 65
  blended with R, 128
  vowels after final L, 39
  written upwards, 8, 39

-lessness as suffix, 244
Lesson preparation, 267
London Chamber of Commerce and Industry, 212
-ly as suffix, 244

M, 8
  before and after O, 22
  blended with B, 242
  blended with F, 138
  blended with R, 127
Magna, magne, magni as prefix, 175
Measurements, how to write, 200
Medial indicators, 25
Medical Secretaries, 216
  Association of, 216
  prefixes, 217
  suffixes, 218
Months of the year, 101
Multi as prefix, 246

N, 8
  after O, 22
  blended with D or T, 141
  blended with P, 146
  blended with R, 74, 97
  blended with V, 150
  blended with W, 150
  blended with X, 151
  lightly sounded, 239
  written in T position for '-tion', 162
'Nation' words, 246
NTH blend, 241

O, 8
  before and after M, 22
  before N, 22
  used for -ONG, 49
  writing -ONK, 58
-obility as suffix, 181
-oble as suffix, 181
Of, of-the omitted, 252
-olity as suffix, 243
-ological as suffix, 182
-ologist as suffix, 182
-ology as suffix, 181
OO, OU, 36
-ority as suffix, 243
Outlines, size of, 264
Over as prefix, 170

P, 8
  blended with B, 241
  blended with N, 146
  blended with V, 31, 65
  following U, 22

Paper for note-taking, 257
Pen control, 44, 139
Per cent, how to write, 201
PL principle, 237
Prefixes, 170, 245
Punctuation, 19, 260

Q, 8
    position of, 8
    used for QU, 8

R, 8
    always shown, 25
    before M, 127
    blended with D, 108, 138
    blended with F, 97
    blended with L, 128, 138
    blended with M, 127, 138
    blended with N, 74, 97
    blended with T, 103, 138
    blended with W, 128
    joined to B, 8
    principle of intersecting or disjoining, 114, 138
Reading back, 263
Recording for dictation, 86
RFR not blended, 98
Royal Society of Arts, 214

S, 9
    before and after U, 19
    methods of writing, 9, 11, 66
    substituted for Z, 14
Self as prefix, 171; as suffix, 244
Semi as prefix, 245
-ses, -sis as suffix, 245
SH, 29
-shal as suffix, 187
-ship as suffix, 244
Special forms, 18
    list of, 274
Specimen examination papers, 211, 220
    223, 234
Speed building, 87, 96, 113, 125, 149,
    160, 161, 169, 178, 195
Speed examinations, 265
    mental requirements for, 268, 269
Spelling, ignoring double and 'silent' letters, 1, 3
    substitution of F for GH, PH, 3
    substitution of I for Y, 4
    use of G for DG, 3
Suffixes, 179, 243
Super as prefix, 175

T, 9
    after upward L, 39, 64
    after M, 64
    after R, 12
    before and after D, 12
    before and after F, 12
    position, 9, 63
Teaching, 267
TH, 29
Than in word groups, 254
Thing, think in word groups, 253
Time in word groups, 253
Time-study into hand movements, 259
-tion, 162
T-tion, 166
-tial as suffix, 187
-tivity as suffix, 245
Towns in the UK and Eire, 283
TR blend, 103
    extended use of, 239
Trans as prefix, 155
TRN blend, 142
Typewriting, 272

U, 13
    before P, 22
    before and after S, 19
    indicator used for -UNG, 50
    writing -UNK, 58
-ubble, -bly as suffix, 182
UN before W, 151
Under as prefix, 170
United Kingdom, towns in, 283

V, 14
    blended with H, 30
    blended with N, 150
    blended with P, 31, 65
Vowels
    between B and C, G or N, 25
    between J and B or C, 25
    combined, 247
    disjoined, 17
    double (AU, EI, etc.), 36
    indicators, 5, 48
    indicators used for -ANG, etc., 48
    initial and final, 3
    omission, 1, 3, 16, 17
    smaller than consonants, 5, 16

W, 14
    blended with F, 138
    blended with N, 150
    blended with R, 128
    following a vowel, 25
    used for OO, OU, 37

-ward, etc., as suffix, 188
　in groupings, 188
Weights, how to write, 198
WH, 29
Word groups
　simple, 47
　advanced, 248

X, 14
　blended with N, 151
　blended with other letters, 15, 92, 138

Y, 14
　substituting I for Y, 4
　used for OY, 4
Years, how to write, 199

Z, 14
　position of, 5
　substituted by S, 14